Svalbard (Norv.)
Mer du Groenland
Jan Mayen (Norv.)
Cercle Polaire Arctique
ISLANDE
Îles Féroé (Dan.)
NORVÈGE
Oslo
Mer du Nord
GRANDE-BRETAGNE
DANEMARK
Copenhague
LETTONIE
LITUANIE
IRLANDE
Londres
P.-B.
Berlin
POLOGNE
BIÉL.
ALLEMAGNE
LUX.
R. TCH.
SLOVA.
UKR
Paris
SUISSE
AUTR.
HONGR.
M.
FRANCE
SL.
ROUM.
CR.
B.-H.
Y.
BULG.
M.
ITALIE
A.
Madrid
Rome
M.
PORTUGAL
ESPAGNE
ALB.
GRÈCE
Athènes
Alger
Tunis
MALTE
Rabat
TUNISIE
MAROC
Tripoli
Le Caire
ALGÉRIE
LIBYE
ÉGYPTE
Sahara
MALI
NIGER
SOU
Sahel
Khartoum
TCHAD
Niamey
BURKINA
N'Djamena
NIGERIA
BÉNIN
CÔTE D'IVOIRE
TOGO
Abuja
RÉP. CENTRAFRICAINE
GHANA
Porto-Novo
CAMEROUN
Bangui
Moscou
Mer Noire
ARMÉNIE
Ankara
TURQUIE
SYRIE
Damas
JORDANIE
ARABIE
Nil
Mer Rouge
Asmara
ÉRYTHRÉE
ÉTHIOPIE

— IL EST ESSENTIEL QUE LE DESIGNER AIT POUR OBJECTIF D'HUMA- NISER LA VILLE.

VOULOIR CRÉER UNE ŒUVRE D'ART EST SANS DOUTE LE PREMIER REPROCHE QUE JE FERAIS À CERTAINS DONT LES CONCEPTIONS ONT POUR BUT D'ATTIRER L'ATTENTION, AU POINT DE FATIGUER AU LIEU DE REPOSER. LE BON DESIGN NE SE VOIT PAS, IL SE SENT.

Marc Kandalaft, directeur artistique, Paris

—GOOD DESIGN IS A BALANCING ACT. IT'S ABOUT KNOWING WHEN TO CHANGE THINGS AND WHEN TO LEAVE THEM ALONE. A DESIGN CITY SHOULD, IDEALLY, CREATE SITUATIONS (THROUGH ZONING, TAX INCENTIVES, PUBLIC WORKS, ETC.) THAT ENCOURAGE CHANGE IN SOME AREAS AND ALLOW OTHER AREAS TO BE LEFT ALONE. A DESIGN CITY SHOULD BE A PLACE WHERE THE MOST STYLISH DISTRICTS AND BUSINESSES STAND OUT, IN PART BECAUSE LESS STYLISH NEIGHBOURHOODS CAN CONTINUE TO EXIST AND THRIVE.

Karrie Jacobs, journalist, New York

NEW DESIGN CITIES

NOUVELLES VILLES DE DESIGN

under the direction of
sous la direction de
MARIE-JOSÉE LACROIX (Montréal)
in collaboration with
in collaboration avec
LAETITIA WOLFF (New York)
JOSYANE FRANC (Saint-Étienne)

— UNE VILLE DESIGN, ET NON PAS UNE VILLE DE DESIGN, EST UNE VILLE PLURIELLE OÙ LE CITOYEN PEUT CHANGER D'ATMOSPHÈRE EN TOURNANT LE COIN D'UNE RUE. ELLE EST TOUTEFOIS ET SURTOUT DOTÉE D'UN FIL CONDUCTEUR QUI PEUT SE DÉFINIR PAR UNE STANDARDI- SATION DE L'AMÉNAGEMENT DE L'EMPRISE PUBLIQUE ET DE SON MOBILIER. SES LAMPADAIRES, POUBELLES, ABRIS, ETC. SONT DISCRETS : ILS PARTICIPENT AU CONCEPT DE POLLUTION VISUELLE ZÉRO ET À L'IDENTITÉ DE LA VILLE, EN LAISSANT L'ARCHITECTURE DES IMMEUBLES SE RÉVÉLER.

Mario Brodeur, architecte, Montréal

— JE DIS OUI AU DESIGN COMME OUTIL DE MIEUX VIVRE,
DE MIEUX ÊTRE DANS LA VILLE, COMME MOYEN
D'EXPRESSION CULTUREL ET ÉCONOMIQUE À L'ÉCHELLE
DE LA RUE ET DU CITOYEN. ADOPTÉ DANS LE QUOTIDIEN
PAR DE PETITES INTERVENTIONS APPRÉCIÉES ET UTILISÉES
DE TOUS —, CE QUI NE DEVRAIT JAMAIS EMPÊCHER
L'AUDACE, L'INNOVATION, LA MODERNITÉ OU L'HUMOUR.
Sylvie Berkowicz, reporter en design, émission d., MusiquePlus, Montréal

—THE PUBLIC AUTHORITIES HAVE A VERY IMPORTANT RESPONSIBILITY. SUPPORTING PROGRESSIVE ARCHITECTURE AND DESIGN OFTEN INVOLVES TAKING RISKS, BOTH FINANCIALLY AND POLITICALLY— AND EVEN AT TIMES GOING AGAINST POPULAR OPINION TO SERVE FUTURE PURPOSES. PRIVATE ENTERPRISES CANNOT ALWAYS BE COUNTED ON TO TAKE THESE NECESSARY RISKS. POLITICAL LEADERS OFTEN HAVE TO MAKE UNPOPULAR DECISIONS TO COUNTERACT THE NEGATIVE EFFECTS OF PRIVATE ENTERPRISES IN THE DESIGN FIELD.

Claes Britton, editor-in-chief of the magazine *Stockholm New* and CEO of Britton & Britton

— FLÂNER, RENCONTRER QUELQU'UN PAR HASARD OU SE DONNER RENDEZ-VOUS, OBSERVER, COURIR D'UN ENDROIT À L'AUTRE, TRAVERSER L'ESPACE PUBLIC OU S'ARRÊTER : CES ACTIONS DEVRAIENT ÊTRE LE POINT DE DÉPART DE LA COMPOSITION DE L'ESPACE PUBLIC.

Siglinde Spanihel, designer industriel de formation et professeur titulaire à l'Académie des Arts Appliqués, Offenbach, Allemagne

—IT IS CRUCIAL TO INCREASE AWARENESS, AMONGST THE LEADERS OF OUR COMMUNITIES AND BUSINESSES, OF THE BENEFITS OF AND METHODS FOR INTE-GRATING DESIGN INTO CITY PROJECTS. IT IS IMPORTANT TO FACILITATE THOSE LEADERS' UNDER-STANDING OF *HOW* WE SHOULD INTEGRATE GOOD DESIGN PROCESSES AS WELL AS *WHY*.

Amanda Cockroft, design innovation consultant, Glasgow

CONTENTS
SOMMAIRE

LES NOUVELLES VILLES DE DESIGN

MARIE-JOSÉE LACROIX
> **Commissaire au design, Ville de Montréal**

Ce livre est le fruit d'une complicité développée ces dernières années entre Montréal et Saint-Étienne. ✕ Tout a commencé lors de la Biennale Internationale Design de Saint-Étienne 2002 : le Centre de Design de l'Université du Québec à Montréal, sous la direction de Marc Choko, y présentait une exposition du design québécois. J'étais invitée à donner une conférence sur le programme Commerce Design Montréal à la Chambre de Commerce et d'Industrie. De cette double participation montréalaise à la Biennale 2002, et en particulier de notre rencontre avec Josyane Franc, chargée des relations publiques et internationales de l'École des Beaux-arts et de la Biennale de Saint-Étienne, sont nées plusieurs collaborations entre nos villes, fortement soutenues par le Centre Jacques Cartier[1]. Depuis, entre autres, un accord de transfert d'expertise pour la reprise du concept Commerce Design par la Ville de Saint-Étienne a été signé et deux éditions de ce concours réalisées, de même que deux colloques organisés dans le cadre des 16e et 17e Entretiens Jacques Cartier[2]. Le premier atelier, tenu à Saint-Étienne en décembre 2003, explorait les frontières entre l'artisanat et le design. Le second, tenu en octobre 2004 au Centre Canadien d'Architecture, à Montréal, et à l'origine de ce livre, portait sur les nouvelles villes de design.

NOUVELLES VILLES DE DESIGN : LE COLLOQUE

Le design, dans sa définition large et inclusive de toutes les disciplines[3], est une activité d'idéation, création, planification, production et gestion qui façonne la qualité de notre cadre de vie, contribue à la compétitivité de notre économie, participe à l'expression culturelle de notre pays, renforce l'identité de nos régions, de nos villes et de nos entreprises. Partant de ce postulat, le colloque Nouvelles villes de design visait à débattre des différentes stratégies de positionnement et de croissance des villes par le design et à en évaluer les impacts. ✕ Aujourd'hui, à l'heure où la concurrence entre les villes se joue de plus en plus sur la notion de «Quality of Place»[4], où leur attrait est mesuré selon leur potentiel créatif ou indice bohémien[5], où les médias associent design et qualité de vie, où l'on confie aux experts en marque de commerce l'identité des centres urbains[6], devenir une ville, une métropole ou, mieux encore,

THE NEW DESIGN CITIES

MARIE-JOSÉE LACROIX
› **Design Commissioner, City of Montreal**

››

This book is the result of a partnership that has developed in recent years between Montreal and Saint-Étienne. ✕ It all started with the 2002 Biennale Internationale Design de Saint-Étienne, where an exhibition of Quebec design was presented by the Centre de Design of the Université du Québec à Montréal, directed by Marc Choko, and I was invited to give a speech on the Commerce Design Montréal program to Saint-Étienne's chamber of commerce and industry. Out of this twofold participation by Montreal at the 2002 Biennale, and in particular thanks to our meeting with Josyane Franc, public and international relations officer of Saint-Étienne's school of fine arts and biennale, a number of joint projects between our cities were born that were strongly supported by the Centre Jacques Cartier.[1] Among other things, the two cities signed an agreement for transfer of expertise so that Saint-Étienne could adopt the Commerce Design concept, two editions of the competition were produced, and two symposia were organized as part of the 16th and 17th Entretiens Jacques Cartier.[2] The first, held in Saint-Étienne in December 2003, explored the boundaries between craft and design. The second, held in October 2004 at the Canadian Centre for Architecture in Montreal (and the subject of this book), discussed new design cities.

NEW DESIGN CITIES: THE SYMPOSIUM

Design, by definition broad and inclusive of all disciplines,[3] is an activity of ideation, creativity, planning, production, and management that shapes the quality of our living environment, contributes to the competitiveness of our economy, is part of our national cultural expression, and strengthens the identity of our regions, cities, and enterprises. Starting from this hypothesis, the New Design Cities colloquium debated cities' different strategies for positioning and growth through design, and evaluated the impact of these strategies. ✕ Today, competition between cities is increasingly played out through the notion of "Quality of Place:"[4] their attractiveness is measured according to their creative potential or Bohemian Index,[5] the media make an association between design and quality of life, and trade-mark specialists are asked to create an identity for cities.[6] Being designated a design city, design metropolis, or, best of all, design capital provides both a powerful communications tool and a positioning that encourages economic growth. ✕ How can design quality and talented designers contribute to the competitiveness of cities? How can cities encourage design quality by all the actions they take within their borders? How can they stimulate the development of the design sector? What incentives do they have at their disposal to do this? And, more broadly, how can design support the sustainable development of cities? ✕ But also, what is a design metropolis? What does it do? How does a city become one? What makes Barcelona and Milan worthy of the status of design capitals? Is it the quality of their living environment, the visibility for designers, and the abundant design production? Is it the high concentration of reputable design institutions and their internationally renowned major events? To these questions and many others, there are at least as many answers that help to define the polysemous concept of "design city." ✕

une capitale du design offre un puissant levier de communication, mais aussi un positionnement porteur de croissance économique. ✗ Comment la qualité en design et le talent des designers peuvent-ils contribuer à la compétitivité des villes? Comment les villes peuvent-elles favoriser la qualité en design sur l'ensemble des actions portées sur leur territoire? Comment peuvent-elles stimuler l'épanouissement du secteur du design? De quels moyens incitatifs disposent-elles pour le réaliser? Et plus largement, comment le design peut-il soutenir le développement durable des villes? ✗ Mais aussi, qu'est-ce qu'une métropole du design? Comment l'est-on? Comment le devient-on? Pourquoi Barcelone ou Milan sont-elles des capitales du design? Qu'est-ce qui leur confère ce statut : la qualité du cadre de vie; la notoriété des designers et une abondante production en design; une forte concentration d'institutions réputées en design; la renommée et la portée internationales des grands événements qui s'y déroulent? Autant de questions et de réponses possibles pour cerner ce concept polysémique de «villes de design». ✗

Montréal et Saint-Étienne, instigatrices du colloque et de cette publication, ont en commun qu'elles ont mis en place au cours de la dernière décennie, avec l'aide des gouvernements supérieurs, des stratégies municipales volontaristes pour se positionner comme villes de design sur l'échiquier international. Alors que pour certaines, l'heure est au bilan, d'autres sont en phase d'incubation. L'idée de cette première rencontre internationale était motivée par notre envie de mettre en commun ces expériences de même que celles d'autres villes ou territoires, telles qu'Anvers, Glasgow, Lisbonne, Stockholm et Times Square New York, qui se démarquent depuis quelques années sur la scène du design. ✗

Le colloque a été construit autour de la présentation d'études de cas, c'est-à-dire d'actions et d'événements à l'origine de l'émergence de ces sept villes, en tant que villes de design. Ces exemples pragmatiques ont été éclairés par les réflexions de trois éminents théoriciens de la ville contemporaine : François Barré (Paris); Saskia Sassen (Chicago) et John Thackara (Amsterdam et Bangalore). ✗ Ce rendez-vous, qui a réuni plus de 30 conférenciers et quelque 200 participants, a permis de porter un regard critique sur les politiques et programmes menés par ces «nouvelles villes de design», puis d'évaluer l'impact de ces stratégies sur la qualité, l'humanité et l'originalité du cadre de vie, la force d'attrait et de rétention des entreprises, le rayonnement international et le tourisme, la notoriété des designers et la croissance de leurs marchés... ✗ Comme le souligne dans sa synthèse Denis Lemieux, qui agissait à titre de rapporteur lors du colloque (voir p. 22), deux consensus émanent distinctement de cette première rencontre internationale : l'inévitable corrélation entre «ville de design» et «design de ville», et l'importance d'une adhésion partagée du politicien, de l'expert/designer et du citoyen, au projet de ville de design. ✗ Les conclusions du colloque ont fortement influencé la conception de ce livre.

Common to Montreal and Saint-Étienne, the organizers of the collo-quium and producers of this book, is that over the last decade they have instituted, with the help of higher levels of government, deliberate municipal strategies to position themselves as design cities on the international scene. For some, the time has come to take stock, while others are still in an incubation phase. The idea for this first international symposium arose from our desire to pool our common experiences as well as those of other cities or districts that have been outstanding presences on the design scene for a number of years, such as Antwerp, Glasgow, Lisbon, Stockholm, and Times Square New York. ✕

The symposium, bringing together more than thirty speakers and some two hundred attendees, was built around the presentation of case studies—that is, actions and events behind the emergence of these seven cities as design cities. These pragmatic examples were analyzed by three eminent theorists of the contemporary city: François Barré (Paris), Saskia Sassen (Chicago), and John Thackara (Amsterdam and Bangalore). The colloquium also cast a critical eye at the policies and programs undertaken by these "new design cities," then evaluated the impact of their strategies on the quality, humanity, and originality of the living environment, the power to attract and retain businesses, international promotion and tourism, visibility of designers and growth of their markets, and other factors. ✕ As Denis Lemieux, who acted as reporter for the colloquium (see p. 23), emphasizes in his summary, two separate points of consensus emerged from this first international encounter: the inevitable correlation between "design city" and "design of the city," and the importance of a shared sense of membership among politicians, experts/designers, and citizens in the "design city" project. ✕ The conclusions of the colloquium strongly influenced the conception of this book.

NEW DESIGN CITIES: THE BOOK
Antwerp, Glasgow, Lisbon, Montreal, Saint-Étienne, Stockholm, and Times Square New York are the cities and districts discussed in this book. Each one is introduced by a brief description of its history and its main design assets. The papers presented by the experts at the colloquium (design promoters and theorists) are complemented by the points of view of the cities' mayors, well-known or emerging designers, and involved citizens. ✕ Thus, *New Design Cities* is intended not only as a record—the proceedings—of the colloquium, but, above all, as a reflection of the main points of consensus that it generated. The book is also intended as a tool for guidance and a source of inspiration for everyone involved in, or affected by, urban development: municipal elected officials and managers responsible for improvements, cultural development, economic growth, and design-promotion programs; experts in international and tourist-promotion marketing; designers of all disciplines; teachers and researchers; and, of course, urban tourists and city residents. ✕ *New Design Cities* confirms the status of these young design metropolises and constitutes a second step, after the symposium, in the formation of a synergy and visibility network, which future design cities are invited to join. ✕ Our thanks go to all who worked on this book for their enthusiastic collaboration.

NOUVELLES VILLES DE DESIGN : LE LIVRE

Anvers, Glasgow, Lisbonne, Montréal, Saint-Étienne, Stockholm et Times Square New York sont au cœur de cet ouvrage. Les caractéristiques historiques et principaux actifs en design ouvrent la présentation de chaque ville/territoire. Les textes des experts réunis en colloque (diffuseurs et théoriciens du design) sont par ailleurs complétés, dans le but d'enrichir les portraits de ville, par des points de vue recueillis auprès des maires, designers réputés ou émergeants et citoyens engagés des villes ciblées. Ce faisant, Nouvelles villes de design se veut un témoignage — les actes — du colloque, mais plus encore, le reflet des principaux consensus qui s'en dégagent. ✕ Au-delà de la trace, le livre se veut aussi un outil de réflexion et une source d'inspiration pour tous les acteurs du développement urbain : élus et responsables municipaux de l'aménagement, du développement culturel, de la croissance économique et des politiques d'achat; urbanistes; gestionnaires de politiques et programmes de promotion du design; experts en marketing international et promotion touristique; designers de toutes les disciplines; enseignants et chercheurs; et, bien sûr, touristes urbains et citadins. ✕ Cette publication confirme le statut de ces jeunes métropoles de design et constitue une deuxième étape, après le colloque, dans la mise en place d'un réseau de synergie et de notoriété, auxquelles de futures villes de design sont invitées à se joindre. ✕ Merci à tous les artisans de cet ouvrage pour leur enthousiaste collaboration.

〉〉〉

1. Le Centre Jacques Cartier est un centre d'études, d'échanges et de recherche situé à Lyon (France). Créé en 1984, il a pour vocation l'établissement et le développement de partenariats scientifiques et culturels entre la région Rhône-Alpes et le Québec, et plus largement, entre la France, le Canada et le monde. ✕ 2. Depuis 1987, le Centre organise annuellement les Entretiens Jacques Cartier, un événement international de très haut niveau, regroupant un ensemble de colloques et séminaires, qui, selon les années, se déroulent en Rhône-Alpes ou au Québec. ✕ 3. Dans le cadre de cette publication, le design est défini dans son sens large, incluant toutes les disciplines de la création qui confectionnent et ont le pouvoir de qualifier, d'enrichir notre cadre de vie : architecture de paysage, design urbain, architecture, design d'intérieur, design industriel, design graphique. ✕ 4. Florida, Richard (2002) *The Rise of The Creative Class*, New York : Basic Books. ✕ 5. *op.cit.* ✕ 6. Julier, Guy (2005) Urban Designscapes and the Production of Aesthetic Consent, *Urban Studies*, 42(5/6), pp. 869-887

〉〉〉

〉〉〉

1. The Centre Jacques Cartier, in Lyon, France, is an institute for study, exchange, and research. Created in 1984, it has the mission of establishing and developing academic and cultural partnerships between the Rhône-Alpes region and Quebec and, more generally, among France, Canada, and the world. ✕ 2. Since 1987, the Centre has annually organized the Entretiens Jacques Cartier, a high-level international event featuring a series of colloquia and seminars. The location of the event alternates between the Rhône-Alpes region and Quebec. ✕ 3. For the purpose of this publication, design is defined to include all creative disciplines that have the power to provide quality and enhancement to our living environment: landscape architecture, urban design, architecture, interior design, industrial design, graphic design. ✕ 4. Richard Florida, *The Rise of The Creative Class* (New York: Basic Books, 2002). ✕ 5. *Ibid.* ✕ 6. Guy Julier, "Urban Designscapes and the Production of Aesthetic Consent," *Urban Studies*, Vol. 42, No. 5/6 (2005): 869–87.

〉〉〉

—TO ME THE THING THAT WAS MOST STRIKING AT THE CONFERENCE IS THE EXTENT TO WHICH DESIGN HAS BECOME PART OF BIENNALE CULTURE. I HAD ALREADY BEGUN NOTICING THAT THE NUMBER OF ART BIENNALES AROUND THE WORLD HAS GROWN EXPONENTIALLY IN RECENT YEARS. A GREAT MANY CITIES AND MUSEUMS, LARGE AND SMALL, BELIEVE THAT AN ART BIENNALE WILL PUT THEM ON THE CULTURAL MAP. BUT THE PRESENTATIONS OF THE REPRESENTATIVES OF LISBON AND SAINT-ETIENNE MADE ME REALIZE THAT, ALONG WITH BETTER ESTABLISHED DESIGN BIENNALES (ARCHITECTURE IN VENICE, GRAPHICS IN BRNO), THERE IS A WIDESPREAD MOVEMENT TO BUILD MAJOR CULTURAL FESTIVALS AROUND THE DESIGN DISCIPLINES.

Karrie Jacobs, journalist, New York

— UNE VILLE DE DESIGN N'EST PAS UNE «VILLE À THÈME». QUALIFIÉE AINSI, ELLE SERAIT ANALOGUE À UN PARC D'ATTRACTIONS, TEL UN «CABINET DE CURIOSITÉS» DU XVIIIᵉ SIÈCLE... UNE VÉRITABLE «VILLE DE DESIGN» EST UNE VILLE PRÉOCCUPÉE PAR SON BIEN-ÊTRE, UNE VILLE QUI CONSTRUIT ACTIVEMENT SON IDENTITÉ, SON ÂME ET SON CADRE DE VIE. MAIS PLUS QUE CELA, C'EST UNE VILLE DONT LE DESSEIN EST LE PROJET PLURIEL.

Philippe Poullaouec-Gonidec, titulaire de la Chaire UNESCO en paysage et environnement, à l'Université de Montréal

NOUVELLES VILLES DE DESIGN
— SYNTHÈSE ET CONSENSUS DU COLLOQUE
PAR DENIS LEMIEUX

› Architecte, Direction des politiques et de la propriété intellectuelle,
  ministère de la Culture et de Communications du Québec

De diverses manières, les conférenciers ont parlé du projet de (re)faire la ville ou de revenir à une «culture du projet», comme le mentionnait François Barré («réapprenons le projet d'habiter la ville… réapprenons la relation et le lien.»). Mais que veut dire (re)faire la ville et quelle est la valeur du design dans ce projet? ✘ Faire la ville, c'est la comprendre, la concevoir, la construire et la communiquer : quatre actions aussi importantes l'une que l'autre, caractérisées par un processus continu d'échanges et d'interactions. ✘ Lors du colloque, les discussions ont davantage porté sur le concevoir et le communiquer, sans doute les deux fonctions où des améliorations doivent être apportées afin de mieux faire la ville. ✘ Ainsi, concernant le concevoir, certains ont dit que la ville devait devenir un laboratoire d'expérimentation, de création et d'innovation, puis privilégier l'utilisation de processus favorisant le dialogue et la participation «publique». Plusieurs exemples ont été donnés : les ateliers professionnels, les appels d'offres «stylistiques», les concours servant à sélectionner le projet à construire, les concours visant à valoriser le projet construit, etc. ✘ Concernant le communiquer, les exemples ont démontré que l'acte de « communiquer » devait être à la base du processus de faire la ville, en lien étroit avec l'acte de «concevoir». On a aussi dit que l'événement (biennale, exposition, etc.) était une composante essentielle de la vie urbaine, mais un événement qui doit être au service du projet (de faire la ville), comme à Saint-Étienne, Lisbonne et Glasgow. ✘ Mieux encore, on a parlé du projet qui devient événement, à l'instar d'Emscher Park en Allemagne (IBA — Exposition internationale d'architecture 1989-1999), illustration parfaite de l'intégration entre le comprendre, le concevoir, le construire et le communiquer. ✘ Dans le projet de faire la ville, plusieurs ont fait état des rôles du politicien, du designer et du citoyen, alors que d'autres parlaient de maître d'ouvrage, maître d'œuvre et maître d'usage. Mais, selon certains, il manque un lien essentiel dans cette relation triangulaire : le rôle joué par le «maître de design» (Dorian Van der Brempt), agent de liaison, accompagnateur, facilitateur et animateur de cette «bottom up platform for social innovation» que mentionnait John Thackara. ✘ En ce sens, le colloque était une illustration intéressante du rôle essentiel joué par les maîtres de design (François Barré, Guta Moura Guedes, Marie-Josée Lacroix, Tim Tompkins, etc.). Cependant, il ne faudrait pas que la compréhension du rôle joué par ces intervenants reste en vase clos car, actuellement, sa valeur est inconnue du citoyen, méconnue du politicien et, parfois même, injustement reconnue par le designer.

NEW DESIGN CITIES—ANALYSIS AND CONSENSUS OF THE SYMPOSIUM

DENIS LEMIEUX

› **Architect**
› **Direction des politiques et de la propriété intellectuelle, ministère de la Culture et de Communications du Québec**

〉〉

In various ways, the speakers discussed projects to (re)shape the city or return to a "project culture," as François Barré mentioned it ("Let us learn again the project of living in the city… let us learn again the relationship and the connection"). But what does it mean to (re)shape the city, and where does the value of design fit in with such projects? ✗ To shape the city is to comprehend, conceive, construct, and communicate it: four equally important activities, characterized by a continuous process of exchange and interaction. ✗ During the colloquium, the discussions focused on the aspects of conception and communication aspects as functions within which improvements must be made in order to better shape the city. ✗ With regard to conception, some opined that the city should first be a laboratory for experimentation, creativity, and innovation, then become an advocate for processes favouring dialogue and "public" participation. A number of examples were given: workshop for professionals, calls for "style-based" bids, design competitions for projects to be built, competitions aimed at highlighting the built project, and so on. ✗ With regard to communication, the examples given at the colloquium showed that the act of "communicating" should be at the core of the process of shaping the city, in close collaboration with the act of "conception." It was also mentioned that events (biennale, exhibition, etc.) are an essential component of urban life, but that they must advance the project (of shaping the city), as is done in Saint-Étienne, Lisbon, and Glasgow. ✗ Projects that become events, such as Emscher Park in Germany (IBA— International building exhibition, 1989–99), were discussed as a perfect illustration of the integration between understanding, conception, construction, and communication. ✗ In the project of shaping the city, a number of people noted the roles of the politician, the designer, and the citizen, while others used terms such as the master owner, the master contractor, and the master user. But, according to some, there is an essential link missing in these triangular relationships: the role played by the "master designer" (Dorian van der Brempt), the liaison agent, guide, facilitator, and host of what John Thackara termed a "bottom-up platform for social innovation." ✗ In this sense, the colloquium provided an interesting illustration of the essential role played by the "master designers" (François Barré, Guta Moura Guedes, Marie-Josée Lacroix, Tim Tompkins, etc.). The role played by these actors must not remain hidden; currently, its value is unknown to citizens, little known to politicians, and sometimes not well recognized even by designers.

〉〉

ANT
WER
PEN

F

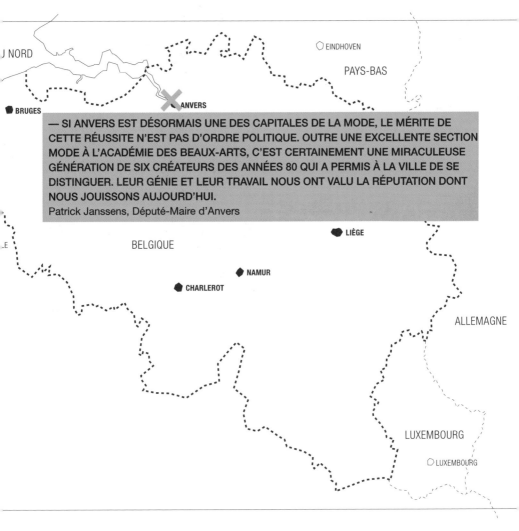

U NORD

○ EINDHOVEN

PAYS-BAS

● BRUGES

ANVERS

— SI ANVERS EST DÉSORMAIS UNE DES CAPITALES DE LA MODE, LE MÉRITE DE
CETTE RÉUSSITE N'EST PAS D'ORDRE POLITIQUE. OUTRE UNE EXCELLENTE SECTION
MODE À L'ACADÉMIE DES BEAUX-ARTS, C'EST CERTAINEMENT UNE MIRACULEUSE
GÉNÉRATION DE SIX CRÉATEURS DES ANNÉES 80 QUI A PERMIS À LA VILLE DE SE
DISTINGUER. LEUR GÉNIE ET LEUR TRAVAIL NOUS ONT VALU LA RÉPUTATION DONT
NOUS JOUISSONS AUJOURD'HUI.
Patrick Janssens, Député-Maire d'Anvers

● LIÈGE

LE

BELGIQUE

◆ NAMUR

● CHARLEROT

ALLEMAGNE

LUXEMBOURG

○ LUXEMBOURG

POR-
TRAIT

〉〉

POPULATION

Anvers compte 500 000 habitants qui se
mêlent au presque million d'habitants dans
ce que l'on appelle le «Grand Anvers».

〉〉

〉〉〉

HISTORIQUE DES
ÉVÉNEMENTS FONDATEURS

La ville a été créée à l'époque romaine, mais ce n'est qu'à la fin du XIIe siècle qu'elle sera protégée par une muraille. Au XVIe siècle, Anvers est une ville importante. Son port et sa situation stratégique lui donnent une importance économique évidente. ✕ Anvers a toujours été une ville de commerce. Son port, à 80 kilomètres de la mer du Nord, est capital pour sa croissance économique. Au XVIe siècle, Anvers est l'un des centres financiers et économiques de l'Europe. L'importation de textiles anglais, le négoce de produits métalliques allemands et d'épices du Portugal composent les bases des activités portuaires. Aujourd'hui, le port d'Anvers est l'un des trois plus importants ports de container au monde. L'imprimeur Plantin, dont le musée, son hôtel particulier, peut toujours être visité, est un acteur principal pour la diffusion des idées. Le Congo belge sera à l'origine d'échanges commerciaux fructueux : coton, café, bois et caoutchouc sont les nouveaux produits exportés par la colonie. La pétrochimie, la chimie et le diamant constituent les secteurs industriels de l'essor belge du XXe siècle. La création, particulièrement la mode, est le dernier secteur qu'Anvers a développé à notre époque.

✕ L'histoire d'Anvers est celle d'une ville qui doit sa richesse à son port. Ses activités commerciales se sont toujours combinées à une effervescence culturelle dont Rubens, Jordaens et Van Dyck sont les ambassadeurs. Anvers a depuis la réputation d'être une ville de plaisir, qui aime la fête. ✕ Les Espagnols pillent Anvers en 1576. Anvers se rend, et l'Escaut, son fleuve, est fermé. Puis, Napoléon découvre les valeurs stratégiques de la ville et en fait un port de guerre. En 1920, Anvers accueillera les VIIe Jeux Olympiques modernes. Quelques années plus tard, une exposition universelle exprime l'espoir. En 1945, plus d'un million de Juifs Européens prennent le bateau au port d'Anvers à destination de l'Amérique du Nord.

〉〉〉

DESIGNERS RÉPUTÉS

On trouve quelques designers importants. Le premier était Rubens, pas seulement peintre baroque, mais en même temps conseiller et décorateur des rois. La réputation actuelle d'Anvers est surtout liée à la mode. Dries Van Noten, Ann De Meulemeester, Walter Van Beirendonck, Véronique Branquino, Raf Simons, etc. sont devenus des ambassadeurs de la ville. Un personnage Anversois de marque est Axel Vervoort maître du bon goût en décoration intérieure, l'antiquaire qui amuse et qui habille.

NOMBRE DE DESIGNERS

La création mode, grâce à l'excellente Académie de la Mode, regroupe une centaine de créatifs et un nombre 10 fois plus important de fournisseurs. L'École de design industriel jouit d'une solide réputation. ✕ Plusieurs cabinets d'architecture sont installés à Anvers. Ce monde de créateurs représente de 1200 à 1500 personnes.

PRINCIPAUX ÉVÉNEMENTS EN DESIGN

Anvers ne réalise pas à proprement parler d'initiatives répétitives et concertées de design. Il y a en septembre un «Laundry Day», où les boutiques de la Kammenstraat (Quartier mode design) occupent la rue. Dans notre histoire récente, il y a eu des «Week-end du Design». Toutefois, ils n'ont pas connu le succès attendu. ✕ Ce n'est probablement pas un phénomène seulement anversois, mais la majorité des manifestations restent des initiatives privées qui ne relèvent pas d'une politique à long terme et qui ne partagent pas de réel dénominateur commun. Avec l'esprit de concurrence et la méfiance naturelle des designers flamands, la vie du design est moins animée par une dynamique de groupe qu'une rencontre informelle et sans schéma précis. La guérilla du design, le hasard et la nécessité de chaque initiative ne se laissent pas gérer facilement. ✕ Événements récents qui se répéteront peut-être : Open Ateliers (septembre), Vitrine (septembre), Vizo Ladders Zat (été), Laundry Day (automne).

〉〉

ÉCOLES ET PROGRAMMES DE DESIGN

Maîtrise en gestion axée sur l'industrie culturelle et la mode. Ce programme est organisé par l'Institut de Gestion de l'Université d'Anvers (Universiteit Antwerpen Management School). C'est un nouveau programme — lancement octobre 2006 — qui vise à former les gestionnaires de la mode et du design. Le secteur de la mode est à l'origine de cette initiative parce qu'«Anvers ville de la Mode» est plus représentative et plus spectaculaire en ce jour qu'«Anvers Ville de Design». ✕ L'Académie de la Mode, est une section importante d'une école supérieure que nous ne qualifions pas d'universitaire. Cette qualification a engagé une longue discussion sémantique et émotionnelle. Au sein de cette Haute École (Hogeschool), il y a plusieurs programmes regroupés sous le chapitre des «Sciences de la Création» (Ontwerpwetenschappen). On y trouve des formations (niveau bachelier) en mode, architecture, design industriel, design graphique.

Sites de références
〉 Académie de la Mode
www.academieantwerpen.ha.be/modeontwerpen
〉 Institut de Gestion de l'Université d'Anvers
www.uams.be
〉 École de design industriel
www.ontwerpwetenschappen.ha.be/modeontwerpen

〉〉

INSTITUTIONS

Le MOMU est un excellent musée de la mode, il offre chaque année différentes expositions à thème. Son atelier de restauration et sa bibliothèque spécialisée en mode sont exceptionnels. Le Flanders Fashion Institute cohabite avec le MOMU et l'Académie de la Mode. ✕ Le Musée du Diamant permet aux créateurs de bijoux de montrer leur savoir-faire. ✕ Betet Skara est un atelier de création et de tissage qui renoue avec le savoir-faire assyrien. Cette initiative est soutenue par un programme socioéconomique.

Sites de références
〉 MOMU
www.momu.be
〉 Flanders Fashion Institute
www.ffi.be
〉 Le Musée du Diamant
www.diamantmuseum.be
〉 Betet Skara
www.betetskara.com

〉〉

STRATÉGIES DESIGN

Il n'y a pas de stratégie de design précise. La province d'Anvers est probablement l'acteur principal du design. Le MOMU, le Musée de l'Argenterie (Kasteel Rivierenhof) et le Musée du Diamant prennent des initiatives locales. La Ville d'Anvers est très active dans la communication.

〉〉

Portrait d'Anvers
Renseignements colligés par
DORIAN VAN DER BREMPT
〉 Professeur, Design Academy de Eindhoven

PATRICK JANSSENS

**DÉPUTÉ-MAIRE D'ANVERS
DEPUIS 2003**

Gérald Tremblay, Maire de Montréal
Michel Thiollière, Sénateur-Maire de Saint-Étienne

Anvers le 13 mars 2005,

Messieurs,
J'ai appris avec plaisir l'intérêt que vous avez pu exprimer pour la ville d'Anvers et je vous en remercie. Je suis heureux de participer au débat que vous avez organisé et qui nous a permis de rencontrer des interlocuteurs de qualité, comme les intervenants à Montréal, New York, Lisbonne, Saint-Étienne et Glasgow. ✕ Anvers est une ville qui a toujours accueilli des créateurs et qui a souvent été le berceau d'initiatives innovantes aussi bien politiques que culturelles. Le port d'Anvers est probablement la métaphore de générosité et de tolérance d'une ville dont les habitants sont connus pour leur personnalité particulière («*Envers soi et contre tous*»). Peut-être ce trait de caractère est-il issu de l'époque espagnole dont nous avons hérité le titre de «Sinjoren» (Seigneurs)? ✕ Aujourd'hui, Anvers est une ville de taille moyenne où cohabitent 140 nationalités. Entre nouveaux venus, nouveau-nés et moins jeunes, je gère et j'organise ce bouillon de cultures. ✕ Les arts plastiques, le théâtre et la littérature ont toujours habité Anvers. Comme toute ville à succès, Anvers a toujours été aimée, détestée et intensément visitée. On pourrait paraphraser Sacha Guitry quand il parlait des femmes, et dire qu'il y beaucoup de monde contre Anvers, tout contre. ✕ Si Anvers est désormais une des capitales de la mode, le mérite de cette réussite n'est pas d'ordre politique. Outre une excellente section mode à l'Académie des Beaux-Arts, c'est certainement une miraculeuse génération de six créateurs des années 80 qui a permis à la ville de se distinguer. Leur génie et leur travail nous ont valu la réputation dont nous jouissons aujourd'hui. ✕ Une initiative importante de la Ville a été la création du Centre de Design Winkelhaak (L'équerre). Nous y offrons un premier studio à loyer modéré aux jeunes diplômés des écoles de design industriel ou graphique. ✕ La mise à disposition d'espaces de travail, d'expositions et de présentations est très importante pour les jeunes créateurs et pour la ville. Le mètre carré dans nos villes n'est presque plus abordable. Il est essentiel que nous intervenions afin de garder cette présence artistique, symbole d'une ville qui crée. ✕ Anvers a une activité culturelle impressionnante. Capitale culturelle de la Flandre, elle fut nommée capitale mondiale du livre par l'UNESCO en 2004, titre qui a d'ailleurs été décerné l'année suivante à Montréal! Anvers jouit par ailleurs de réels atouts touristiques. Les musées et galeries, les arts de la scène, la mode et ses boutiques et la gastronomie qui réunit tout le monde offrent l'embarras du choix et de la qualité. ✕ Anvers, ville de design est un titre dont je suis fier. La ville le mérite, car elle s'est réalisée selon l'éventail éclectique des talents présents, comme autant de strates qui recouvrent le mot «design». Anvers offre plusieurs lectures, d'où l'intérêt de la découvrir progressivement, sous un angle, puis un autre pour enfin la saisir dans sa globalité. ✕ À dire vrai, Anvers n'a pas de politique de design précise. De bonnes écoles ont formé de bons designers. La ville essaie de communiquer avec tous ses citoyens. C'est une entreprise dans laquelle les designers jouent et joueront leur rôle. ✕ Je vous invite toutes et tous à visiter Anvers, la ville qui a l'ambition de toujours vous étonner, de vous raconter à chaque visite une nouvelle histoire.
Bien à vous

››

– LE DESIGN A LA QUALITÉ TRÈS PARTICULIÈRE D'INSPIRER DES INDIVIDUS DE CULTURES DIFFÉRENTES À SE RETROUVER, À SE MÉLANGER SANS SE PERDRE LES UNS DANS LES AUTRES. LE DESIGN, C'EST AUSSI LE RESPECT ET LE CULTE DE LA DIFFÉRENCE, LA CÉLÉBRATION DU MERVEILLEUX ÉTRANGER.

Dorian Van Der Brempt, Professeur, Design Academie de Eindhoven, Pays Bas

01

ANVERS, NOUVELLE VILLE DE DESIGN?

PAR DORIAN VAN DER BREMPT
> **Professeur, Design Academy de Eindhoven, Pays Bas**

〉〉

Anvers est une ville à la mode et une ville de la mode. *Newsweek*, dans un article paru en 2004, en parlait comme l'une des 10 villes influentes dans le domaine culturel. Disons plutôt, une des 10 villes surprenantes du moment. Je ne sais pas exactement ce que signifie l'expression «ville de design». Si ce colloque parle de «nouvelles villes de design» en opposition à «anciennes villes de design», ces dernières devraient pouvoir s'inscrire dans l'histoire et y occuper une place toute particulière. ✕ J'ai donc suivi la piste historique et me suis posé la question suivante : À quoi pourrait correspondre une ancienne ville de design? Une courte balade dans l'histoire de l'Europe me fait découvrir ce que j'oserais appeler les premières villes de design. Les villes andalouses des XIVe et XVe siècles, au-delà de leur grand âge, sont des villes de design dans l'acceptation moderne du terme. ✕ La qualité de la vie à Toledo, Cordoba et Granada était à l'époque d'un extrême raffinement et d'une sensualité fort développée. Le choix et l'usage de matériaux ainsi que de techniques de construction, afin de créer des courants d'air frais et d'eau fraîche, dans une région aux étés tropicaux, relevaient de la plus haute technologie esthétique et hédoniste. L'architecture et le design des objets de la vie domestique andalouse combinaient des éléments orientaux et occidentaux, juxtaposant esthétique musulmane et imagerie chrétienne. Cette architecture et ce design sont probablement à l'origine des premières communautés multiculturelles. Multiculturelles non pas dans le sens d'une assimilation, mais dans un respect des valeurs et normes de chacun. Longtemps avant l'Andalousie, la Mésopotamie était également un bouillon de culture, ce qui place la barbarie actuelle dans une perspective encore plus triste. Anvers est aujourd'hui une ville où plus de 120 nationalités cohabitent. Cette rencontre entre cultures, religions et coutumes n'est pas toujours facile, mais c'est un défi permanent. ⨯ La différence capitale entre l'Andalousie des XIVe et XVe siècles et, par exemple, les États-Unis d'aujourd'hui tient dans ce constat : les conseillers des rois andalous étaient jadis des poètes, des artistes et des savants qui ont été remplacés, aux côtés de George Bush, par des commerçants qui ne comprennent plus et ne reconnaissent plus l'intérêt général. Et voilà une première définition ou direction : une ville de design était et sera une ville où l'intérêt général occupe une valeur égale ou supérieure aux intérêts particuliers. ⨯ Le design peut être compris comme une certaine sensibilité appliquée au contenant et au contenu des choses. Un mobilier public bien conçu est une invitation à la rencontre et au dialogue. Le design peut avoir une dimension politique. Il y a des exemples classiques dans la politique de notre époque. John F. Kennedy et François Mitterrand sont deux présidents précurseurs qui se sont fait remarquer pour avoir été conseillés par des designers. Le premier par Raymond Loewy et le second par Philippe Starck. ⨯ Mon pays, la Flandre, est un pays où l'on peut trouver des villes qui correspondent à l'idée de «vieilles villes de design». Bruges, Gand, Anvers sont des villes qui, du XIVe siècle au XIXe, étaient des villes de design avant même que l'expression soit définie comme elle l'est aujourd'hui. ⨯ Rubens n'était pas seulement peintre et diplomate, il était aussi le maître de la cérémonie commerciale et de la vie élégante. À ce titre, il décorait les palais des rois, des nobles et des commerçants richissimes qui se préparaient déjà à prendre leur place. Dans la ville actuelle d'Anvers, le souvenir et la tradition se mêlent et inspirent la créativité contemporaine. La cathédrale Notre-Dame d'Anvers reçoit 300 000 visiteurs par an pour voir entre autres *La Descente de la Croix*. ⨯ Désormais, Axel Vervoort, maître décorateur et antiquaire, qui habille les maisons des princes et des princesses ainsi que celles de musiciens pop anglais qui s'installent en Toscane, Jan Fabre, artiste plasticien et homme de théâtre, et Dries Van Noten, couturier célèbre, sont les nouveaux châtelains d'Anvers. ⨯ Pour preuve, ces trois créateurs ont acquis des châteaux afin d'y vivre. Quand la noblesse perd sa fortune, les créateurs *prédateurs* prennent leur place. C'est probablement la première fois dans l'histoire de l'humanité

que certains artistes, créateurs, et ceux que j'appelle les grands amuseurs (sportifs, musiciens pop, acteurs de cinéma), profitent de récompenses extrêmes que le système capitaliste a développées. La créativité, ou une certaine créativité, n'a jamais payé comme elle paie en 2004. Si l'artiste ex-saltimbanque faisait dessiner hier la porcelaine de son jet privé, cette logique rejoint celle pratiquée au Québec. Le Cirque du Soleil prouve que le design est également un des vecteurs de l'exportation des villes. ⨯ Les explosions commerciales de certaines formes d'innovation ne sont pas sans risques, bien entendu. Oscar Wilde nous avait prévenus que viendrait le jour où nous connaîtrions les prix sans connaître la valeur. Le prix est la limite de la valeur. Parler de design, c'est parler de valeur et non de prix. Le magasinage design est l'un des atouts touristiques majeurs. Les boutiques modes autour du MOMU, le Musée de la Mode, valent le déplacement. La librairie spécialisée Copyright, qui y est installée, offre un choix exceptionnel.

〉〉

Pour parler de cette valeur appelée design, j'aimerais proposer l'idée suivante : Le design est un acte politique. La ville design est aujourd'hui une ville qui se soigne, qui se conserve bien. Elle fait du sport, se lave, se parfume délicatement et s'habille comme il faut avec le charme discret de la bourgeoise. C'est une ville qui aime recevoir et qui a une réputation de générosité bien organisée. La ville design invite, aime être entourée. Conditionner la ville, l'équiper afin qu'elle soit à la fois belle et pratique, agréable et sécurisante, sympathique et décidée sont des décisions politiques et des décisions de politique de design. L'espace public, les transports en commun, l'offre culturelle, les services d'éducation et de soins (et la communication entre toutes ces bonnes choses et les habitants) sont les domaines où une bonne et juste dose de design peut faire la différence. Aux femmes et aux hommes politiques de le comprendre. À nous de leur expliquer qu'un mauvais choix de luminaire s'avère aussi coûteux qu'un bon. Qu'un mobilier urbain bien pensé et bien fabriqué n'est pas plus cher que la variante banale. Le secteur public, du local au national, est le plus grand consommateur de biens et de services. Il va de soi qu'une discipline et qu'une méthodologie efficace de commandes publiques constituent une garantie pour améliorer la qualité de notre biotope humain, trop souvent urbain. ⨯ C'est pour cela que nous avons suggéré prudemment d'envisager la création d'un maître de design dans l'administration de la ville. Aujourd'hui, tout le monde comprend qu'une ville a droit à une administration qui se concentre sur l'architecture et l'urbanisme, mais peu de politiciens considèrent la création et le développement de produits comme suffisamment importants. Pour achever la création du grand frère Architecture, il faut que la petite sœur Design puisse se manifester et être influente. ⨯ Si «ville de design» est synonyme de «ville de qualité», il est évident que d'ici quelques années, nous verrons une nouvelle formation universitaire qui produira des «maîtres en design public». C'est avec une formation classique combinée de sciences sociales que le designer contribuera à la création de produits et services qui ont l'ambition de servir l'intérêt général de la ville autant que l'intérêt particulier de l'utilisateur. Par boutade, je dirais que le designer public soigne les utilisateurs quand le designer privé s'occupe des consommateurs.

Le design est la rencontre du bon goût et du bon sens. UNE INTERVENTION DE DESIGN DEVRAIT ÊTRE «NORMALE». IL NE S'AGIT PAS D'UNE RECHERCHE SOPHISTIQUÉE POUR SE FAIRE REMARQUER À TOUT PRIX. LES BONNES INTERVENTIONS DE DESIGN SONT SOUVENT DISCRÈTES. Le choix intelligent de matériaux est aussi important que celui des formes. Un excès est permis de temps en temps. Lorsque le baron Empain, en 1935, importe des châssis de fenêtre en acier de Belgique pour construire le premier centre de magasinage à Sainte-Marguerite du lac Masson, vous pouvez imaginer que c'est là une histoire belge. Mais c'est avant tout une intervention de design. Certes, elle est un peu plus de «bon goût» que de «bon sens». Mais dans l'élan de cette famille d'entrepreneurs parfois farfelus et de décideurs dignes de ce nom, une certaine dose de folle imagination est permise. N'oublions pas que Louis Empain était aussi l'inventeur d'un certain tourisme de neige. ⨯ C'est grâce à la mode, grâce à l'Académie d'Anvers, que notre ville est aujourd'hui perçue comme une ville de design. Est-ce le hasard qui voulait que six jeunes créateurs, il y a 20 ans, tous étudiants en dernière année de mode, combinent toutes les qualités requises? Ils étaient très travailleurs, extrêmement ambitieux et très différents les uns des autres. Chacun avait une excellente dose de pragmatisme et du flair. De plus, les décideurs politiques étaient conscients de leur existence et créaient un peu plus tard le Flandres Fashion Institute. ⨯ Installé dans le MOMU, c'est l'institut qui combine culturel et commercial. La mode est l'un des secteurs de la créativité les plus volages. Deux fois par an, la distribution attend les créateurs pour leur offrir ces quelques instants de jugement qui décideront du semestre ou de l'année à venir. Cette tension intense, cette obligation de succès pour survivre est l'un des fils rouges de cette industrie culturelle. ⨯ Je vous raconte cela comme un incident ou un effet du hasard, car je suis convaincu que le hasard est tout aussi présent que la nécessité. Je crois que l'on peut stimuler, encourager et faciliter la création ou le design, mais le premier signal doit venir des créateurs. Ce sont eux qui doivent s'imposer, qui doivent convaincre les mondes politique, financier et commercial qu'une occasion se présente. Dries Van Noten est probablement le créateur de mode le plus remarquable de sa génération. Il continue la tradition familiale en y ajoutant une nouvelle dimension. La reconnaissance internationale de Van Noten et d'autres a donné à Anvers une nouvelle réputation de ville de design.

Le design est parfois l'expression culturelle du nouveau riche, le faux code du bourgeois avant-gardiste. Il y a 15 ans, un petit théâtre new-yorkais avait transformé le *Bourgeois Gentilhomme* de Molière en obsédé d'avant-garde. Il ne s'entourait que d'objets dits de design, visitait les expositions d'art conceptuel qu'il n'aimait pas et vivait dans une maison qui ne faisait plaisir qu'à l'architecte et aux décorateurs qui avaient conseillé notre pauvre bourgeois. J'ai vu à Houston des immeubles bien dessinés à la silhouette élégante. Béton, acier et verre se filaient en dentelle à l'horizon. Mais ces perles d'architecture étaient occupées par des messieurs qui portaient des bottes et des chapeaux qui nous incitaient à chercher l'endroit où ils avaient bien pu parquer leur cheval. Au 26e étage, les bureaux étaient équipés de fausses cheminées qui offraient un faux feu de bois. Quand le design triche, le résultat est triste. Le design est une méthode et une vitamine, ce n'est pas un antibiotique. Il en faut de petites doses régulières et permanentes. Une intervention rapide restera superficielle.

Le design va au-delà de l'identité. Il donne aux femmes et aux hommes de demain une dimension cosmopolite. Dans un monde globalisant, il va de soi qu'il y a des influences globales. Le goût n'est pas international, mais global. Cela veut dire que de nouvelles communautés se forment. L'appartenance à ces communautés signifie partager un même intérêt ou un goût particulier. Ainsi, 100 000 adeptes d'une musique, d'une expression plastique ou d'un texte ne vivent plus nécessairement dans une même ville ou un même pays. La communication nouvelle permet de partager une intimité du goût à distance. Je parle de ces communautés, car nous ne pouvons pas oublier que ceux qui participent activement à la fête du design composent un nombre limité de privilégiés. ✕ Le design est aussi un langage qui dépasse celui des mots. C'est un moyen de communication et un vecteur d'échanges. Grâce à leurs propres magazines et à leur communication électronique, des Japonais fous de mode et très informés débarquent à Anvers et trouvent le quartier de la mode dont ils avaient d'ailleurs une parfaite image avant de venir. Le design a la qualité très particulière d'inspirer des individus de cultures différentes à se retrouver, à se mélanger sans se perdre les uns dans les autres. Le design, c'est aussi le respect et le culte de la différence, la célébration du merveilleux étranger. ✕ Je ne serai jamais cynique parce que la vie ne me le permet pas, mais aujourd'hui, le plus grand parti politique qui oblige tous les autres à former une coalition de force, est hélas une formation d'extrême droite. Dans ma bonne «nouvelle ville de design», un Anversois sur trois a voté pour une formation qui prêche des valeurs qui ne sont pas les miennes, qui ne sont pas les nôtres. Je n'ai pas de réponse précise à cette question qui hante. Je cherche la réplique. Je me demande comment je peux récupérer les déçus, les fous et les furieux. ✕ Parce que le vrai défi, c'est celui-là. Comment transformer les «nouvelles villes de design» en «nouvelles villes» tout court. Le design doit être une méthode, un mode et un parcours, mais jamais un but. L'art pour l'art ne peut être suivi aujourd'hui par la variante postmoderne : «le design pour le design». ✕ Le designer transforme le monde, change la ville. C'est une belle démarche de sensibilité, car elle a pour seule ambition d'augmenter la qualité de la vie. Mais si l'intention peut être ambitieuse, le designer et le politicien qui l'accompagnent ne pourront parler de triomphe ni même de succès si la majorité des citadins des villes de design ne peuvent participer à cette transformation, à cette belle fête du bon goût et du bon sens. ✕ Anvers vaut le détour. C'est un demi-chauvin qui vous le dit. Je suis un Anversois content et comblé car je me rends compte que je suis gâté. Je n'ai pas encore rencontré une ville aussi facile et agréable à vivre, qui a tant à offrir. Aussi bien l'art contemporain que l'art ancien sont représentés dans les musées et la galeries. Les arts de la scène, résultats d'une excellente politique flamande, nous invitent aux meilleures productions de danse et de théâtre. ✕ Anvers est une ville pour jouisseurs. Il faut la visiter pour comprendre.

〉〉〉

01 Graffiti, la rue comme impression et comme expression

〉〉

AXEL ENTHOVEN
〉 Designer industriel
〉 Président d'Enthoven Associates
  design consultants, Anvers, Belgique.

〉〉

**EN MATIÈRE DE DESIGN,
QUELLES SONT LES AMÉLIORATIONS
QUE VOUS AIMERIEZ OBSERVER?**
Que les commanditaires/clients soient for-
més, qu'on les amène à formuler adéquate-
ment les descriptifs de leurs commandes.

**QUE VOUDRIEZ-VOUS VOIR CONSTRUIT
OU AMÉLIORÉ DANS VOTRE VILLE?**
Actuellement, s'il manque quelque chose à
Anvers, c'est un bâtiment-phare. Le nouveau
Palais de justice aspire à ce statut, mais il
était bien plus attrayant en maquette qu'en
réalité. Il est clair que nous avons besoin
d'un pont puissant qui relierait les deux parties
de la ville rationnellement et émotivement
comme alternative à nos tunnels. Il pourrait
assurément devenir mon endroit préféré.

〉〉

01 Tram pour la ville et les communes d'Anvers, design: Enthoven Associates Design Consultants, constructeur : Bombardier

01

〉〉〉〉〉〉〉〉〉〉〉〉〉〉〉〉〉〉〉〉〉〉〉〉〉〉〉〉〉〉〉〉〉〉〉〉〉〉〉

**EVERT CROLS, DIRK ENGELEN
ET SVEN GROOTEN**

〉 B-architecten, Anvers, Belgique

〉〉〉〉〉〉〉〉〉〉〉〉〉〉〉〉〉〉〉〉〉〉〉〉〉〉〉〉〉〉〉〉〉〉〉〉〉〉〉

En novembre 1997, Evert Crols, Dirk Engelen
et Sven Grooten fondent B-architecten, un
bureau de design indépendant situé à
Anvers, en Belgique. ✕ Les trois architectes
se sont rencontrés au cours de leurs études
à Anvers et à Amsterdam. Inscrits au Berlage
Institute,un laboratoire international d'études
avancées en architecture aux Pays-Bas, ils y
ont découvert leurs intérêts communs en
matière de design. ✕ B-architecten est une
équipe qui œuvre de façon novatrice à divers
projets : construction, concours de design et
études. Ces projets sont réalisés en partenariat avec d'autres bureaux au besoin.

〉〉〉〉〉〉〉〉〉〉〉〉〉〉〉〉〉〉〉〉〉〉〉〉〉〉〉〉〉〉〉〉〉〉〉〉〉〉

SVEN GROOTEN

1971 〉 naissance à Beveren-Waas.

1995 〉 diplôme d'architecte du Henry van de
Velde Instituut, Anvers.

1995

1997 〉 études avancées au Berlage Institute,
Amsterdam.

1997 〉 architecte au bureau
Driesen-Meersman-Thomaes, Anvers.

1997 〉 ouverture du bureau de design
B-architecten en compagnie d'Evert
Crols et de Dirk Engelen.

〉〉〉〉〉〉〉〉〉〉〉〉〉〉〉〉〉〉〉〉〉〉〉〉〉〉〉〉〉〉〉〉〉〉〉〉〉〉

〉〉〉〉〉〉〉〉〉〉〉〉〉〉〉〉〉〉〉〉〉〉〉〉〉〉〉〉〉〉〉〉〉〉〉〉〉〉〉

**QUELS ENDROITS PUBLICS D'ANVERS
PRÉFÉREZ VOUS ?**

Mon premier choix se porte sur le
«Linkeroever» (la rive gauche de la rivière
Schelde). De là, vous avez une vue extraordinaire de la silhouette de la ville. À l'heure
actuelle, pour beaucoup de gens, le
«Linkeroever» ne fait pas véritablement
partie de la ville. ✕ En second, je choisis
le port, l'un des plus grands du monde.
Le sillonner en bateau la nuit, au milieu de
navires énormes, de millions de lumières,
de gigantesques flammes dégagées par
les industries, c'est fantastique!

**EN MATIÈRE DE DESIGN,
QUELLES SONT LES AMÉLIORATIONS
QUE VOUS AIMERIEZ OBSERVER ?**

Les quais de la rivière. On y trouve aujourd'hui
d'immenses aires de stationnement pour
automobiles, camions et autobus. Il est
honteux que ces espaces ne soient pas
traités comme un lieu public.

**QUE VOUDRIEZ-VOUS VOIR CONSTRUIT
DANS VOTRE VILLE ?**

Un pont traversant la rivière pour relier
les deux rives. Et j'aimerais bien en être
le designer.

〉〉〉〉〉〉〉〉〉〉〉〉〉〉〉〉〉〉〉〉〉〉〉〉〉〉〉〉〉〉〉〉〉〉〉〉〉〉〉

01 Hall central du Beursschouwburg, centre culturel de la Communauté flamande, Bruxelles, 2004.
Design: B-architecten et DHP-architecten

— UNE VILLE DE DESIGN, EST UNE VILLE INACHEVÉE, À LA RECHERCHE D'ELLE-MÊME ET QUI SE RÉINVENTE PARFOIS. LES CRÉATEURS, JEUNES ET MOINS JEUNES, QUI COHABITENT ET TRA-VAILLENT À ANVERS, LUI DONNENT UNE NOUVELLE DIMENSION, UNE REMISE EN QUESTION PERMANENTE. ANVERS, C'EST LA VILLE DE LA CATHÉDRALE GOTHIQUE, DE L'ÉGLISE BAROQUE CAROLUS BOROMÉUS ET DE LA MAISON DE RUBENS. MAIS C'EST AUSSI LA VILLE OÙ L'ON RENCONTRE UNE ARCHITECTURE CONTEMPORAINE, COMME LE NOUVEAU PALAIS DE JUSTICE DE RICHARD ROGERS ET LA NOUVELLE BIBLIOTHÈQUE DE LA VILLE, AU MILIEU D'UN QUARTIER DÉFAVORISÉ. — C'EST UNE IMPLANTATION RISQUÉE ET OSÉE, MAIS RAISONNABLE ET RÉUSSIE.

Wivina Demeester, ancien ministre de la Belgique et de la Flandre, Anvers

GLAS
GOW

—GLASGOW WISHES TO FOSTER AND ATTRACT CREATIVE INDUSTRIES AND TO PROMOTE THOSE THAT SEE DESIGN AS INTEGRAL TO THEIR WORK AND WHO REPORT ITS DIRECT AND POSITIVE IMPACT ON THEIR BUSINESS PERFORMANCE.
Liz Cameron, Lord Provost of Glasgow

DESIGN POR- TRAIT

〉〉

POPULATION

Glasgow's population is 700,000; the metro-politan population is 1.5 million.

〉〉〉

〉〉

YEAR OF FOUNDATION

Glasgow grew up around the cathedral founded by St. Mungo in the sixth century, and its university was founded in 1451.

〉〉

STRENGTHS AND CHALLENGES

Glasgow's prosperity grew in the eighteenth century because of the American tobacco trade, and the city continued to prosper in the nineteenth century as a centre of textiles, shipbuilding, heavy engineering, and coal and steel manufacturing. It was a major centre of the Industrial Revolution and the Second City of the British Empire. In the first half of the twentieth century, Glasgow prospered from its munitions industries; the city supplied ships and arms for the two world wars. However, after the Second World War it went into post-industrial decline. That decline was arrested by, for example, developing the service industries and promoting the creative industries, including design. The city is also a major education, TV/media, and music centre.

〉〉

〉〉

SIGNIFICANT EVENTS

Major international exhibitions were held in 1881, 1888, 1901, and 1938. More recently, the city celebrated the Glasgow Garden Festival (1988), was nominated the European City of Culture (1990), staged the International Design Festival (1996), and was the UK's City of Architecture and Design (1999). All of these events left their mark on the development of the city, helping Glasgow re-brand itself and accelerating its urban regeneration.

〉〉

NUMBER OF DESIGNERS

There are approximately three hundred design companies in Glasgow, including one hundred architecture practices.

〉〉

01 Students at the Glasgow School of Art 02 Glasgow, bird's-eye view 03 The Clyde made Glasgow and Glasgow made the Clyde. On the eve of World War I a third of the world's shipping was built on the River Clyde, but after the end of World War II the river and its industry went into decline. The city which literally turned its back on the river is now investing in its rejuvenation with major architectural projects including the Glasgow Science Centre, a new headquarters for the BBC by David Chipperfield, and extensions to his Conference Centre by Norman Foster.

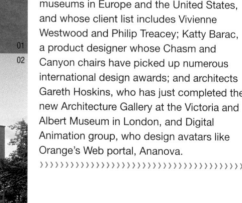

RENOWNED DESIGNERS
Glasgow's most famous designer was Charles Rennie Mackintosh, although his wife, Margaret Macdonald, was a significant designer in her own right. His name prevails today, but it should be pointed out that Mackintosh was part of a large circle of creative people in Glasgow at the beginning of the twentieth century. ✕ Contemporary designers continue to contribute to the city, including Timorous Beasties, textile designers whose work may be found in major museums in Europe and the United States, and whose client list includes Vivienne Westwood and Philip Treacey; Katty Barac, a product designer whose Chasm and Canyon chairs have picked up numerous international design awards; and architects Gareth Hoskins, who has just completed the new Architecture Gallery at the Victoria and Albert Museum in London, and Digital Animation group, who design avatars like Orange's Web portal, Ananova.
>>>

01
02

›››››››››››››››››››››››››››››››››››››››

ANNUAL DESIGN EVENTS

In September Glasgow runs the annual architecture festival called Block. This coincides with Doors Open Day, when many Glasgow buildings are open to the public. In addition, an annual international design conference is usually held in the spring and hosted by The Lighthouse.

›››››››››››››››››››››››››››››››››››››››

DESIGN INSTITUTIONS

As Scotland's National Centre for Architecture and Design and the City, as well as the hub for Scotland's creative industries, The Lighthouse is instrumental in the promotion of national architecture policy through exhibitions, education, events, and B2B activities. It works in association with the Royal Incorporation of Architects in Scotland (RIAS), the Chartered Society of Designers (CSD), and the Design Business Association (DBA). It also works closely with the UK Design Council, Design Partners, and the UK Architecture Centre Network. Internationally, The Lighthouse is involved with the European Design Forum (EDF), a network of design centres; the Bureau of European Design Association (BEDA); The GAUDI Network; and the European Forum on Architecture Policies.

›››››››››››››››››››››››››››››››››››››››

›››››››››››››››››››››››››››››››››››››››

DESIGN SCHOOLS

Glasgow has two schools of architecture as well as the Glasgow School of Art (GSA), all of which run degree, post-graduate, and research programs. GSA covers the full range of design courses—graphics, product, textiles, jewellery, interior, and so on. In addition, the universities of Strathclyde and Glasgow Caledonian have degree and master's courses in product, digital, and interior design. A wide range of vocational design courses at the pre-degree level is also offered at local colleges.

›››››››››››››››››››››››››››››››››››››››

DESIGN STRATEGIES

Glasgow City Council recently produced a creative industries strategy aimed at the promotion of key sectors like design. The city was also the first to produce its own design directory, listing design businesses and tracking the status of the industry within Glasgow.

›››››››››››››››››››››››››››››››››››››››

Design portrait of Glasgow
Information provided by The Lighthouse, Scotland's Center for Architecture, Design and the City

01 Charles Rennie Mackintosh's room, Glasgow School of Art 02 Charles Rennie Mackintosh, House for an Art Lover

LIZ CAMERON

LORD PROVOST OF GLASGOW SINCE 2003

〉〉〉

WHAT IS YOUR PERSONAL DEFINITION OF A DESIGN CITY?
A design city is one that demonstrates quality of life through design decisions such as the improvements to the built environment or the development of design industries. It is a city that strives to link people, products, and places, celebrating design while encouraging economic growth. It is a sustainable city, integrating the social, economic, and environment needs of its citizens and visitors. Creativity and innovation are principles that are encouraged and fostered there by developing physical projects, increasing intellectual capital, and promoting the involvement of all sectors.

WHY DO YOU CONSIDER YOUR CITY TO BE A NEW DESIGN CITY?
Glasgow is recognized as a design capital. The creative industries play a big part in the dynamics of the city, from design consultants advancing the quality of products and services, to the provision of interesting lighting and streetscape upgrades. We are looking to further develop the connections between all aspects of the design and creative industries by participating in the Design Festival program being developed for various cities in Scotland. ✕ Design is fundamental to the continuous development of Glasgow as a city. Glasgow has changed to reflect different economic circumstances, and this legacy of innovation and celebration is visible in its built heritage. ✕ "Let Glasgow Flourish," the City Council motto, encapsulates the vibrant nature of the city while promoting the idea of building on the past to create a city for the future. We pay careful attention to the city's image to attract investors and visitors, and to make it a place that people are happy to live in. ✕ The current marketing campaign labels the city as "Glasgow: Scotland with Style," epitomizing the way in which design is important in placing Glasgow within a wider context. ✕ The regeneration of the River Clyde

Corridor as a focal point through the city is a visionary project that is transforming living and working environments. It is an exciting, internationally competitive, twenty-first century environment connecting the city and the river. It involves approximately 300 hectares of prime riverfront land, and £2 billion of investment is being targeted at the River Clyde Waterfront and Clyde Gateway Project.

WHAT HAS BEEN YOUR PERSONAL CONTRIBUTION IN FACILITATING THE EMERGENCE OF YOUR DESIGN CITY?

I am keen to promote my city in every way I can. I play a big part in negotiating with partners, agencies, and new investors to get them to consider quality design. I am particularly proud of the investment of nearly £28 million drawn from different partners to refurbish the impressive Kelvingrove Art Gallery and Museum. This renovation project has been carried out with extensive consultation with the public to give them a say in the new collection displays. This project, due to re-open in 2006, is a perfect example of how to learn from our past in order to create a twenty-first century museum in Glasgow's favourite Edwardian building.

WHY DO YOU BELIEVE THAT POSITIONING YOUR CITY THROUGH DESIGN IS IMPORTANT?

Glasgow is building upon a number of design initiatives that have taken place in the recent past, such as the Festival of Architecture and Design in 1999, the European Year of Culture, and last year's Architecture Festival, which focused on exploring the city. These initiatives reflect the potential that we wish to develop in the long run, as well as the already achieved improvements in the quality of the place. ✕ Employment in the creative industries is rising—recent figures show that in Glasgow employment in this sector rose from 22,000 to 27,000 over the period 1999–2001. Glasgow wishes to foster and attract creative industries and to promote those that see design as integral to their work and who report its direct and positive impact on their business performance. ✕ Design talent is fostered in Glasgow through the internationally recognized academic institutions, such as the Glasgow School of Art and the universities, and The Lighthouse Centre for Architecture and Design. Internationally renowned architects have been involved in the city by developing key projects, like the recently commissioned £50 million Museum of Transport (Zaha Hadid + Event Communications). Sir Norman Foster built the Clyde Auditorium, and Sir Richard Rogers is designing a new bridge across the River Clyde. Piers Gough developed the master plan and some of the buildings for the regeneration of the Gorbals neighbourhood. David Chipperfield architects are developing the BBC site as part of the media campus on the River Clyde.

01 Kelvingrove Art Gallery and Museum

01 Glasgow School of Art 02 The Lighthouse 03 Royal Exchange Square

**WHAT EXAMPLES OF DESIGN PROMOTION STRATEGIES DEVELOPED
IN OTHER CITIES INSPIRE YOU?**

We have strong international links that build upon Glasgow's competitiveness and enhance its position in the global economy. We have twinning arrangements with Nurenberg (Germany), Turin (Italy), Rostov-on-Don (Russia), Dalian (China), and Havana (Cuba). We were inspired to develop Glasgow, City of Light, a city-wide lighting strategy. We now lead the Culture and Lighting Commission for LUCI (Lighting Urban Community Initiative), which has brought us into contact with lighting specialists from many parts of the world. The challenges of the design and build industry were recently discussed in Chicago. All of these contacts help us foster relationships while keeping us inspired by the work of others.

**WHAT SHOULD BE THE ROLES OF THE CITIZEN, THE DESIGNER,
AND THE POLITICIAN IN THE DEVELOPMENT OF A DESIGN CITY?**

Everyone can have a say in good design. Citizens can help to influence what is good design by their use of products and by being actively engaged in their neighbourhood improvements. ✕ Designers can inspire and bring joy to the lives of others. They can challenge concepts and develop new ways of thinking. They help to develop the culture of the design city. ✕ Politicians also have a fundamental role in developing the design city. Public expenditure across all sectors is affected by design decisions, so our continued support of investment in innovative ways of delivering projects, products, and services is vital. Glasgow recently appointed a design advisor to promote quality in design across all development sectors.

03

GLASGOW, DESIGN CITY

BY DR STUART MACDONALD

⟩ Director, The Lighthouse, Scotland's Center for Architecture, Design and the City, Glasgow

⟩⟩

THE NINETIES: A VIRTUOUS CIRCLE OF CREATIVITY

Whether your abiding memory of the last decade is Diana or the Dome, retro or reality TV, it was in the nineties that we learned to love our old industrial cities. What became a global phenomenon—the post-industrial transformation of cities through design and cultural regeneration—is the mark of how Glasgow, after its reign in 1990 as the European City of Culture, used design to define a decade. The timing was crucial. Helped by Roger Hargreave's graphics and the marketing acumen of its civic leaders, Glasgow, once the Second City of the British Empire, commenced its long and painful journey out of the gloom of its industrial past with the renowned "Glasgow's Miles Better" campaign of the mid-eighties. It lead to one of the biggest urban ground shifts in history. ✗ With its associated inward investment and cultural strategies—the Garden Festival, the opening of the Burrell Collection (a landmark building predating Bilbao's Guggenheim by a decade)—that campaign secured the 1990 European City of Culture crown and created a virtuous circle of design creativity that included the 1996 International Design Festival and lead to the prize of UK City of Architecture and Design 1999 and the opening of The Lighthouse as Scotland's Centre for Architecture, Design and the City. What is the role of design in terms of Glasgow's past, present, and future, now that the design decade of the nineties has given way to more recent notions such as the creative industries and the creative city?

⟩⟩

THREE PILLARS OF WISDOM

There are at least three prevailing pieces of wisdom about the impact of design and cultural developments on Glasgow in the nineties, and within the first two is an inherent cynicism that I am sure is transferable to other cities. The first is that the City of Culture 1990 and the ensuing design-led initiatives had little effect—at most, 6,000 jobs were created in the creative sector and most of them were temporary. The second is that 1990 sparked a renaissance in the city's economic growth by creating a platform for the emerging creative industries—media, design, architecture, and music—set up by a growing army of cultural entrepreneurs. ✗ The reality is that elements of both are true. The third 1990 story is that repositioning Glasgow as a City of Design did amount to more than hype. Of course, it didn't solve all of the city's problems but it did drive a process of adaptation and self-learning in which the city (in other words, the public sector) in conjunction with the private sector sought to develop Glasgow's cultural assets and creative economy. This is very important in terms of differentiating cause and effect relative to today's debate and the emergence of Richard Florida's creative class.[1] Another important aspect in our sorting of hype from reality and cause from effect is the actual impact and role of design, as opposed to the more generic role of the arts, within that process of regeneration. ✕ Certainly in the case of Glasgow that debate began in earnest with Design Renaissance, the International Design Congress staged in the city in 1993. It marked a moment when designers stopped showing each other pretty pictures and started talking about the more far-reaching, contextual issues of their work. Predating Florida by ten years, Janice Kirkpatrick, a Glasgow designer, declared that investing in people and not iconic projects was the way forward.[2] Also significant was the fact that artists were emerging in Glasgow as important protagonists not just for enhancing place quality (a bi-product), but also for delivering stinging (and often unwelcome) critiques of urban regeneration. All these attitudes contributed to Glasgow's edgy reputation as a creative city. ✕ However, if any help is needed in this exercise, one only has to try to envision what the city would have been like had there been no investment in Glasgow as a City of Design—the outcome, quite frankly, is unimaginable. Glasgow is, in fact, a model; its momentum-building techniques have been copied elsewhere in Europe. The place-marketing that started with Glasgow's Miles Better campaign and was multiplied by the City of Culture event[3] carried through to the 1996 and 1999 city design festivals that focused on narrowing the gap between hype and reality. It also projected Glasgow as an innovative city, earning it a "can do" reputation, as the developments in design and the visual arts demonstrate. ✕ With Tramway (1990), the city launched the then-largest performance and exhibition space in Europe. The transformation of Tramway from industrial to contemporary art space was widely copied, notably by the Palais de Tokyo in Paris, the Friche in Marseilles, and the Baltic in Gateshead. Tramway was recently revamped at a cost of £2.8 million. Glasgow also opened a Gallery of Modern Art (GOMA), which now attracts half a million visitors a year. The recent £7-million rehabilitation of the Centre for Contemporary Art (CCA) consolidates Glasgow at the cutting edge of the contemporary art scene. But, and this relates to the need to understand how strategies are promoted, the provision of physical spaces goes hand in hand here with artist-led or "soft" initiatives: exhibitions, of course, but also non-gallery and public art projects, magazines, records, posters, prints, graphics, flyers, graffiti, DJ/VJs, demos, clubs, talks, readings, polemics, and

01 View of Glasgow 02 These huge watertowers dominate the approaches to Glasgow and its peripheral housing estates. Loved by architects and hated by locals, they have now been transformed into gigantic works of art and lighting design.

so on. And, for example, relative to the size of the city, Glasgow artists have trumped their rivals in the UK's Turner and Becks awards, therein gaining international exposure.[4] These cultural assets not only enhance the visual arts, they are crucial in attracting and retaining Florida's "creative class," that new breed of designers, architects, and artists who, in Leadbeater's words, "create wealth from thin air."[5] They represent a contrast to the earlier, failed examples of event-led urban regeneration that focused on physical manifestations and of which international examples abound, not least in North America.

〉〉〉

GLASGOW: UK CITY OF ARCHITECTURE AND DESIGN

One of the most important staging posts for Glasgow as a design city was its reign, on the eve of the millennium, as UK City of Architecture and Design. Described by one national newspaper as a "shimmeringly successful year," its exhibitions attracted over 1 million people, 40 percent of whom had never before been to an exhibition on architecture or design, with thousands more taking part in education and community events. Among the actual build projects were Homes for the Future, an innovative, mixed, private and social housing project in a historically deprived area of the city, and a project called 5 Spaces that set out to achieve a sense of place in pretty inhospitable territory. All of this, the exhibitions, events, and other projects, increased investments in the design community in terms of commissioning design, graphics, exhibitions, and buildings. Fifty percent of design companies in Glasgow believed that their turnover would increase as a result of the festival, and it did. There was also a hard-nosed economic development project in industrial design, The Glasgow Collection, that sought to promote innovation by subsidizing the costs of developing new products and encouraging emerging graduates to stay in the city. In fact, because of the combined capital and revenue investment of £27.5 million, the impact of UK City of Architecture and Design 1999 was closely monitored, and it has been estimated that the event generated £60 million, in addition to the indirect impacts.

〉〉〉

THE LEGACY: NEW MODELS FOR CULTURE AND THE ECONOMY

Glasgow's reputation for innovation linked to the creative economy accelerated with The Lighthouse, the £12 million conversion of Charles Rennie Mackintosh's former Glasgow Herald building to Scotland's Centre for Architecture, Design and the City, and the £40 million Science Centre on the former site of the Glasgow Garden Festival. Both projects demonstrate the continuity of the change mentality. As well as being about cultural tourism they sit on the crossover from cultural consumption to cultural production, design being the connective tissue that joins science, technology, and art. The Lighthouse—with its mix of exhibitions, events, education, design into business, and the creative industries network—is on the com-

01 The Lighthouse is the legacy of Glasgow's reign as UK City of Architecture and Design 1999. Originally Charles Rennie Mackintosh's Glasgow Herald newspaper office and converted by Page and Park, it is now Scotland's National Centre for Architecture and Design and the hub for the country's creative industries. 02 Science Centre

mercially active side of the arts-economy equation. Termed a creative industry in the United Kingdom, The Lighthouse is establishing a new business model and tools for the design sector, in keeping with one of the real legacies of the nineties design decade. Research on what a design museum for the twenty-first century might be like has focused on The Lighthouse as a design centre that has created a distinctive local identity but is, at the same time, located in an international context.[6]

>>>

CREATIVE CITIES AND CREATIVE INDUSTRIES

Numerous commentators, including Florida and in the UK people like Leadbeater, Bentley,[7] and Landry,[8] have made careers from talking about the creative economy and the importance of place in sustaining cities. The development of the creative industries, which are inexorably linked to sustainable city development, emerged as a UK government priority in 1998 and has been a strategic focus for the devolved Scottish government since 2000. Indeed, Scotland's First Minister recently called for Scotland to become universally recognized as a "creative hub." ✕ The creative industries are one of the fastest growing economic sectors in the United Kingdom and Scotland. In the United Kingdom, they are worth over £94.5 billion and account for over 5 percent of GDP, and in Scotland they represent £8.2 billion in investment and employ 150,000 people out of a total population of 5 million. Importantly, in terms of the urban context, 10 percent of these jobs are in Glasgow. More interestingly, according to a recent publication on the creative industries, Glasgow has the largest share of them, with strong concentrations in film, TV, publishing, and cultural industries, that is, galleries and museums. It also has the strongest design base outside London. And Time magazine recently called Glasgow the new music capital of the world—the New Detroit. ✕ Recent research has asked whether the city's concentration of creative industries is the basis for the strength of its international visual arts culture, the so-called Glasgow Miracle.[9] In Glasgow, design, which is perceived as the invisible thread that permeates and interconnects architecture, publishing, music, software, and games, may be responsible for the vigour of its cultural community, which, in turn, is responsible for attracting other categories of people and investment. To put it another way, design and the creative industries are indeed the cause, and not simply the effect, as theorized by Florida. Design may be playing a bigger role in urban regeneration than the commentators have given it credit for.

>>>

CITY STRATEGIES FOR DESIGN
The Lighthouse for Design

This concentration creates a rich urban ecology. It is a bilateral ecology in that it enhances place quality and improves competitiveness. The design-led festivals and other cultural initiatives of the nineties in Glasgow promoted this advance, but they were accompanied by large-scale public and capital investment projects and by grassroots visual arts phenomena, in accordance with Florida's thesis. The Lighthouse is the physical manifestation of all this; it intersects both national and local government policies and strategies. For example, The Lighthouse underpins the delivery of Scotland's architecture policy, acts as a hub for the nation's creative industries, promotes internationalism, and is currently heavily involved in the development of a design strategy with local and national dimensions. ✕ Central to the latter are the issues of talent creation and retention, creative business development and innovation, and design promotion and international networking. Specifically, while showcasing local design talent like Timorous Beasties, textile designers whose work is in the collection of the Victoria and Albert Museum in London and the Cooper Hewitt National Design Museum in New York, we send exhibitions to places such as the Milan Fair and the Venice Architecture Biennale. This entails networking on a national and European scale. We run a Creative Entrepreneurs Club for professionals and students that offers advice, training, and support and also develops digital educational materials for use in schools, colleges, and universities. In other words, The

Lighthouse aggregates value by promoting design as an interconnected social, educational, cultural, and economic concern transecting both public and professional groups.

Collaborations

The Lighthouse transects local and national strategy on design, making partnership development one of its key elements. One example is the multi-layered collaboration with the National Endowment for Science Technology and the Arts (NESTA). NESTA commissioned a major research project on the creative industries which concluded, among other findings, that there was a need for greater collaboration between investors, the public sector (including education), and creative entrepreneurs. Key to that was "investor readiness" amongst young or starting-up designers and design companies. Thus, The Lighthouse is now involved with NESTA on several projects: Insight Out is a mentoring scheme for recent design graduates of the Glasgow School of Art that provides them training and help taking their ideas to market. IdeaSmart is a high-risk fund sponsored by a range of partners that offers grants to designers and provides collateral support and advice on business planning, marketing, and presentation. The UK-wide Graduate Pioneers program is supported by The Lighthouse and aims to take the very best design graduates in the United Kingdom and nurture, harvest, and distribute their ideas. In addition, NESTA supports The Lighthouse's Creative Entrepreneurs Club, a networking scheme focusing on collaboration within a disparate sector of SMEs (small and medium-sized enterprises) that operate solo or as freelancers. ✕ All of these collaborative initiatives point to a need for:
> graduates and businesses knowing what is possible and what is expected of them
> investors understanding the real commercial potential of early-stage creative businesses
> policy and decision-makers recognizing the significance of partnerships,
   sectoral intelligence, and leadership for a growing creative industries sector

Creative Hub

New strategies are being formulated in Glasgow that incorporate the development of the creative industries and the interconnection with the creative city posited by Florida et al.[7] These take the form of five key themes:
> creative infrastructure
> creative business
> creative workforce
> internationalization
> creativity and innovation

In terms of infrastructure, a creative industries hub had been proposed for Glasgow's Merchant City, its former warehouse area, which is currently undergoing a physical and symbolic transformation into a creative quarter. There is also a need to provide specific business support, and the role of The Lighthouse is changing to take on the account management of design / architecture practices—for a design centre, an evermore interesting meld of culture and business. New kinds of training and professional development have also been identified that require new forms of educational brokerage to offer a sustainable ladder of support, and The Lighthouse's work with NESTA and various academic partners are examples of this. ✕ Internationalization is central to the future strategy. In 2004, The Lighthouse took exhibitions to the Milan Fair, London's 100% Design, the Venice Biennale, and to Utrecht and Marseille. As well as creating routes to market for designers, these events play a critical role in promoting the city and its image. Another critical and significant challenge is to nourish creativity and innovation through partnerships with academic research institutes, especially with respect to defining what knowledge transfer is in the creative industries. However, most important is creating an environment in which creativity and innovation can flourish. For Glasgow, a post-industrial city on the edge of Europe, this means avoiding parochialism by showcasing design and architecture talent from elsewhere. The Lighthouse thus plays a singular role by staging exhibitions and events that draw on the best of what is going on around the world.

>>

SUMMARY

In the twentieth century there were various attempts to define design, with many different interest groups claiming hegemony over the process. The design of spacecraft, aircraft, weapons, and ships has always been a matter of specialized technical expertise, and often the process was anonymous. Only in fashion, cars, furniture, and luxury goods has design been associated with individual personalities and even hero figures, the efforts to define it in terms of regional difference and national and urban identity being relatively new. In terms of the consumer, design is governed by polls, surveys, focus groups, and, more recently, the demand for differentiation and customization. Nonetheless, marketing and the power of the brand hold sway. What is salient is that cities—and the Cities of Design are one indicator of this trend—are now being discussed in the same terms. Does any of this matter in the twenty-first century? Can we define design in a relevant way for the new century? It didn't begin with technology or artifacts, nor with their creators, appreciators, users, or consumers. ✕ In English "design" is both a noun and a verb referring to intentions and plans, as well as to fashioning and concocting. The word is also connected (and this tells you a lot about the English language) with deception and cunning. "Craft," which is also a noun and a verb, has as its adjective "crafty," which also means cunning. According to the philosopher Vilem Flusser, designers are like cunning plotters because they bridge art and technology to overcome or deceive nature. This is perhaps not the place to open up a sterile semantic or philosophical debate; the point is that, at the beginning of the twenty-first century, we are better able to see behind artifice or trickery. Our education and access to communications technology mean that we can interrogate claims about "weapons of mass destruction," the inequities or benefits of globalization, ethical or environmental matters linked to industrial development, issues relating to our identity, and, for that matter, to urban development. Propelled not only by pressure groups, eco-warriors, and global protestors but also by post-industrial change, we now seek, it would seem, the perfect reconciliation of needs with resources. Design—the process that is—is one way to achieve that. ✕ Nonetheless, in the creative economy uniqueness and innovation are the ultimate keys. They make Glaswegians as unique as Londoners or Milanese, and Glasgow as intriguing as Barcelona or Montreal. Glasgow, Europe's City of Culture for 1990, spun that identity, and can rightly lay claim to kick-starting the rise of the creative city.
>>

REFERENCES 1. Richard Florida, *The Rise of The Creative Class* (New York: Basic Books, 2002). ✕ 2. J. Myerson (ed.), *Design Renaissance* (London: Chartered Society of Designers, 1993). ✕ 3. P. Booth and R. Boyle, "See Glasgow, see Culture," in F. Biancini and M. Parkinson (eds.), *Cultural Policy and Urban Regeneration* (Manchester: Manchester University Press, 1993). ✕ 4. Sarah Lowndes, *Social Sculpture* (Glasgow: StopStop, 2004). ✕ 5. Charles Leadbeater, *Up the Down Escalator* (London: Penguin/Viking, 2002). ✕ 6. D. Charny, "Collection of Thoughts," *Blueprint* (December 2004 / January 2005). ✕ 7. Tom Bentley and Kimberley Seltzer, *The Creative Age* (London: DEMOS, 1999). ✕ 8. Charles Landry, *The Creative City* (London: Comedia, 2000). ✕ 9. Lowndes, *op. cit.* ✕ 10. Florida, *op. cit.*
>>

01

01

WHAT'S YOUR FAVOURITE PUBLIC PLACE IN YOUR CITY?

Grounds for Play, Bellahouston Park: a designed grassy place with rambling bumps, play areas, seating areas, and playthings for local adults and children to enjoy.

DO YOU CONSIDER YOU LIVE IN A DESIGN CITY? IF SO, WHY? IF NOT, WHAT IS MISSING?

A variety of exciting design courses at the undergraduate and post-graduate level, as well as The Lighthouse, make Glasgow a magnet for new design companies and a hub for designers. A history of manufacturing along with a wealth of retail, entertainment, and media businesses make it feel possible to find work and find ways to produce new things, here. Design festivals over the years have encouraged citizens to feel proud of their "design city" and to appreciate good design—to feel that design is both accessible and something to be celebrated.

FOR A DESIGN CITY TO EMERGE, DO YOU THINK IT NEEDS A SPECIAL SOCIAL BACKGROUND, A POLITICAL TRADITION, A CERTAIN INDUSTRIAL OR CREATIVE HISTORY?

A design city needs higher educational courses which train designers in a city that they have chosen to live in, at least for the length of their course (and therefore potentially for longer). These people and their tutors create social groups, supportive networks for each other, that can survive and thrive.

IF YOU WERE A POLITICIAN WHO WANTED TO TRANSFORM HIS OR HER CITY INTO A DESIGN CITY, WHAT ACTIONS WOULD YOU TAKE?

I would generate:
> a festival for promotion
> a development fund for clients and designers to develop relevant, market-researched products / buildings for the long-term benefit of those companies and the city
> a research archive for designers and clients to use, meet, and network

KATTY BARAK
> Designer, One Foot Taller product and interior design, Glasgow.

01 Undulate seats, design: Katty Barak

〉〉

JANICE KIRKPATRICK

〉 Creative director of the cross-disciplinary
design consultancy Graven Images
〉 Governor of Glasgow School of Art,
Glasgow, Scotland.

〉〉

Janice Kirkpatrick is a graphic designer,
chairman of The Lighthouse, and a governor
of Glasgow School of Art. In 1986, with her
partner Ross Hunter, she founded the cross-
disciplinary design consultancy Graven Images,
where she functions as creative director.

〉〉

〉〉

**WHAT ARE YOUR TWO FAVOURITE
PUBLIC PLACES IN YOUR CITY?**

Glasgow School of Art and The Lighthouse,
Scotland's Centre for Architecture, Design
and the City. All buildings are "public space"
and we live with them every day, whether
they're good or bad. The School is close to
the hearts of Glaswegians, who are proud of
their famous son Charles Rennie Mackintosh.
The building is open to the public, although
there is a charge for tours. The School also
runs many public exhibitions and events,
some of which take place in its facilities. The
Lighthouse is the old Glasgow Herald newspaper building; it was also designed by
Mackintosh and extended by Page & Park
Architects. It is open to the public, who can
visit the shop and tower. ✕ I believe that a
very small amount of great architecture goes
a long, long way. Mackintosh built in Glasgow
for a very short period but the effect of his
work, economically and culturally, is perhaps
greater today than it has ever been.

**WHAT WOULD YOU LIKE TO SEE
IMPROVED DESIGN-WISE?**

I'd like to see more really challenging new
architecture. We live at a time when the risks
associated with creativity are seen as dan-
gerous and must be avoided at all cost, even
if this means living in a boring, litigious world
with insufficient investment in research and
development, and therefore, an uncertain
future. ✕ I'd like to see a better understanding of the economic effects of creativity. I'd
like R&D to be supported and made a priority
in all kinds of businesses. And I'd like design
to be taught in schools as an integral part of
all subjects. That's just for starters.

**WHAT WOULD YOU LIKE TO SEE BUILT
IN YOUR CITY?**

More small-scale office space for sale.

〉〉

02 Collage Bar, Glasgow Radisson SAS Hotel, design: Janick Kirkpatrick, 2002

—THE CITYSCAPE OF
GLASGOW HAS CHANGED
SO MUCH THROUGH
DESIGN, THROUGH NEW
INFRASTRUCTURE, BETTER
STREET LIGHTING, AND
THE CREATION OF NEW
BUILDINGS. RECENTLY,
MANY NEW CITY-CENTRE
APARTMENTS HAVE BEEN
BUILT, ENCOURAGING
PEOPLE TO MOVE BACK
AND LIVE DOWNTOWN.

Sharon Taggart, Audi conference and events manager, Glasgow.

LIS
BOA

— THE DESIGN BIENNALE AND OTHER DESIGN EVENTS HAVE LARGELY CONTRIBUTED TO ELEVATE LISBON AS A CITY DEVOTED TO PROMOTING THE LINK BETWEEN PATRIMONY AND CONTEMPORARY PRODUCTION.
Pedro Santana Lopes, Mayor of Lisbon

Vigo
Orense
Puebla de Truves
Ribadavia
Viana del Bollo
Puebla de Sanabria
Monçao
Valença
Linhosa
Monterey
Caminha
Ruivaes
Chaves
Bragança
Alcaniz
anna do Castello
Braga
ENTRE
TRAS OS MONTES
Pavoa do Varzim
Mirandella
Miranda
DOURO E MINHO
VillaReal
Mogadouro
Hermillo
Mattosinhos
Porto
Penafiel
Torres
Fuen
VillaNova de Gaia
Lamego
San João
Freixo
Feira
Arouca
Trancoso
Salamanq
Ovar
San Pedro
Estarreja
Vizeu
Panhel
Almeida
Aveiro
Manguald
Guarda
Ilhavo
Agueda
Torico
B
E
I
R
A
Pampilhosa
Mondego
Sa Estrella
Seguer
Montemor o Velho
Coimbra
C. Mondego
Soure
Santa Clara
Figueira da Foz
Louriçal
Pedrogao
Castello Branco
Pombal
Proença
Plasen
TUGAL
Leiria
Velha do Rodão
Alcantara
Almonte
Torres Novas
Thomar
Caceres
Obidos
Abrantes
eiro
Valencia
de S. Pedro
Santarem
Tago
Portalegre
Albuquerque
Montes
Vedras
Aviz
Arronches
ESTREM
ira
ESTREMADURE
Campo Maior
Villanuev
ntra
Salvaterra
ALEM TEJO
Montijo
Merida
ca
Alhandra
Estremoz
caes
LISBONNE
Aldeia Gallega
Elvas
Badajoz
Hon Ben
Almada
Barreiro
Ossa
Olivenza
Almendrale
Cezimbra
Setubal
Montemor o Novo
Fuente del Ma
spichel
Alcacer do Sal
Evora
los Santos
Azuag
Casablanca
Moura
Zafre
São Thiago de Cacem
Vianna
Grandola
Ferreira
Llerena
C. de Sines
Sines
Beja
Nova de Milfontes
Casevel
Castro Verde
Odemira
Mertola
Séville
Monchique
Almodovar
Aljezur
Villa Nova
A L G A R V E
Huelva
Utrera
lla do Bispo
Silves
Palos
incent
Sagres
Lagos
Lagoa
Faro

DESIGN POR- TRAIT

〉〉

POPULATION
Lisbon's population is 600,000;
the metropolitan population is 2.5 million.
〉〉

YEAR OF FOUNDATION
Lisbon is a legendary city, founded in the
fifth century B.C. and conquered by the
Moors in 1147.
〉〉

SIGNIFICANT EVENTS
Major international exhibitions were held in
1994, when Lisbon was the European Capital
of Culture, and Expo'98, when Lisbon hosted
the last universal exposition of the twentieth
century. Based on a theme of ocean
conservation, the Expo attracted more
than 10 million visitors. More recently,
Lisbon hosted Euro2004, the European
soccer championship. All of these events
helped Lisbon re-brand itself and
accelerated its urban regeneration.
〉〉

NUMBER OF DESIGNERS (all disciplines)
5,000 in Lisbon
〉〉

**RENOWNED DESIGNERS WHO HAVE
CONTRIBUTED TO OUR DESIGN CITY**
Filipe Alarcão, Pedro Silva Dias, Henrique
Cayatte, Daciano Costa and many others
〉〉

>>
ANNUAL DESIGN EVENTS
ExperimentaDesign—Lisbon Biennale is a Portuguese biennale with an international approach to design, artistic creation, and project culture. It aims to build in the Portuguese capital an international platform open to reflection and experimentation. The biennale explores the idea of design and contemporary culture in areas such as ambient design, architecture, visual arts, cinema, graphic design, industrial design, wearable design, photography, multimedia, music, video, and Web design. The fourth edition will take place in Lisbon from 15 September to 30 October 2005. Within the theme "The medium is the matter," the biennale will present fifteen events in various categories including conferences, screenings, exhibitions, and urban interventions. ✕ Other significant Lisbon design events include IN'Nova, the international fair for global trading that is held every year in September, and Moda Lisboa, a festival that occurs every spring and autumn to promote fashion design made in Portugal.
>>
DESIGN INSTITUTIONS
The CPD (Centro Português de Design) brings together a network for Portuguese designers and promotes design culture to educate the Portuguese industry. The Experimenta Association is dedicated to exploring various fields of artistic intervention by uniting different areas of activity, experience, and knowledge on the basis of common design concerns.
The Design Museum permanently exhibits collections of international design at the CCB (Centro Cultural de Belém).
>>

>>
DESIGN SCHOOLS AND PROGRAMS
The FBAUL (Faculdade de Belas Artes da Universidade de Lisboa) offers degrees in product and graphic design; it is adding a degree in art and multimedia next year. The other public graduate school, FAUTL (Faculdade de Arquitectura da Universidade Técnica de Lisboa), offers degrees in fashion and product design. ✕ IADE (Instituto de Artes Visuais Design e Marketing) is a private institution that offers degrees in design and multimedia, with an emphasis on web design and the visual arts. ✕ In addition, a wide range of vocational design courses at the pre-degree level is offered at local colleges. Private universities also provide courses that explore approaches to design practice (e.g., Universidade Lusíada in Lisbon and Porto).
>>
DESIGN STRATEGIES AND POLICIES
Politicians, institutions, and private companies are hiring more and more designers and architects to solve their problems and to contribute to the urban landscape. A new design block has been created by Norman Foster for Santos, a new pedestrian bridge project is being developed, and the Car Parking Silos, an ongoing project initiated by Experimenta, has been adopted by the city.
>>
Design portrait of Lisbon
Information provided by
Experimenta
ExperimentaDesign—Bienal de Lisboa

CONTEMPORARY LISBON IN THE HEART OF TRADITION

NORMAN FOSTER'S BOAVISTA PROJECT

〉〉〉

The neighbourhood of Santos, located next to the historic centre of Lisbon, has become the design hub of the city. × The first design school in Portugal was located in this neighbourhood; it was followed by the theatre, television, jewellery, and architecture schools. Over the last decade, Santos witnessed a proliferation of modern design stores, galleries, restaurants, and bars, quickly becoming the entertainment centre of Lisbon. × The site for the Boavista Project was built on the River Tagus during the nineteenth century and was formerly occupied by the warehouses that supported the area's industrial activities. As they became obsolete, it was necessary to envisage a new role for the area, one that would harmonize with the development of the city and the character of the surroundings. × Inviting British architect Norman Foster to design the Boavista Project was a choice fuelled by a strong determination to develop a project of modern lines that reflected the city's contemporaneity and also pioneered solutions in environmental sustainability. Simultaneously, it was a way of embracing the old urban mesh of Lisbon's streets, with their pedestrian paths and long tradition of open public spaces, as well as the extraordinary relationship of the city to its river, presently hindered by the railway that runs parallel to the river Tagus. × In order to attract residents and visitors to this newly founded centrality and to encourage a 24/7 activity, Foster proposed a new public square of generous proportions, surrounded by a balanced mix of residential, commercial, and office spaces as well as a boutique hotel, a novelty for Lisbon.

These spaces, with their special calling for design-related businesses and emerging artists, will be complemented by the Design Centre that is being developed in close collaboration with ExperimentaDesign and IADE (Instituto de Artes Visuais Design e Marketing), two of the foremost design institutions in Portugal. × The Design Centre at Centro Cultural de Belém will be a cultural venue that reflects a dynamic and provocative stance intended to fuel expressive and dynamic relationships with the public while highlighting the link between creative designers and consumers. It will be a place for cutting-edge creativity, experimentation, and laboratory work, a place where the cultural and economic worlds can meet, free from preconceptions and with a strategic vision of the future. × The Design Centre will also be a platform for communication with the outside world. It will include exhibition and multi-purpose rooms; space for lectures and workshops; creative studios for all disciplines (industrial and sustainable design, media design, architecture and urban planning, photography and video, digital music and sound design). Its Inspiration Centre will feature a design database—an innovative materials library—showcasing new technologies and current information sources. × Boavista will be a unique space to reflect on, debate about, promote, and trade design in Portugal. It aims to become a gravitational centre and Lisbon's foremost symbol on the international scene.

〉〉〉

01 BoavistaLisbon view 02 BoavistaLisbon section

PEDRO SANTANA LOPES

MAYOR OF LISBON SINCE 2001

WHAT IS YOUR PERSONAL DEFINITION OF A DESIGN CITY?

A city that uses design as a strategy for growth and that recognizes design as a key tool for its sustainable development.

WHY DO YOU CONSIDER YOUR CITY TO BE A NEW DESIGN CITY?

Since 1999 Lisbon has invested heavily in events and structures connected with design. We have ModaLisboa, a fashion design event; the Lisbon Biennale, ExperimentaDesign; and the Design Museum at Centro Cultural de Belém. The Portuguese Design Centre is also based in Lisbon, as are some of the most important design schools. In terms of architecture and urban design, there has been much new investment. You can see it on the streets, in the shops, in public areas.

**WHAT HAS BEEN YOUR PERSONAL CONTRIBUTION IN FACILITATING
THE EMERGENCE OF YOUR DESIGN CITY?**

During my mandate ExperimentaDesign was officially designated the Lisbon Biennale, a move that won unanimous approval from the Municipal Assembly. We also decided to buy the Francisco Capelo Design Collection (fashion and industrial design) that is presently part of the Design Museum at Centro Cultural de Belém. That collection was about to be sold to a foreign country, and we decided to buy it in order to keep it in Portugal. We also invited Frank Gehry to design a new structure of great importance to the city, where design and culture assume a special role, and we are building the Lisbon Car Parking Silos with the contribution of young designers and architects. This project originated, by the way, during the third edition of ExperimentaDesign. We are about to approve a project by Norman Foster in Santos (a Lisbon neighbourhood) that includes a design centre which will be open both to the public and the design community.

**WHY DO YOU BELIEVE THAT POSITIONING YOUR CITY
THROUGH DESIGN IS IMPORTANT?**

With the design biennale and the fashion event, the Portuguese Design Centre and the Design Museum among others, Lisbon is already a hot spot in the design circuit. Design not only improves the quality of life of its citizens, it also helps to promote Lisbon in the tourist and cultural circuits. It contributes a lot to elevating Lisbon as a city devoted to promoting the link between patrimony and contemporary production. In the Iberian context, and that represents a large geographical, political, and economical zone within the European Union, we have assumed a leading role.

**WHAT EXAMPLES OF DESIGN PROMOTION STRATEGIES
DEVELOPED IN OTHER CITIES INSPIRE YOU?**

I definitely prefer to look at Lisbon within the national and international context, of course, and to create a strategy for our own needs and aims. Nevertheless, Milan is obviously an example to be considered…

〉〉

EXPERIMENTA DESIGN, LISBON

BY AUGUSTA REGINA MOURA GUEDES
> Founder and Chairman of Experimenta
> Director of the biennale ExperimentaDesign—Bienal de Lisboa

>>>

Experimenta—the Association for the Promotion of Design and Project Culture—is a non-profit organization founded in Lisbon in 1998. Experimenta is a knowledge and event production unit that uses creativity as its main raw material and works within Portuguese culture to bring about permanent change. Its creativity and its main field of action is culture and culture's permanent transformation. It aims to intervene incisively in the processes of thinking, producing, and promoting culture in Portugal. ✕ Experimenta explores a variety of artistic interventions by bringing together different creative activities, experience, and knowledge, all within a design context. It acts as a strategic partner for anyone—in Portugal and abroad—who looks at culture as a catalyst and an indispensable factor in the development of Portugal, its economy, and its urban fabric. Through its work in the field of contemporary design, it unites brings together culture and commerce, industry and communications, experimentation and development. Experimenta seeks to contribute to the redefinition of the boundaries from which emerge new thoughts, new aesthetic principles for the world, and new opportunities for human development. ✕ Its staff is made up of musicians, architects, and designers of all types—industrial, graphic, image, and sound designers—as well as managers, artists, journalists, engineers, lawyers, and professionals from other disciplines.

>>>

The Experimenta Association is primarily known for:
> ExperimentaDesign—Lisbon Biennale >> Voyager >>> Designwise
among other products and services.

>>>

OBJECTIVES OF EXPERIMENTA

> To conceive and produce ExperimentaDesign for the Lisbon Biennale and to establish this event within the existing international biennale circuit based on the strengths of its alternative and inter-disciplinary character and its original organic development. This biennale launched Lisbon as an international platform, allowing it to develop as a "free zone" in which various cultural products could be designed, built, and shown.

01

> To stimulate and promote creativity and the critical and productive capacities of the Portuguese people, creating conditions for the synergy of Portuguese cultural and economic agents.
> To educate and inform the public about the Association and its activities, since it is as important to promote the education of creators as it is to court potential consumers of cultural products.
> To democratize culture by trying to reach out to as many people as possible and by doing so in a joyous and celebratory manner.
> To create conditions for the setting up of cultural laboratories in the areas that need it most, namely, design and new media. These laboratories must adopt a gradual and sustainable approach based on a network of public institutions, private enterprises, and free agents.
> To provide services in design, architecture, and communications, either in response to direct invitations or as the initiator.
> To internationalize Portuguese cultural production by creating circuits for the presentation of the work abroad and by creating travelling projects.
> To defend art and culture as essential to society and fundamental to its survival and growth.
> To encourage active international collaborations in the areas of design, architecture, and culture by developing projects in partnership with other countries.
> To ensure that the mutability and cross-disciplinary that feed creative processes nowadays do not result in a loss of traditional identities and expressions, but rather that they encourage the discovery of new methodologies as well as openness to new situations and, consequently, new realities.
> To encourage the understanding of art, design, and culture as services provided to society in which the underlining idea of a project is the creative motivator.

01 S*Cool exhibition, ExperimentaDesign 2003

HERMÈS

LXD03
CNAL DE LISBOA
7SET - 02NOV

SHOWINDOWS

EXPERIMENTADESIGN2003

01

02

03

EXPERIMENTADESIGN—LISBON BIENNALE

ExperimentaDesign—Lisbon Biennale was created in Portugal in 1999 by the Experimenta Association. ExperimentaDesign—Lisbon Biennale is an active and dynamic cultural platform with an international dimension of dialogue and reflection. ✕ Every two years this event invades Lisbon, in September and October, to showcase projects of different formats, from conferences and screenings to exhibitions and urban interventions, as well as performances in various spaces. The biennale is based in Lisbon and organized by the people of that city but in collaboration with a network of Portuguese and international creators and partners who have common perspectives and attitudes, and who consider collaboration to be fundamental in today's world. ✕ The Lisbon Biennale's starting point is design: not industrial design or graphic design, not sound design, interior, or environmental design, but design as a working discipline and a methodology: a creative activity and cultural process that brings together economics, aesthetics, ethics, ecology, technology, sociology, functionality, and sustainable development to produce the most appropriate responses to contemporary society's needs. Within this perspective, the Lisbon Biennale integrates architecture, photography, new media, dance, visual arts, cinema, theory, and criticism, among other fields, while exploring various formats for presenting content. ✕ The biennale does not import existing projects; it commissions and creates them from scratch, working non-stop year after year, as it has since 1999. ✕ Above all ExperimentaDesign—Lisbon Biennale is an open event that is constantly evolving and redefining itself.

〉〉〉

FINANCIAL STRUCTURE OF EXPERIMENTADESIGN—LISBON BIENNALE

ExperimentaDesign—Lisbon Biennale is Portugal's largest recurring cultural event. An initiative of the Experimenta Association in partnership with Lisbon City Council, it receives the support of Portugal's Ministry of Culture. Since 2002, the contributions from the Lisbon City Council and the Ministry of Culture have represented 45 percent of the biennale's total budget. The remaining 55 percent is provided by private sponsors and co-productions, both local and international. ✕ Over 95 percent of the Lisbon Biennale's events and publications are free of charge. Since its first edition, the biennale has been designated by the President of the Portuguese Republic as a High Patronage event and has been awarded the Statute of Superior Cultural Interest within the patronage of the Arts Law.

ExperimentaDesign 2003 : 01 Matali Crasset, Showindows 02 Jurgen Bey, Bright Minds, Beautiful Ideas exhibition
03 Thom Faulders – Beige Design, Expanded exhibition 04 Campanas exhibition

EXPERIMENTADESIGN 1999

〉〉〉

THEME — Intersections of and in Design

DATES — September 12 to October 16, 1999

PARTICIPANTS — 130 Portuguese and foreign participants

VISITORS — 29,817

EXHIBITIONS
> Objectos Comunicantes (Convento do Beato)
> Meeting Point (Gare Marítima de Alcântara)
> Design Inserts (Gare Marítima de Alcântara)
> O Futuro é um estado de Alma
  (Sociedade Nacional de Belas Artes)
> Essentials Deluxe (Centro Cultural de
  Belém)
> Archizoom Today (Centro Cultural de Belém)
> Experimentáveis ou Experimentais?
  (Convento do Beato)
> Escala Reduzida (Palácio Pombal)

CINEMA CYCLE — Designmatography (Cinemateca Portuguesa)

PERFORMANCE — Houseware Experience (Central Tejo)

CONFERENCES AND WORKSHOPS
> Lisbon Conferences
  (Centro Cultural de Belém)
> Intersections of and in Design
  —Arrábida Course

OTHER PROJECTS

URBAN INTERVENTIONS

EXPERIMENTADESIGN 2001

〉〉

Modus Operandi

〉〉

September 16 to October 31, 2001

〉〉

180 Portuguese and foreign participants

〉〉

84,142

〉〉

〉 Space Invaders (Central Tejo)
〉 Dieter Rams Haus
   (Centro Cultural de Belém)
〉 Voyager 01 (Pavilhão de Portugal)
〉 A Casa do Coleccionador (FIL)
〉 Designoperandi (Cordoaria Nacional)
〉 After Olympics (Promontório)

〉〉

Designmatography II

〉〉

〉〉

〉 Lisbon Conferences (Centro Cultural de
   Belém and Fundação Calouste Gulbenkian)
〉 O pensamento enquanto Design
   (Universidade de Verão da Arrábida)
〉 1000 Plateaux (Cais da Bica do Sapato)

〉〉

〉 Pixel (CAM/Fundação Calouste Gulbenkian)
〉 Lounging Space (Cais da Bica do Sapato)

〉〉

〉〉

**EXPERIMENTADESIGN 2003
—LISBON BIENNALE**

〉〉

Beyond Consumption

〉〉

September 16 to November 2, 2003

〉〉

376 Portuguese and foreign participants

〉〉

133,483

〉〉

〉 Bright Minds, Beautiful Ideas
   (Centro Cultural de Belém)
〉 Campanas (Valentim de Carvalho, Rossio)
〉 Expanded (Torreão Nascente,
   Cordoaria Nacional)
〉 Design France: Innovation and Inspiration
   (Torreão Nascente, Cordoaria Nacional)
〉 Objectos Cruzados (FIL-Intercasa)
〉 S*Cool (Edifício Record)

〉〉

Designmatography III (Cinema São Jorge)

〉〉

〉〉

〉 1000 Plateaux (Cinema São Jorge)
〉 Lisbon Conferences (Teatro Municipal
   São Luiz / Centro Cultural de Belém)
〉 EXD Masterclasses (Palácio Foz)

〉〉

〉〉

〉 Lounging Space (Cinema São Jorge)
〉 Showindows (Baixa, Av. Da Liberdade)
〉 Voyager 03 (Praça do Comércio)
〉 Super Panorama (Panorâmico de Monsanto)

〉〉

01

02

03

04

VOYAGER–EXPERIMENTADESIGN–LISBON BIENNALE
A SPECIAL INTERNATIONAL COMMUNICATION PROJECT

Voyager is an installation–exhibition on Portuguese creativity that also disseminates information about the Lisbon Biennale. As a communications exhibition, it is designed to be shown at home and abroad. The project offers opportunities for contemporary creation, and all of the showcased content is original. Voyager explores and experiments with new exhibition formats, seeking new and more efficient means of reaching out to the public. It is a creative collaboration strategy; at each presentation it challenges interlocutors and creators and establishes co-operative networks for exchange. × Voyager is characterized by experimentation, exploration, and the integration of various disciplines and dialogues between creators and visitors. It challenges artists and designers to create an image—among the many possible images—of contemporary Portuguese culture. Voyager often investigates movement, displacement, open space, time, and speed.

Voyager 01

Due to its modular concept, Voyager 01 was designed to be presented indoors. It comprised the proposals of eighty creators working in the fields of environmental design, architecture, dance, fashion design, graphic design, industrial design, music, new media, photography, product design, sound design, video, and the visual arts.

Presentations in 2001
> Milan, Fuori Salone, April
> London, The Old Truman Brewery (Brick Lane), June
> Lisbon, Pavilhão de Portugal, September

Presentations in 2002
> Barcelona, upon an invitation by the Spanish Ministry of Culture for Portugal to participate in the Barcelona International Book Salon (12,303 visitors, 535 visitors/day)

Voyager 03

The result of a concept that stressed collaboration, Voyager 03 was designed to be transportable and displayed in public spaces. It presented the proposals of fifty creators working in the fields of architecture, art, photography, graphic design, industrial design, fashion design, product design, video, and music.

Presentations in 2003
> Barcelona, Plaza dels Angels, in front of MACBA, July 3 to 12
  (10,600 visitors, 1060 visitors/day)
> Paris, in front of the city's Musée d'Art Moderne and the Palais Tokyo, July 17 to 27
  (7,400 visitors, 673 visitors/day)
> Madrid, Plaza Santa Isabel, in front of Museu Centro de Arte Reina Sofia, September 10 to 14
  (3,970 visitors, 993 visitors/day)
> Lisbon, Praça do Comércio,September 17 to November 2
  (13,274 visitors, 282 visitors/day)

01 Voyager 2003, Barcelona 02 Voyager, Red Module, 2001 03 Voyager 2003, Lisbon 04 Voyager 2003, Paris

IMPACT OF THE EXPERIMENTADESIGN—LISBON BIENNALE INTERNATIONAL

There are many and different ways of measuring the side effects of ExperimentaDesign. In addition to the growth of jobs in the cultural field, there has been a huge investment in the creative community. The event acts as a launching platform for many Portuguese designers, architects, and other creators—not only in Portugal but also abroad. ✕ The biennale also helps to mark Lisbon as a design city within international tourist circuits, increasing tourism and improving the image of Portugal as a country focused on contemporary creativity and innovation. Finally, it helps to improve the number and quality of design-driven places in the city, such as shops and restaurants. ✕ Perhaps one of the most important outcomes is that some of the ideas generated at ExperimentaDesign—some of the projects presented at biennale events—are actually produced, becoming major transformational factors in our city. Because they go beyond mere ephemeral projects, prototypes, or concepts to become reality, such projects interact multi-dimensionally with the future of Lisbon. The Car Parking Silos are one example. Originally presented within Voyager 03 as a research project by nine Portuguese architecture studios working in urban design, cars, floating population, accessibility, etc., the nine proposals were later adopted by the city, and some of them are now being built. ✕ Launched by Experimenta after the second edition of the biennale, Designwise is an organization that edits, manufactures, and distributes original products created by Portuguese designers. Designwise is not a specialized collection, nor is it dedicated to a specific category of objects: its products span a variety of scales and universes, incorporating different materials, uses, and prices. What brings unity to the seemingly diverse objects is the fact that they all "tell a story," often with unexpected humour. The stories may be imagined by the designer, or simply created by the users when they appropriate the objects into their own personal universes. Designwise is all about Portuguese design and industry, and since 2002 its products have been sold worldwide. ✕ Another dimension of the impact of Experimenta is that Voyager 03 has also been shown in other Portuguese cities, thus expanding the information flow on the biennale and encouraging larger audiences locally and in Lisbon while increasing interest in design and culture. ✕ ExperimentaDesign supports the idea of celebrating culture in festive and democratic ways. It invades Lisbon for one month and a half each year, opening up familiar and unfamiliar places to give, to anyone who wants to take the challenge, an opportunity to discover them. ✕ Finally, ExperimentaDesign is about networking, the fundamental concept of our times and the future, in terms of cities and their roles in sustainable development.

01

02

Car Parking Silos, Voyager 2003, ExperimentaDesign 2003 : 01 Design: Nuno Mateus Guerreiro 02 Design: Emit Flesti

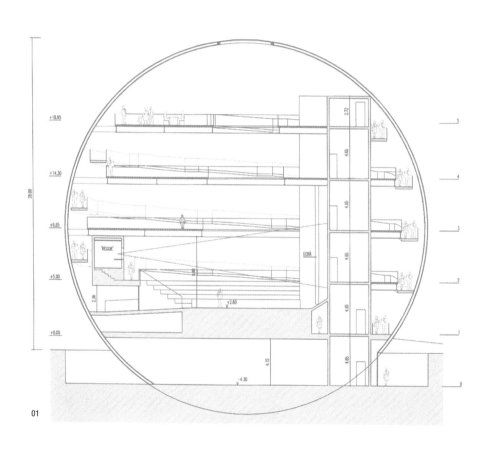

01

01 The project "Global Network Building" is a public building sphere-shaped, an icon for the city where the most varied activities can take place – educational, cultural, scientific

›››››››››››››››››››››››››››››››››››
HENRIQUE CAYATTE
› Graphic designer and advisor
at Henrique Cayatte Studio
› Founder, head designer, and illustrator
of the newspaper *Público*
› President of the Portuguese Design Centre,
Lisbon.
›››››››››››››››››››››››››››››››››››››
Henrique Cayatte, graphic designer, Portugal
Born in Lisbon (1957), Cayatte is president of
the Portuguese Design Centre. In 1991 he
founded the Henrique Cayatte Studio, which
works on cultural, educational, and scientific
design, illustrations and editorial production
and signage and also acts as a multimedia
graphic advisor. Cayatte is the founder, head
designer, graphic editor, and illustrator of the
newspaper *Público*.
›››››››››››››››››››››››››››››››››››››
WHAT ARE YOUR TWO FAVOURITE
PUBLIC PLACES IN YOUR CITY?
The old quarters of Lisbon, including the
Castle and Bairro Alto, and the city's
riverfront, around Terreiro do Paço and
the Expo '98 site.
WHAT WOULD YOU LIKE TO SEE
IMPROVED DESIGN-WISE?
The involvement and social responsibility
of designers. Design in public places
with total access ensured by clear signs
and communication. Support for
design exploration.
WHAT WOULD YOU LIKE
TO SEE BUILT IN YOUR CITY?
First, less and better! Then, a place of
utopia for the twenty-first century.
›››››››››››››››››››››››››››››››››››››

01

〉〉〉

MIGUEL VIEIRA BAPTISTA
〉 Industrial designer
〉〉〉

Born in Lisbon in 1968. Graduated in Industrial Design from IADE in 1990. Obtained a post-graduate degree in Product Design from Glasgow School of Art in 1993. In 1994 started working in product, exhibition, and interior design for companies such as Atlantis, Authentics, Asplund, Loja da Atalaia, ProtoDesign, and Vista Alegre. In 2001 curated and designed the exhibition Dieter Rams Haus at the Centro Cultural de Belém museum, in Lisbon. In 2003 designed the exhibition vehicle Voyager 03, for ExperimentaDesign—Lisbon Biennale; it travelled to several European cities. Between 2002 and 2004 designed twice a year the interiors for the Lisbon Fashion Week.
〉〉〉

WHAT IS YOUR FAVOURITE PUBLIC PLACE IN LISBON?
There is a cedar tree from 1859 in the Principe Real garden. Its branches have spread over the years onto a man-made metal structure, creating a shadow that's 20 metres in diameter. It's a great place for people to rest for a while.
WHAT WOULD YOU LIKE TO SEE IMPROVED DESIGN-WISE?
I'd like to see the city's sidewalks broadened.
WHAT WOULD YOU LIKE TO SEE BUILT IN YOUR CITY?
A new bridge built over the River Tagus.
〉〉〉

01 "Figo" modular carpet in wool, design: Miguel Vieira Baptista, 2003

— ASPIRER À DEVENIR UNE VILLE DE DESIGN, C'EST AVANT TOUT SE PRÉOCCUPER DU BIEN-ÊTRE DE SES CITOYENS, C'EST MILITER EN FAVEUR DE LEUR QUALITÉ DE VIE DANS UNE OPTIQUE DE DÉVELOPPEMENT DURABLE.
Gérald Tremblay, Maire de Montréal

POR-TRAIT

POPULATION

Population de 3,5 millions pour l'aggloméra-tion métropolitaine, dont 34,3% composent plus de 150 communautés culturelles.

ANNÉE DE FONDATION

Fondée en 1642 par des militaires et des religieux français. Conquise en 1760 par l'Angleterre.

HISTORIQUE DES ÉVÉNEMENTS FONDATEURS

À la fin du XIXe siècle, Montréal est la métropole incontestée du Canada. Le développement du chemin de fer transcontinental, les grandes entreprises maritimes qui commercent avec l'Europe et l'Asie, quelques banques tôt concentrées et d'importantes sociétés (fourrure, tabac, farine, sucre, ferronnerie…) ont fait sa fortune. La Seconde Guerre sera l'occasion du développement de fortes industries : aéronautique, optique, biochimie… ✕ Mais le déclin d'après-guerre des indus-tries traditionnelles entraînera la perte de multiples sièges sociaux et d'une partie importante de l'activité financière au béné-fice de Toronto, devenue métropole du Canada. ✕ La reprise de la fin du XXe siècle se produira autour des nouvelles technolo-gies de l'information et des communications, des agences de publicité, et de l'industrie du cinéma, qui font les beaux jours du Montréal contemporain, mais aussi grâce à une très forte activité récréotouristique, notamment autour des festivals internationaux et des plaisirs de la table. ✕ L'exposition universelle de 1967, Expo 67, et la construction du métro, puis les Jeux olympiques de 1976, constituent des moments clés pour le design au Québec. Montréal et ses créateurs vont alors bénéficier d'occasions de travail et d'une ouverture médiatique sans précédent. ✕ Les professions du design, qui avaient commencé à se structurer, acquièrent notoriété et crédibilité. Montréal attire un certain nombre de designers européens qui y feront carrière, et parfois même école.

1933 › Fondation de l'Association des décorateurs d'intérieur du Québec, qui deviendra en 1948, Société des décorateurs-ensembliers du Québec puis, en 1992, Société des designers d'intérieur du Québec et, en 2003, Association des professionnels en design d'intérieur du Québec;

1951 › Formation de l'Art Directors Club de Montréal, suivie en 1974 par celle de la Société des graphistes, qui, 20 ans plus tard, prend le nom de Société des designers graphiques du Québec;

1958 › Fondation de l'Association des designers industriels du Québec;

1966 › Le Conseil national d'esthétique industrielle (fédéral) — Design Canada ouvre un centre de design à Montréal destiné à la promotion du design canadien (fermé en 1970);

1973 › Ouverture d'une section de design industriel à la Faculté de l'aménagement de l'Université de Montréal, puis, en 1974, création des programmes en design graphique et en design de l'environnement (architecture, design industriel et design urbain) à l'Université du Québec à Montréal (UQAM);

1979 › Le Centre Canadien d'Architecture (CCA) est fondé par Phyllis Lambert;

1981 › Création du Centre de design de l'UQAM par un groupe de professeurs;

1983 › Lancement de Via Design, exposition commerciale de design, incluant la mode, qui ne connaîtra que trois éditions;

1984 › La Société des graphistes du Québec lance le concours Graphisme Québec, remplacé en 1997 par les prix Grafika à l'initiative des Éditions Infopresse;

1986 › Deux centres de design (vitrines d'exposition pour les fournisseurs de l'industrie) voient le jour à Montréal : le Centre Infodesign, créé par une promotrice du design, Ginette Gadoury, et fermé en 1988, et le Centre international de design, initié par un promoteur immobilier et fermé en 1989;

Avec la sortie du Rapport Picard en 1986, le design devient l'un des sept axes prioritaires pour le développement économique de la région de Montréal. Les gouvernements du Canada, du Québec et la Ville de Montréal se mobilisent autour de l'objectif de faire de Montréal un centre de design de calibre international. Dans la foulée des recommandations de ce rapport, en :

1989 › Ginette Gadoury et la Société des décorateurs-ensembliers du Québec lancent le Salon international du design d'intérieur de Montréal (SIDIM);

1989 › Agence Liaison Design, un centre d'information et de maillages entre l'offre et la demande en design, est fondé par Marie-Josée Lacroix avec l'appui des associations professionnelles. Liaison Design sera intégré à l'Institut de Design Montréal en 1995;

1991 › La Ville de Montréal innove en Amérique du Nord en créant un poste de commissaire au design, exclusivement consacré au développement et à la promotion du design dans la métropole;

1992 › L'Institut de Design Montréal, dirigé par Elen Stavridou, est mis sur pied sous l'impulsion de la Chambre de commerce du Montréal métropolitain, grâce à des financements des gouvernements fédéral, provincial et municipal;

1995 › Le commissariat au design de la Ville de Montréal lance le concours Commerce Design Montréal;

› Fondation de l'École supérieure de mode par l'UQAM et le Groupe Collège LaSalle;

1998 › Création de l'émission d, entièrement consacrée au design sous toutes ses formes, produite par TVMaxPlus et diffusée entre autres sur TV5 (Sylvie Berkowicz, réalisatrice, et François Guenet, producteur délégué);

Fin des années 90, Le Centre de design de l'UQAM met l'accent sur la reconnaissance du design québécois sur la scène internationale. Grâce au soutien des trois paliers de gouvernement, Montréal 5 — portrait de cinq designers montréalais (sous la direction de Georges Adamczyk), puis une série d'expositions itinérantes (sous la direction de

Marc H. Choko) sont présentées à partir de 1998, en Amérique du Nord, en Amérique latine, en Europe et en Chine ;

2005 › L'installation du siège social de l'International Design Alliance (regroupant l'ICSID et l'ICOGRADA) marque une autre étape de l'ouverture de la ville sur l'international et de la reconnaissance de Montréal dans le domaine du design.

〉〉〉

NOMBRE DE DESIGNERS

Montréal compte environ 20 000 designers et architectes œuvrant dans tous les domaines de la conception. Après un léger exode des créateurs durant la crise économique des années 80, ce phénomène s'est inversé avec une hausse de près de 40 % du nombre de designers au cours des 10 dernières années.

〉〉〉

DESIGNERS RÉPUTÉS

Moshe Safdie, concepteur du complexe Habitat 67, est certainement l'architecte le plus connu sur la scène internationale. Dan Hanganu est le créateur de plusieurs institutions montréalaises d'importance dont l'emblématique Musée d'histoire et d'archéologie de Montréal Pointe-à-Callière. Les architectes Saucier + Perrotte, concepteurs des futures installations du Cirque du Soleil à Tokyo, ont commencé à se faire remarquer, notamment lors de la Biennale de Venise 2004. ✕ En design de produits, Michel Dallaire, concepteur, entre autres, du mobilier de la Grande Bibliothèque du Québec et du mobilier urbain du Quartier international de Montréal, est la figure dominante. ✕ En design graphique, de jeunes agences comme Orangetango et Paprika se distinguent par leurs créations souvent audacieuses, dans les domaines culturel et commercial. ✕ Du côté du design d'intérieur, Jean-Pierre Viau s'impose comme chef de file, du moins en aménagement de commerces, comme en témoignent les nombreux prix qui lui ont été décernés par Commerce Design Montréal. ✕ Enfin, signalons les principales figures actuelles en design de mode, Philippe Dubuc, en architecture de paysage, Claude Cormier, et en design d'exposition, GSM design.

〉〉〉

〉〉〉

PRINCIPAUX ÉVÉNEMENTS EN DESIGN

Plusieurs événements en design se déroulent en mai, baptisé par l'Institut de Design Montréal «Mois du design» : parmi les activités, notons la tenue des expositions des étudiants de toutes les écoles de design montréalaises, le SIDIM, la remise des prix du concours Commerce Design Montréal et celle de l'Institut de Design Montréal. ✕ Depuis 2004, la Biennale internationale de Montréal (arts visuels et architecture) inclut aussi un volet design.

〉〉〉

INSTITUTIONS

Sur le plan des expositions et de la diffusion en design, on retrouve à Montréal l'une des plus importantes collections de design contemporain, de 1935 à aujourd'hui (textiles, arts de la table et mobilier), acquise par la Fondation Stewart pour le Musée des Arts décoratifs de Montréal, maintenant intégré au Musée des Beaux-Arts de Montréal. ✕ Doté d'un fonds d'archives unique, le CCA figure parmi les plus prestigieuses institutions de recherche et de diffusion de l'architecture au monde. ✕ Le Centre de design de l'UQAM présente ou produit des expositions (certaines itinérantes) dans tous les domaines du design depuis 1981. ✕ Monopoli, galerie d'architecture, propose des expositions thématiques depuis 2003.

〉〉〉

〉〉

ÉCOLES ET PROGRAMMES DE DESIGN

Le département Design Art de l'Université Concordia offre un programme d'études de trois ans. Il met l'accent sur l'interdépendance entre le design, les arts et les sciences humaines et appliquées. Il offre également un diplôme d'études supérieures en Design et technologies numériques, ainsi qu'un baccalauréat en Image et son numériques. ✕ L'École de design industriel de l'Université de Montréal offre deux programmes de formation professionnelle en design : Design industriel (quatre ans) et Design d'intérieur (trois ans). Le programme de maîtrise en Design et complexité ainsi que celui du doctorat en Aménagement accueillent les concepteurs désireux de poursuivre des recherches plus poussées. ✕ L'École d'architecture de l'Université de Montréal présente un programme de formation de quatre ans reconnu par l'Ordre des architectes, tout comme l'Université McGill. Enfin, l'Université de Montréal offre également, depuis plus de 30 ans, la seule formation universitaire en Architecture de paysage au Québec. ✕ L'École de design de l'UQAM, créée en 1974, offre trois programmes de premier cycle — Design graphique et Design de l'environnement, et, en collaboration avec le Collège LaSalle, Design de mode (trois ans), ainsi que trois programmes d'études supérieures spécialisés : Connaissance et sauvegarde de l'architecture moderne; Design d'événements et Design d'équipements de transport (un an). L'École organise chaque année une session d'été en Design international.

〉〉

〉〉

STRATÉGIES DESIGN

Les stratégies municipales sont essentiellement axées sur l'amélioration du design de la ville et sur la promotion de Montréal comme Ville de design. ✕ Depuis 1991, par l'action de son Commissariat au design jumelant un travail de communication, des réalisation exemplaires et un rôle d'accompagnement de la commande en design (concours de mobilier pour le Casino de Montréal et pour la Grande Bibliothèque du Québec, atelier pour l'identité du Quartier des spectacles, etc.), la Ville sensibilise les acteurs privés et publics aux bénéfices de la qualité en design. ✕ Après un important effort de sensibilisation, de 1995 à 2004, auprès des commerçants (détaillants, restaurateurs, hôteliers, artisans), au moyen du programme Commerce Design Montréal — dont elle fut l'instigatrice et qui est aujourd'hui repris par d'autres villes du monde —, la Ville élabore sa nouvelle stratégie intégrée «Design de ville | ville de design» visant à introduire la notion d'innovation en design dans l'ensemble des décisions et actions affectant l'environnement bâti, de même qu'à intensifier la mise en réseau internationale du design montréalais.

〉〉

Portrait de Montréal par

MARC H. CHOKO

〉 Professeur titulaire à l'École de design
〉 Directeur du Centre de design de l'Université du Québec à Montréal

〉〉

GÉRALD TREMBLAY
MAIRE DE MONTRÉAL
DEPUIS 2001

〉〉

CONSIDÉREZ-VOUS MONTRÉAL COMME UNE NOUVELLE VILLE DE DESIGN?
Tout d'abord, je crois que pour être une ville de design, il ne suffit pas de le déclarer. Il faut être très prudent lorsqu'on adopte des slogans «Montréal, capitale de ceci ou de cela». Si c'est utile et important pour consolider une réputation, il faut quand même que ce soit le reflet d'une réalité. ✕ Je préférerais donc qualifier Montréal de jeune métropole de design, de ville de design émergente sur la scène internationale. Pourquoi? Parce que Montréal est à la fois une ville où le design et les designers représentent une force dynamique de la vie culturelle et économique, et une ville qui sait de mieux en mieux mettre cette puissance créatrice au service de la qualité de son cadre de vie.

✕ Ville moderne, propulsée sur la scène internationale par l'Exposition universelle de 1967, Montréal suscite aujourd'hui la curiosité et la conquête des amateurs de culture et de design, qui s'y établissent ou qui en font leur destination touristique, les uns attirés par l'accessibilité d'un cadre de vie de qualité, les autres stimulés par la créativité ambiante ou séduits par la diversité de son offre commerciale. Ce sont autant de motivations à l'origine de la récente décision de l'International Design Alliance (secrétariat conjoint de l'ICSID et de l'ICOGRADA) d'établir son siège social à Montréal. Ce choix s'est fait parmi une trentaine de villes candidates. Nous en sommes très fiers. ✕ Montréal bénéficie de certains atouts majeurs : présence de plusieurs designers, institutions de formation performantes et centres de diffusion réputés. Mais selon moi, ce qui fait notre principale force et notre différence comme ville de design tient avant tout à la dissémination de la créativité en design et en architecture partout dans la ville, sans égard à la taille ou à la nature des projets. Cette omniprésence subtile de la création — discrète ou éclatante — résulte d'un travail de démocratisation du design trop souvent réservé à l'élite ou aux limites convenues des centre-villes. ✕ Grâce à des initiatives telles que Commerce Design Montréal et à celles de plusieurs partenaires engagés dans cette même mission de sensibilisation, LE DESIGN À MONTRÉAL N'EST PAS SEULEMENT SPECTA-CLE, IL EST SOURCE DE MIEUX-ÊTRE AU QUOTIDIEN ET DEVIENT UNE VALEUR POUR LES MONTRÉALAISES ET MONTRÉALAIS. AINSI PORTÉE PAR SES CITOYENS, MONTRÉAL S'AFFIRMERA FORCÉMENT COMME VILLE DE DESIGN.

QUELLE FUT VOTRE CONTRIBUTION PERSONNELLE À L'ÉMERGENCE DE MONTRÉAL COMME VILLE DE DESIGN?

En premier lieu, je dirais que je crois profondément en l'importance du design. Et cette conviction n'est pas née d'hier. Lorsque j'étais ministre de l'Industrie, de la Science et de la Technologie du Québec, de 1989 à 1994, j'ai créé le crédit d'impôt au design, une mesure fiscale déterminante pour stimuler les investissements privés dans la recherche et l'innovation en design, encore en vigueur. Cet incitatif a développé le marché pour les designers du Québec, dont près des deux tiers sont concentrés à Montréal. Sous l'initiative de Bernard Lamarre, j'ai aussi soutenu la création de l'Institut de Design, qui a pour mission de promouvoir le design en tant que valeur économique et faire de Montréal un centre de design de calibre international. ✕ Comme maire, mes fonctions m'amènent à prendre quotidiennement des décisions qui ont un impact sur le design de la ville. Il m'incombe d'en être conscient et de savoir m'entourer des compétences indispensables pour éclairer mes jugements. À ce titre, nous avons mis en place plusieurs instances qui jouent ce rôle de conseiller, dont le Conseil du patrimoine et, plus singulier, le Commissariat au design. ✕ À cet égard, la Ville de Montréal est la seule ville canadienne à s'être dotée d'une fonction de commissaire, exclusivement consacrée à la promotion du design. Ce poste, créé par mes prédécesseurs il y a 15 ans, a beaucoup contribué à la croissance du design montréalais. Ma contribution aura sans doute été de reconnaître immédiatement l'importance stratégique de cette fonction au sein de l'appareil municipal et d'en soutenir les actions et interventions. Le défi est désormais d'élargir la portée de l'intervention du Commissariat au design de la Ville par une approche intégrée de valorisation du design à l'ensemble de nos actions sur le territoire. La Ville, comme institution, doit elle-même montrer l'exemple et innover dans ses façons d'agir, être un meilleur client pour que les designers puissent nous aider à mieux «faire» la ville.

01

02

01 Vue de Montréal à partir du Pont Champlain 02 Parc du Mont-Royal

POURQUOI CROYEZ-VOUS IMPORTANT DE POSITIONNER VOTRE VILLE PAR LE DESIGN ?

Le design n'a de sens que lorsqu'il permet aux humains de mieux vivre, de s'épanouir. L'importance du design vient de son immense impact sur nos vies. Pensons par exemple à la conception des produits de toutes sortes, des environnements de travail, des maisons, des parcs, des rues. ✕ Ainsi, aspirer à devenir une ville de design, c'est avant tout se préoccuper du bien-être de ses citoyens, c'est militer en faveur de leur qualité de vie dans une optique de développement durable. ✕ ✕ D'AILLEURS, LE DESIGN CONSTITUE UN OUTIL EXTRAORDI-NAIRE D'INCLUSION SOCIALE. NOS VILLES OCCIDENTALES SONT EN PHASE DE REQUALIFICATION (RECYCLAGE, RÉUTILISATION, RESTAURATION, RÉHABILITATION), DANS UN CONTEXTE DE MUTATION SOCIOCULTURELLE SANS PRÉCÉDENT, QUI NÉCESSITE UNE COHABITATION TOUTE NOUVELLE DE POINTS DE VUE ET VALEURS. ✕ Récemment, un atelier de design a été organisé pour choisir une équipe de concepteurs dans le but de développer l'identité du Quartier des spectacles de Montréal. Plus qu'un simple processus de sélection de professionnels qui a conduit au choix du designer suisse Ruedi Baur et du montréalais Jean Beaudoin du réseau international Intégral, cet exercice de design contextuel a surtout offert une plateforme pour enrichir la réflexion sur les attentes et besoins des différents groupes d'intérêts, parfois divergents, qui occupent ce territoire, puis générer parmi eux une vision commune inclusive indispensable à la réussite du projet. ✕ Miser sur le design pour l'avenir de Montréal, c'est saisir l'occasion que nous offre ce puissant processus de conception pour [re]faire la ville avec et pour celles et celles qui y vivent.

DES STRATÉGIES DE PROMOTION DU DESIGN INITIÉES PAR D'AUTRES VILLES VOUS ONT-ELLES INSPIRÉS ?

Montréal est active dans divers réseaux internationaux de villes (Metropolis, Association Internationale des Maires Francophones (AIMF), Cités et Gouvernements Locaux Unis (CGLU)), et nous avons signé des protocoles de partenariat avec plusieurs villes du monde. Ces relations alimentent constamment notre réflexion et enrichissent nos pratiques. Le design étant une fonction transversale qui touche plusieurs dimensions de la vie municipale, nous avons été inspirés par de nombreuses actions menées par nos collègues des autres villes, comme le plan lumière de la Ville de Lyon. ✕ La Biennale Internationale Design Saint-Étienne a aussi représenté une importante source d'inspiration pour nous. Animée par une forte volonté de démocratisation du design, nous aimerions que certains éléments fondateurs de ce concept stéphanois donnent naissance à une biennale similaire montréalaise centrée sur les Amériques. ✕ Et plus récemment, dans le cadre de nos réflexions visant à doter Montréal d'une stratégie intégrée de valorisation du design articulée autour de l'idée d'une «plateforme d'innovation en design», le modèle britannique CABE (Commission for Architecture and the Built Environment) nous a beaucoup inspirés. Nous sommes entre autres convaincus de la pertinence de former des «design champions», ces indispensables relais sur le terrain, pour promouvoir la qualité en design dans tous les arrondissements de Montréal.

QUELS DEVRAIENT ÊTRE LES RÔLES RESPECTIFS DU CITOYEN, DU DESIGNER ET DE L'ÉLU DANS LE DÉVELOPPEMENT D'UNE VILLE DE DESIGN ?

Le citoyen doit être critique et exigeant. Il doit savoir reconnaître, apprécier et réclamer un design et une architecture de qualité. Il doit aussi être responsable face à son milieu de vie. Le designer doit être un initiateur de nouvelles idées et un médiateur. Il est l'expert qui inspire tout en assumant pleinement son leadership. Il doit savoir traduire, mettre en forme et projeter les aspirations des élus et des citoyens. ✕ Quant à l'élu, il doit faire preuve d'une vision rassembleuse et prendre le risque de l'innovation tant dans le choix des projets qui lui sont présentés que dans la mise en place des processus.

>>>

COMMERCE DESIGN MONTRÉAL : IMPACTS SUR LA VILLE

PAR MARIE-JOSÉE LACROIX

> **Commissaire au design, Ville de Montréal**

›››

Une ville de design est non seulement une ville qui communique autour du design, mais aussi — et peut-être même surtout — une ville en projet, une ville de projets, qui reflète ce souci de qualité et d'innovation en design dans tout ce qu'elle offre à vivre et à voir : bâtiments, rues, parcs, signalisation, affichage, mobilier urbain, musées, écoles, transports en commun, aéroports, habitations, hôpitaux, commerces… ✕ La Ville de Montréal s'intéresse avant tout au design pour sa contribution à la qualité du milieu de vie, facteur décisif de la localisation des entreprises, mais aussi élément important de différenciation et d'attrait touristique. ✕ L'action municipale vise donc d'abord à encourager la participation des designers à la «confection» de la ville, à stimuler des efforts de qualité en design chez les promoteurs — tant publics que privés –, dont les projets définissent et influencent notre environnement bâti, tout en servant de vitrines d'expérimentation et de diffusion aux designers d'ici et d'ailleurs. ✕ Commerce Design Montréal est né en 1995 de cette volonté municipale d'encourager la qualité en design sur son territoire en ciblant en priorité les commerçants qui, par leur omniprésence dans la ville, ont un impact énorme sur l'attrait de Montréal.

›››

POURQUOI CIBLER LE COMMERCE?

S'il est un secteur d'activité qui influence notre expérience quotidienne de la ville — qu'on y vive, travaille ou la visite –, c'est bien celui du commerce de détail et de la restauration. Lieux d'échanges et d'humanité, les magasins, boutiques et autres ont toujours été et resteront l'âme d'une cité. Lorsqu'ils sont beaux et animés, la ville l'est tout autant… et vice versa. ✕ *A priori*, la Ville en tant qu'institution dispose de très peu de moyens pour promouvoir la qualité en design de commerces. À Montréal, comme partout en Amérique du Nord, la notion d'intérêt public diffère grandement de l'Europe. Chez nous, les droits individuels dominent largement. ✕ De plus, le commerce est ici extrêmement éphémère. La notion de fonds de commerce — et de legs en général — n'existe pas. Les artisans bouchers peuvent succéder à des pharmaciens, eux-mêmes ayant suivi des bistrotiers. Sauf exception, les commerces changent de propriétaire, de vocation et de décor à un rythme effréné. Dans une certaine mesure, chacun peut faire ce qu'il veut à l'intérieur de son établissement, même si, dans bien des cas, la vitrine du commerce — parfois tout en transparence — a autant d'impact visuel sur la rue, du moins pour le piéton, que la façade entière. ✕ Dans un environnement aussi libéral et individualiste, la qualité en architecture et en design peut difficilement être dictée par un cadre réglementaire. Tout devient donc une question de culture. Pour la développer, il faut y être exposé. Personnellement, je ne crois pas à la promotion du «beau», du «bon goût» ou de l'excellence dans l'absolu. Surtout dans une ville courtepointe comme Montréal, dont l'intérêt et l'identité reposent précisément sur le caractère hétérogène, la pluralité des approches, des styles et des regards. ✕ Dans ce contexte, pour instaurer une culture du design et de l'architecture, j'ai confiance en l'immense pouvoir de l'exemple, de l'exemple accessible qui inspire le plus grand nombre. Je crois à l'apprentissage par mimétisme… si ce qui est promu en exemple a du sens culturellement et socialement. L'innovation suivra. ✕ Les Québécois ont fait des pas de géant dans plusieurs domaines où la question des sens et la culture du goût étaient interpellées. Qu'on pense à la gastronomie ou à l'œnologie. Le bilan des 10 ans de Commerce Design Montréal et les récents débats publics sur la question du beau et du laid dans la ville nous indiquent que nous développons aussi un goût pour l'architecture et le design.

01-02 Exemples de commerces de quartier

COMMERCE DESIGN MONTRÉAL — LE CONCEPT

Commerce Design Montréal est donc un concours que nous avons lancé en 1995 pour encourager les collaborations entre les professionnels du design et les commerçants montréalais. L'idée de base était de récompenser ceux et celles qui, par leur talent et leurs judicieux investissements en architecture et en design de commerces, rendent la métropole stimulante, unique et attirante pour les résidants et les gens de passage. Notre objectif était non seulement de récompenser, mais d'en persuader plusieurs autres. ✕ Véritable laboratoire d'expérimentation en matière de stratégies de communication du design, ce colloque a offert une occasion propice d'en partager les principaux enseignements avec d'autres personnes qui, ailleurs dans le monde, dans d'autres villes, travaillent au développement d'une culture du design et de l'architecture. ✕ Après une décennie et près de sept millions $, principalement publics, investis dans ce programme, nous tenions à en mesurer la portée le plus précisément possible. Nous disposions à cet effet d'un corpus unique et abondant de données constitué au fil des ans. Le programme s'est toujours nourri de son autoévaluation pour ajuster ses stratégies. Ces évaluations de rendement et remises en question annuelles de nos outils et actions de promotion nous ont non seulement permis de faire évoluer le concept, de le rendre plus efficient, mais aussi d'en documenter les impacts. ✕ Nous avons fait la somme et la synthèse de cette documentation cumulée au fil des 10 ans dans un rapport intitulé *Commerce Design Montréal 1995-2004 – Rapport décennal* afin de rendre des comptes et de les rendre publics. En voici les faits saillants.

PRINCIPES FONDATEURS

L'objectif premier de ce concours est de créer un effet d'entraînement, de convaincre d'autres commerçants du bien-fondé du design pour leur succès en affaires et d'avoir un impact structurant sur la revitalisation des rues commerciales. ✕ Le principe est de sensibiliser le plus grand nombre par la promotion de cas exemplaires. La campagne promotionnelle et publicitaire entourant les établissements primés se trouve, par conséquent, au cœur de la stratégie préconisée par les organisateurs. Les commerces honorés sont abondamment promus comme des exemples de succès dans les médias grand public pour démontrer aux commerçants avoisinants que la qualité en design est rentable. ✕ La sélection des établissements récompensés est aussi fondamentale à l'atteinte des objectifs de sensibilisation : les commerces primés annuellement doivent refléter plusieurs réalités commerciales de façon à ce que la majorité des commerçants puissent se reconnaître dans l'un ou l'autre des établissements promus. La sélection doit offrir des contre-exemples pour défaire les préjugés et prouver que le design n'est pas un style d'aménagement (moderne et branché), qu'il est abordable et rentable pour tous les commerces, quels que soient leurs produits ou services, leur taille, leur localisation et leur clientèle cible. Il ne s'agit pas de décerner un prix d'excellence absolue en design de commerces, mais 20 prix *ex æquo* d'excellence relative au contexte urbain, au domaine d'activité des commerces et aux ressources disponibles pour leur aménagement. En effet, ce concours est basé sur l'idée que l'on bâtit une ville sur la somme des efforts individuels et non pas sur des cas d'exception. De ce fait, il récompense aussi bien des projets spectaculaires, extrêmement novateurs et à grands budgets que des réalisations beaucoup plus modestes, qui démontrent un souci de qualité d'aménagement et que l'on aimerait voir se multiplier dans tous les quartiers et secteurs d'activité commerciale. ✕ Si les commerces primés sont de bons ambassadeurs dans leur milieu, les consommateurs le sont tout autant, sinon plus. En effet, pour amener les commerçants à investir dans la qualité du design de leur établissement, il faut avant tout qu'ils en sentent le besoin et donc que leur clientèle le réclame. Le concours comporte ainsi, depuis 1998, un vote public, complémentaire à celui du jury, qui invite la population à évaluer les commerces en lice, à porter un regard critique sur les aménagements réalisés et à choisir ses préférés.

01 Salon funéraire Alfred Dallaire, design : Richer-Noël architectes, 2000 02 H₂0 Laundromat et cie, design : Bosses Design, 2001

CHOIX DES LAURÉATS

En tout, 20 grands prix *ex æquo* sont attribués chaque année par un jury d'experts composé de professionnels des différentes disciplines — architecture, design d'intérieur, design graphique, design urbain — et présidé par une personnalité publique du monde des affaires (Louise Roy, consultante internationale), des communications (Jean-Jacques Stréliski, publicitaire ; René Homier-Roy, animateur à la radio de Radio-Canada), des arts (Denys Arcand, cinéaste, *Les invasions barbares*) ou de la culture (Lise Bissonnette, présidente de la Grande Bibliothèque du Québec ; Claude Gosselin, directeur général et artistique de la Biennale de Montréal). Puis, la population est invitée à choisir son commerce préféré parmi ces 20 sélections du jury.

CAMPAGNE DE PROMOTION

Commerce Design Montréal est une activité de promotion du design basée sur les communications auprès du grand public. ✕ Le concours ne distribue pas de récompenses pécuniaires aux commerçants ou aux professionnels de l'aménagement. Il investit plutôt dans la campagne de promotion des lauréats comme des exemples à suivre. Il contribue ainsi à leur notoriété et à l'accroissement de leur volume d'affaires tout en maximisant l'effet de contagion recherché. ✕ Le succès du programme repose essentiellement sur la promotion entourant les 20 ambassadeurs et sur sa capacité de toucher les commerçants ainsi que le public. La campagne promotionnelle comporte deux volets : l'un qui nécessite une communication de proximité auprès des Montréalais et l'autre destiné à l'international. Les deux visent autant un public de non-initiés que de spécialistes. Plusieurs outils de communication ont été élaborés et raffinés au cours des 10 ans du concours. ✕ À l'origine, le programme se limitait à l'attribution de prix et mentions pour souligner la qualité en aménagement commercial. L'événement a vite pris de l'envergure par l'ajout progressif d'une foule d'activités périphériques : vote du public, publication d'un guide de design, site Internet, circuits de visites commentées, animation sur rue avec participation à des braderies, relations de presse nationales, puis internationales, etc. Ces outils et stratégies permettent de toujours mieux promouvoir les commerces lauréats pour qu'ils en influencent d'autres, de sensibiliser

01-02 **Affichage dans la ville**

le public afin qu'il réclame plus de qualité en design, de confirmer et faire émerger des talents québécois en design et de positionner Montréal comme une métropole du design. Dix ans plus tard, Commerce Design Montréal est l'une des plus importantes opérations de promotion du design au Québec. D'autres villes s'en inspirent.

〉〉

FINANCEMENT
Commerce Design Montréal est une initiative du Commissariat au design de la Ville de Montréal. Réalisé par une équipe de direction composée de 5 personnes, le programme regroupe depuis quelques années plus de 30 consultants qui assument des mandats spécialisés et ponctuels. Ce capital humain, cette intelligence en design de commerces, plus globalement en communication du design, développé sur plusieurs années, est au cœur de la croissance et du succès du programme.

〉〉

PARTICIPATION DES MILIEUX
Le projet a rapidement et durablement reçu l'appui des réseaux professionnels et d'affaires visés par son action. Les associations professionnelles, chambre de commerce et regroupements de commerçants soutiennent l'activité par une commandite financière ou en services. Ils sont, depuis le début, les principaux relais sur lesquels s'appuie Commerce Design Montréal pour se faire connaître et recruter les candidatures au concours.

〉〉

MOBILISATION DE L'ÉTAT ET DU PRIVÉ
Commerce Design Montréal est basé sur deux grands types de partenariat : de financement et de diffusion. Ils ont joué des rôles essentiels et complémentaires dans l'évolution du programme, en favorisant sa croissance et en optimisant son rendement. ✕ Cette logique de partenariat fait partie intégrante de la stratégie de Commerce Design Montréal. Plus généralement, tous les partenaires sont sollicités en raison de la pertinence de leur contribution potentielle face aux objectifs du programme. ✕ La recherche de pertinence et de synergie entre les partenariats ne limite en rien l'étendue des domaines auxquels ils appartiennent. Au contraire, la diversité est au rendez-vous : Hydro-Québec, Société des alcools du Québec, Société de transport de Montréal, Air Canada, Tourisme Montréal, MusiquePlus… ✕ De même, le positionnement stratégique de Commerce Design Montréal, à la croisée des enjeux urbains, économiques et culturels, bénéficie d'un accueil favorable du gouvernement du Québec. Le caractère transversal du programme mène à l'engagement coordonné de trois ministères directement intéressés à la promotion du design de commerces à Montréal : du Développement économique et régional et de la Recherche ; des Affaires municipales, du Sport et du Loisir ; et de la Culture et des Communications.

〉〉

BUDGET
Commerce Design Montréal a connu une croissance constante et a généré des investissements en promotion du design de presque sept millions $: près de deux millions $ (1 973 465 $) de la Ville de Montréal et environ cinq millions $ (4 907 304 $) des partenaires extérieurs. ✕ En 1995, seule la Ville de Montréal, instigatrice du concours, a fourni l'effort initial en finançant la totalité des coûts directs et indirects de sa réalisation. Dès sa deuxième édition, le programme a commencé à diversifier ses sources de financement. En moyenne, sur les 10 ans, les secteurs parapublic et privé ont financé 39 % des coûts de réalisation de Commerce Design Montréal, les gouvernements 21 %, la Ville de Montréal 41 %. Toutefois, depuis 2000, la proportion des investissements des gouvernements et de la Ville de Montréal s'établit à environ 30 % pour chacun. Depuis 1995, le budget annuel du programme a été multiplié par 15 et dépasse un million $ depuis 2001.

ÉVOLUTION DU CONCOURS

CONTEST EVOLUTION

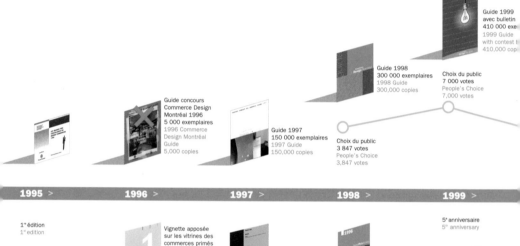

Guide concours
Commerce Design
Montréal 1996
5 000 exemplaires
1996 Commerce
Design Montréal
Guide
5,000 copies

Guide 1997
150 000 exemplaires
1997 Guide
150,000 copies

Guide 1998
300 000 exemplaires
1998 Guide
300,000 copies

Choix du public
3 847 votes
People's Choice
3,847 votes

Choix du public
7 000 votes
People's Choice
7,000 votes

Guide 1999
avec bulletin
410 000 exe
1999 Guide
with contest b
410,000 copi

1995 >	1996 >	1997 >	1998 >	1999 >

1ʳᵉ édition
1ˢᵗ édition

Vignette apposée
sur les vitrines des
commerces primés
Electrostatic stickers
displayed in winners'
businesses

Lancement du vote
« Choix du public »
Inauguration of
People's Choice vote

5ᵉ anniversaire
5ᵗʰ anniversary

Hors-série
1995-1999
220 000 exer
Retrospective
1995-1999
220,000 copi

Choix du public 58 725 votes
People's Choice 58,725 votes

Circuits Commerce Design Montréal
Commerce Design Montréal
Guided Tours

Choix du public
37 298 votes
People's Choice
37,298 votes

Choix du public
38 346 votes
People's Choice
38,346 votes

Ventes trottoirs
Sidewalk sales

Choix du public
23 777 votes
People's Choice
23,777 votes

Circuits touristiques du
Montréal Design
Design à la Montréal
Guided Tours

CommerceDesign Saint-Étienne

Franchise du concept «Commerce
Design» à Saint-Étienne (France)
«Commerce Design Saint-Étienne»
Commerce Design concept licensed
to Saint-Étienne, France, "Commerce
Design Saint-Étienne"

Colloque Nouvelles
Villes de design
New Design Cities symposium

Site Internet
Web site

Guide 2000
500 000 exemplaires
2000 Guide
500,000 copies

Dépliant de vote 2001
228 500 exemplaires
2001 voting leaflet
228,500 copies

Dépliant de vote 2002
225 000 exemplaires
2002 voting leaflet
225,000 copies

Dépliant de vote 2003
205 000 exemplaires
2003 voting leaflet
205,000 copies

Dépliant de vote 2004
210 000 exemplaires
2004 voting leaflet
210,000 copies

Trophée
Trophy

Trophée
Trophy

Trophée
Trophy

Trophée
Trophy

du public
votes
's Choice
votes

Guide 2001
140 000 exemplaires
2001 Design
Montréal Guide
140,000 copies

Guide 2002
140 000 exemplaires
2002 Guide
140,000 copies

Guide 2003-2004
150 000 exemplaires
2003-2004 Guide
150,000 copies

Guide 2003-2004
35 000 copies
2003-2004 Guide
35,000 copies

0 >   2001 >   2002 >   2003 >   2004 >

Affiche
Poster

Affiche
Poster

Affiche
Poster

Affiche
Poster

Passeport
t Passport

des retombées du
urs de 1995-1999
of Commerce Design
éal's impact from 1995-1999

Rayonnement international
insertion du Guide Design Montréal
dans le magazine Metropolis
International exposure from
insertion of Design Guide in
Metropolis magazine

Insertion dans Metropolis
Insertion in Metropolis

Mise à jour des sondages
et instruments de mesures
Updating of surveys and impact
measurement tools

Prix de l'International Downtown
Association "Outstanding
Achievement Award"
"Outstanding Achievement Award"
from the International Downtown
Association

Insertion dans Metropolis
Insertion in Metropolis

Mise à jour des sondages
et instruments de mesures
Updating of surveys and impact
measurement tools

Franchise du concept
«Commerce Design»
à Times Square, New York
«Design Times Square»
Commerce Design concept
licensed to Times Square,
New York, "Design Times Square"

10e anniversaire
10th anniversary

Commerce+design
Les clés du succès

10+1 Designers Commerce
Design Montréal

Élaboration de sondages et
d'instruments de mesures
Elaboration of surveys and
impact measurement tools

International Downtown
Association

Franchise du concept
«Commerce Design» à
Trois-Rivière (Québec)
«Séduction Design»
Commerce Design concept
licensed to Trois-Rivières,
Québec,"Séduction Design"

DESIGN
TIMES SQUARE

Franchise du concept
«Commerce Design»
à Lyon (France) «Grand Prix
du design Points de vente»
Commerce Design concept
licensed to Lyon, France, "Grand Prix
du design Points de vente"

Grand Prix
du Design

1995-2004

1995-2004 Commerce
Design Montréal

Boîte
de votes
Ballot box

séduction
design

COMMERCE DESIGN MONTRÉAL — LES IMPACTS

Dix ans, c'est peu pour développer une culture de la qualité en design chez les commerçants, changer les mentalités, défaire les préjugés, sensibiliser, intéresser et «éduquer» tous les publics visés. Mais 10 ans, c'est beaucoup et rare pour une initiative publique de promotion du design aussi particulièrement ciblée. Peu de programmes au Québec ont connu cette longévité. Généralement, ils sont abandonnés prématurément : les financeurs — gouvernements et commanditaires — se retirent progressivement (principe de non-récurrence, de diversification de leur soutien, de renouvellement des projets); les pouvoirs politiques changent et misent sur la nouveauté; les organisateurs s'essoufflent et les experts se dispersent à la recherche d'emplois stables. La force de Commerce Design Montréal est certainement d'avoir réussi à perdurer, tout en conservant et en élargissant son équipe, ses partenaires et ses commanditaires. ✕ Il importe aujourd'hui d'en évaluer les retombées. A-t-on atteint les objectifs qui motivent, depuis le début, la tenue annuelle de cette activité? Les impacts recherchés ont-ils été réalisés?

Impacts pour le secteur du commerce

Décentralisation du design

Alors que les candidatures lors des premières éditions du concours provenaient d'entreprises situées essentiellement dans les quartiers centraux de Montréal, on constate sur la cartographie des 10 ans de participation une décentralisation progressive des projets vers des quartiers périphériques. Le consommateur, de plus en plus intéressé au design et à la recherche de lieux distinctifs, incite les commerçants excentrés à offrir des environnements de vente compétitifs à ceux du centre-ville.

Effet d'entraînement de proximité

La qualité attire la qualité. Les commerces innovants, primés ou non, ont un réel impact sur leur environnement immédiat en incitant, par leur seul exemple, la concurrence à investir dans la qualité en design. Ainsi, 40 % des commerçants primés estiment représenter une source d'inspiration pour leurs voisins.

Les atypiques deviennent typiques

Le recours au design n'est plus réservé qu'aux établissements du centre-ville. Il s'étend à des types de commerces pour lesquels, il y a 10 ans, la qualité en design était loin de constituer une priorité. Certains, identifiés comme «atypiques» durant la période 1995-2000, se retrouvent aujourd'hui parmi les commerces qui recourent fréquemment au design, notamment les boutiques de téléphonie, les librairies, les institutions financières et les «dépanneurs» (petites épiceries de quartier ouvertes 24 heures sur 24 pour «dépanner» les résidants). ✕ À la lumière de cette diversification, il est évident que le programme a élargi le marché en design de commerces en réalisant des percées auprès de secteurs auparavant indifférents à la qualité en aménagement.

01   02   03

Du bon design «à tous prix»

Contrairement à l'idée encore largement répandue que le design coûte cher, la participation au concours depuis 2001 indique que le nombre de projets à petits budgets, de moins de 70 $ le pied carré reste la moyenne la plus forte (39 %), même si, avec la popularité et la notoriété grandissantes du concours, les designers et commerçants ont tendance à s'autoexclure de la compétition lorsqu'ils jugent leur projet trop modeste. Commerce Design Montréal a contribué à défaire ce préjugé en primant des commerces qui démontrent que le bon design à faible coût est possible.

Le design est payant

Enfin, le concours crée vraiment un effet d'entraînement chez les commerçants, de plus en plus nombreux à constater que le design est payant :
› 46 % observent une augmentation de leur achalandage
› 40 % constatent une augmentation de leur vente
› 51 % affirment attirer une nouvelle clientèle.

Impacts pour le milieu du design

Retombées d'affaires tangibles pour les professionnels

Les 10 ans de Commerce Design Montréal ont aidé à sensibiliser et à défaire les préjugés des commerçants à l'égard du design. Ils sont plus nombreux à considérer que l'aménagement d'un lieu de vente ou d'un restaurant nécessite des compétences précises et doit être confié à des spécialistes. De nouveaux secteurs se préoccupent désormais de la qualité en aménagement, tant pour des projets à petits qu'à grands budgets. Par conséquent, Commerce Design Montréal a eu un impact sur le développement de nouveaux marchés pour les professionnels en design de commerces. ✕ 80 % des professionnels primés par Commerce Design Montréal affirment avoir créé de nouveaux contacts d'affaires grâce à leur distinction au concours ; ✕ 46 % disent que ces contacts ont entraîné des contrats générant des revenus d'affaires (de 50 000 $ à 200 000 $).

01 Waxman, design : Krief Design, 1999 02 Hôtel Gault, design : YH2 + Paul Bernier architecte + Fournier, Gersovitz, Moss et associés architectes, 2003 03 Les touilleurs, design : Louise Savoie, 2003 04 Restaurant Les Chèvres, design : Jean-Pierre Viau Design, 2004 05 Les gourmets pressés, design : Abbruzzo Design, 2004

De plus en plus de designers connus et reconnus

Le concours contribue aussi à la découverte, l'affirmation et la confirmation de talents québécois en design de commerces sur les scènes nationale et internationale. Chaque année, près de la moitié (46 %) des projets soumis au concours proviennent de professionnels — architectes et designers d'intérieur — n'ayant jamais participé. Cette compétition ne récompense pas toujours les mêmes candidats, car, en moyenne, près de 60 % des professionnels primés annuellement sont lauréats du concours pour la première fois, contribuant ainsi au rajeunissement, au renouvellement et à l'enrichissement constants de la liste des créateurs québécois en design de commerces.

Impacts pour le public

Un public qui augmente et se diversifie

Depuis que le vote du public a été instauré, en 1998, le nombre de votants est passé de 3 847 à 58 725 en 2004. En 2004 alors qu'aucun changement n'a été apporté à la campagne de l'année précédente, 20 000 personnes de plus ont voté. ✕ Cette hausse fulgurante démontre clairement l'intérêt grandissant du public à l'égard du design en général et du concours en particulier. ✕ Non seulement la population participe-t-elle de plus en plus au volet «Choix du public», mais l'événement attire — et donc sensibilise — de nouveaux consommateurs chaque année. En moyenne, au cours des années 2002 et 2003, 77 % des votants participaient pour la première fois.

Impact médiatique chiffré

La sensibilisation du public au design se mesure également par l'intérêt que portent les médias au sujet et le nombre de personnes touchées par les retombées médiatiques du concours. ✕ Ces évaluations plutôt conservatrices, réalisées sur la base de coefficients d'équivalence monétaire des couvertures de presse obtenues révèlent que l'impact médiatique du concours connaît une croissance remarquable. Il touche, depuis 2001, plus de 12 millions de personnes par année (12 562 155 en 2003), individuellement exposées à la qualité en design de commerces montréalais, dont près de 2 millions à l'extérieur du Québec (Canada, États-Unis, Europe).

Impacts pour Montréal

Une telle mission de valorisation de la qualité du cadre de vie par le design de commerces revient naturellement aux villes. Il est en effet légitime qu'une municipalité souligne, incite et récompense les efforts déployés sur son territoire qui contribuent directement à la rendre plus compétitive. C'est dans cette optique que la Ville de Montréal consacre des ressources professionnelles et matérielles considérables à Commerce Design Montréal depuis 1995. Après deux millions $ de fonds municipaux investis dans ce programme, quels bénéfices Montréal en retire-t-elle aujourd'hui?

Amélioration du cadre de vie

Le premier bénéfice de ce programme a été de générer des investissements en design de commerces, lesquels ont eu un effet notoire sur l'embellissement et la revitalisation des rues commerciales.

Investissements rentables

Pour la Ville de Montréal, Commerce Design Montréal a généré une source d'investissements externes de plus de 626 000 $ par année en moyenne. Ces revenus ont bonifié substantiellement le budget municipal annuel alloué aux communications avec les citoyens. Grâce à cette activité, la Ville de Montréal profite aujourd'hui d'un vaste et solide réseau de partenaires sensibilisés et responsabilisés, avec lesquels elle peut poursuivre, étendre et renforcer sa mission de valorisation de la qualité en design.

Montréal, destination design

Commerce Design Montréal a contribué au positionnement de la métropole comme une destination d'intérêt pour les amateurs de design. ✕ Entre autres, avec l'envoi du Guide Design Montréal aux 15 000 abonnés du magazine américain Metropolis, opération répétée au cours des trois dernières années, Commerce Design Montréal a fait découvrir Montréal sous l'angle de son design de commerces. En s'adressant à ce public spécialisé en design de l'est des États-Unis, le but était de classer la métropole comme une ville de design et d'en inciter la découverte. ✕ Si Commerce Design Montréal a investi dès 1998 dans des actions de promotion à l'international (diffusion à bord d'Air Canada, partenariat de Tourisme Montréal, accueil de journalistes étrangers, création d'un site Internet), la distinction décernée par l'International Downtown Association en 2002 (Washington D.C.) et les licences accordées aux autres villes en 2003 ont nettement renforcé l'attrait de Montréal comme ville de design auprès de la presse internationale.

〉〉

UNE STRATÉGIE QUI FAIT ÉCOLE

En effet, repris à ce jour par une seule ville du Québec (Trois-Rivières en 2002 — Concours Séduction Design), le concept Commerce Design se voit aujourd'hui exporté. ✕ En 2003, trois licences complètes ou partielles ont été accordées à la demande de la Ville de Saint-Étienne (première ville européenne à reprendre le concept), de la Chambre de commerce et d'industrie de Lyon et du District de Times Square, à New York. Bratislava (Slovaquie), Zagreb (Croatie), Genève (Suisse), Paris (France) et Philadelphie (États-Unis) étudient, elles aussi, la possibilité de reprendre le concept du concours. ✕ Ces ententes génèrent de stimulantes demandes de transfert de compétences et des occasions de partenariats avantageuses pour la mise en réseau internationale de Montréal.

〉〉

DIX ANS DE COMMERCE DESIGN MONTRÉAL EN PERSPECTIVE

Les principes fondateurs sur lesquels repose la spécificité de Commerce Design Montréal (démocratisation du design, opération de valorisation dirigée vers le commerçant et mobilisation de la population) sont à l'origine du succès du programme désormais reconnu au Québec et à l'étranger. ✕ Les données confirment que les objectifs visés par la Ville de Montréal au départ ont été atteints : effet d'entraînement tangible auprès des commerçants, création de nouveaux marchés pour les designers, développement de l'intérêt et des exigences du public, renforcement de l'attrait touristique de Montréal. ✕ Cette initiative, basée sur l'éducation des commerçants et du public, dont l'impact repose sur la persévérance et la récurrence d'un même message sur plusieurs années, a nettement porté ses fruits. ✕ Le design de commerces est en voie d'intégration durable et profonde dans la culture montréalaise, en tant que facteur déterminant de compétitivité économique, de qualité de vie et d'identité urbaine. Il constitue déjà clairement une composante avantageuse de l'image publique de Montréal. ✕ En d'autres termes, Commerce Design Montréal a eu un effet structurant et tangible à la fois sur la ville et sur l'image de la ville, contribuant ainsi à faire pleinement de Montréal une jeune métropole de design.

〉〉

Commerce**Design**Montréal

01 Trophée Commerce Design Montréal, design : Claude Mauffette

〉〉

PHYLLIS LAMBERT
〉 Directeur, fondateur et président du conseil des fiduciaires, Centre Canadien d'Architecture (CCA)

〉〉

Fondé en 1979, le Centre Canadien d'Architecture (CCA) a pour mission de sensibiliser le public
à l'architecture, promouvoir la recherche de haut niveau dans ce domaine et favoriser l'innovation
dans la pratique du design.

〉〉

QUELLE EST VOTRE DÉFINITION D'UNE VILLE DE DESIGN ?
Une ville de design sous-entend une politique municipale qui touche tous les aspects du quotidien : transports, enjeux patrimoniaux, graphisme, signalisation, aménagement des rues,
mobilier urbain, éclairage, etc.

**POUR QU'UNE VILLE S'IMPOSE COMME VILLE DE DESIGN, DOIT-ELLE POSSÉDER
UN CONTEXTE SOCIAL HISTORIQUE PARTICULIER, UNE TRADITION POLITIQUE OU
INDUSTRIELLE SPÉCIFIQUE ?**
Une ville de design ne peut exister sans la créativité des individus. Les villes ne dépendent
plus de leurs industries comme source de revenus, mais plutôt des services qu'elles offrent et
de leurs secteurs culturels. Elles évoluent et atteignent leur maturité uniquement dans un contexte politique ouvert et démocratique. Une ville doit entretenir une tradition de créativité.

COMMENT LE DESIGN PEUT-IL AMÉLIORER LA QUALITÉ DE VIE DANS LA VILLE ?
Récemment, il y a eu des discussions à propos de l'éclairage, pas seulement des rues, mais
plus largement de l'utilisation de la lumière pour créer des lieux de rassemblement nocturne.
Les lieux publics doivent être envisagés comme des «endroits inspirants», qui laissent place
tant à la contemplation qu'à la stimulation, et qui confèrent une identité propre aux différents
secteurs de la ville. Il nous faut une stratégie d'ensemble qui générera une continuité d'espaces
publics variés, dispersés dans toute l'île, donnant ainsi une structure globale à la ville entière.
J'ai exposé ce concept de la nécessité de «lieux inspirants» au symposium Montréal 2017, à
la Chambre de commerce, en mai 2002.

01 Hall d'entrée du Centre Canadien d'Architecture

QUELS SONT LES RÔLES RESPECTIFS DES CITOYENS, DES DESIGNERS ET DES POLITICIENS DANS LE DÉVELOPPEMENT D'UNE VILLE DE DESIGN?
Le rôle du citoyen est de militer pour le bon design. La consultation du public par des audiences publiques bien structurées a prouvé que les citoyens sont les acteurs les plus efficaces dans les questions urbaines. Les idées proviennent de la base et font leur chemin jusqu'au sommet. Le designer travaille avec les citoyens et politiciens à l'évaluation du programme, du contexte, des contraintes et des possibilités. Le design qui en découle est soumis aux audiences publiques; les politiciens établissent les règlements puis, le cycle recommence.

EN QUOI MONTRÉAL A-T-ELLE LE MIEUX PROFITÉ DU CCA?
Le CCA a assuré une présence constante et une compréhension civique et critique de l'architecture dans la société d'aujourd'hui. Grâce à ses riches programmes d'expositions et de conférences, grâce aux concerts qui mettent en lien architecture et musique, grâce à son dynamique Centre d'étude et à sa collaboration avec les écoles, le CCA a redonné à Montréal son statut international. Certains changements qui ont eu lieu dans la ville ne se seraient pas produits sans le CCA.

QUELS ONT ÉTÉ LES PRINCIPAUX OBJECTIFS DES PROGRAMMES PUBLICS DU CCA À CE JOUR?
Les expositions et publications ont soulevé une série de questions urbaines, que je qualifie de «points névralgiques», en se servant de la ville et de l'évolution de son paysage urbain comme d'un livre ouvert permettant de déchiffrer la culture de notre pays. Des enjeux majeurs qui touchent à l'environnement ont été abordés par l'entremise de nos programmes publics, comme la ville du futur, les processus de préservation et d'évolution urbaines (du passé colonial aux années 60), la viabilité sociale face à la viabilité écologique, ainsi que d'autres questions soulevées tant par les architectes les plus influents du XXᵉ siècle (de Mies à Frank Lloyd Wright) que par des grandes figures contemporaines, comme Peter Eisenman.

〉〉

〉〉〉

RALPH DFOUNI
〉 directeur de la création, président
  et fondateur, Bluesponge, Montréal
〉〉〉

〉〉〉

QUELS ENDROITS PUBLICS DE MONTRÉAL VOUS PRÉFÉREZ-VOUS?

Le mont Royal dans son ensemble, y compris le cimetière et, plus particulièrement, la piste mauve; on s'y sent si loin de la ville, c'est incroyable. ✕ Les rues secondaires de Montréal, diverses, éclectiques, sont accueillantes pour le promeneur. On y trouve, en outre, des bijoux architecturaux, si l'on prend la peine de lever les yeux de temps à autre.

EN MATIÈRE DE DESIGN, QUELLES AMÉLIORATIONS AIMERIEZ-VOUS OBSERVER?

L'accès aux rives. Évidemment, il faudrait d'abord assainir l'eau. Bien que Montréal soit une île, cette réalité paraît absurde aux citoyens, étant donné qu'ils sont très éloignés de l'eau qui les entoure. On devrait faire entrer le fleuve dans l'âme de la ville, ce qui pourrait être réalisé en procurant aux citadins des accès aux berges multiples et variés.

QUE VOUDRIEZ-VOUS VOIR CONSTRUIT DANS VOTRE VILLE?

Une pyramide... ou, si c'est un peu exagéré, il faudrait réhabiliter le tramway! Montréal n'est pas une ville de monuments. Sa convivialité et son charme sont faits de petites choses, de détails. C'est ce qui lui donne un air de village et y rend la vie agréable.

DE QUELLE FAÇON VOTRE SITE MADEINMTL ABORDE-T-IL LE DESIGN DANS LA VILLE?

MadeinMTL.com est une tentative pour recréer et représenter certains aspects d'une ville (en l'occurrence Montréal) sur un écran d'ordinateur à l'aide d'une gamme d'outils qui rendent le contenu accessible au visiteur. MadeinMTL est à la fois un espace et un instrument; il véhicule l'esprit, l'atmosphère de la ville, par des accents sur ses lieux les plus intéressants ou pittoresques, des sonorités, des images et des couleurs. La poésie de la ville se trouve contrebalancée par la navigation pragmatique proposée. Flanqué d'un moteur de recherche algorithmique, que nous appelons «itinérateur», le site permet à ses visiteurs de créer des itinéraires sur mesure dans la ville et, grâce à son riche contenu médiatique, de vivre l'expérience virtuelle d'y habiter avant d'y être vraiment.

〉〉〉

×

— MONTRÉAL S'EMBELLIT DEPUIS UNE VINGTAINE D'ANNÉES. LES MÉGALOMANES FOUS DE BÉTON ET D'AUTOS ONT FAIT PLACE À DES CONCEPTEURS SOUCIEUX DE LAISSER LEUR MARQUE SUR DES PROJETS QUI AMÉLIORENT LE PAYSAGE URBAIN. ET CELA N'EST PAS UNE MINCE TÂCHE EN RAISON DE L'HÉTÉROGÉNÉITÉ DE LA VILLE. À LA DIFFÉRENCE DES VILLES RÉPUBLICAINES, QUI ONT LONGTEMPS VALORISÉ UNE CERTAINE HOMOGÉNÉITÉ, MONTRÉAL POSSÈDE UNE INTENSITÉ ARCHITECTURALE COMME ON EN TROUVE PEU DANS LE MONDE. UN ATOUT, MAIS AUSSI UN DÉFI POUR LES DESIGNERS, URBANISTES ET ARCHITECTES.

François Cardinal, éditorialiste au quotidien La Presse, Montréal.

— EN FAISANT SE RENCONTRER, IL Y A PLUS DE DEUX SIÈCLES, L'ART ET L'INDUSTRIE, EN INVENTANT DES OBJETS FONCTIONNELS MAIS TRAVAILLÉS DANS UN SOUCI ARTISTIQUE, SAINT-ÉTIENNE A FAIT GERMER LES RACINES DU DESIGN FRANÇAIS ET, PAR CE STATUT DE PRÉCURSEUR, A ANTICIPÉ SUR SON AVENIR.
Michel Thiollière, Sénateur de la Loire, Maire de Saint-Étienne

POR-
TRAIT

〉〉〉

POPULATION

Avec quelque 185 000 habitants, Saint-Étienne
est la deuxième ville de la région Rhône-Alpes
au cœur d'une agglomération qui compte
elle-même 400 000 résidants. Au total, Saint-
Étienne Métropole rassemble 43 communes.

〉〉〉

01

02
03

〉〉

FONDATION

Saint-Étienne se présente aux portes de l'histoire au XIIIᵉ siècle sous le nom de paroisse Sanctus Stephanus de Furano. Au XVᵉ siècle, c'est un minuscule bourg de paysans et de forgerons. Au XVIᵉ siècle, Saint-Étienne prend son essor grâce à l'industrie des armes blanches et des armes à feu, à la quincaillerie et à la rubanerie. Quant à la Manufacture Royale d'Armes, elle fut créée en 1764.

〉〉

DÉFIS

Le Grand Siècle de Saint-Étienne, c'est le XIXᵉ siècle qui voit s'affirmer cette expansion industrielle autour de la mine (charbon), de la métallurgie, des cycles, des armes, de la mécanique et de la fabrique de rubans, qui connaît son âge d'or. Saint-Étienne est alors le cœur du plus important bassin industriel de France. ✕ Audacieuse, Saint-Étienne est la première ville à accueillir le chemin de fer (la liaison est établie entre Saint-Étienne et Andrézieux en 1827 ; puis entre Saint-Étienne et Lyon en 1832). Elle sera également la première à offrir à ses concitoyens le tramway dans la ville. L'inventivité stéphanoise s'est également déployée par la vente par correspondance avec Manufrance et son catalogue mythique, puis par la grande distribution avec Casino. ✕ À cette période, elle construit l'École Régionale des Beaux-Arts dès 1857 et le Musée d'Art et d'Industrie en 1889, exprimant déjà sa volonté d'une culture plurielle. ✕ Les crises économiques de la deuxième moitié du XXᵉ siècle ont contraint la ville à développer de nouveaux axes économiques et pôles d'excellence : industrie optique, mécanique, technologies médicales, enseignement supérieur et design.

〉〉

〉〉

HISTORIQUE DES ÉVÉNEMENTS FONDATEURS

1947 〉 Inauguration de la Comédie de Saint-Étienne. Centre Dramatique National dirigé par Jean Dasté qui a œuvré toute sa vie pour la création en province d'un théâtre de qualité pour tous.

1968 〉 Ouverture de la Maison de la Culture

1987 〉 Ouverture du Musée d'Art Moderne

1991 〉 Ouverture du Musée de la Mine

1998 〉 Saint-Étienne accueille la Coupe du Monde de Football

1998 〉 Première Biennale Internationale Design Saint-Étienne

2000 〉 Deuxième Biennale Internationale Design Saint-Étienne

2002 〉 Troisième Biennale Internationale Design Saint-Étienne

2004 〉 Quatrième Biennale Internationale Design Saint-Étienne

2005 〉 Les Transurbaines, Fête de la ville

〉〉

NOMBRE DE DESIGNERS

On trouve à Saint-Étienne 200 designers et agences de communication, parmi lesquels œuvrent 150 architectes.

〉〉

›››››››››››››››››››››››››››››››››››››
DESIGNERS CONNUS

Dans la métropole de Saint-Étienne, se trouve un site unique en Europe : l'ensemble architectural de Le Corbusier à Firminy-Vert. Il comporte une unité d'habitation, une maison de la culture, un stade, une piscine et une église. L'achèvement des travaux de l'église Saint-Pierre s'est produit en 2005 par l'architecte franco-américain José Oubrerie. ✕ Oser une architecture forte, exemplaire et audacieuse constitue un choix récent pour Saint-Étienne. ✕ Didier Guichard a signé le Musée d'Art Moderne et Jean-Michel Wilmotte a réhabilité le Musée d'Art et d'Industrie. ✕ Plusieurs projets sont en cours : › Le Zenith, signé Fosters et Partners ›› La Cité du Design, œuvre de l'Agence LIN-Finn Geipel et Giulia Andi ››› Le siège social de Casino, imaginé et créé par Architecture Studio ✕ Parmi les designers, nommons François Bauchet, Éric Jourdan, Laurent Gregori, Sylvie Fillère, Jean-François Dingjian, Céline Savoye, Patrick de Glo de Besses et Bertrand Voiron. ✕ L'Atelier Espace Public, animé par Jean-Pierre Charbonneau, regroupe des jeunes designers, architectes et artistes qui travaillent avec les techniciens de la ville à la rénovation des espaces de proximité.

›››››››››››››››››››››››››››››››››››››››

Fondée en 1998, la Biennale Internationale Design Saint-Étienne est la plus importante manifestation publique de design international organisée en France. Placée sous l'égide de la Ville de Saint-Étienne, elle est organisée par l'École Régionale des Beaux-Arts de Saint-Étienne avec de nombreux partenaires. Elle propose un éclairage sur la diversité du design dans le monde par un foisonnement d'objets qui permet de décrypter la pensée et les enjeux de notre temps. ✕ La première édition du concours Commerce Design Saint-Étienne est organisée en 2003 en partenariat avec la Ville de Montréal.

›››››››››››››››››››››››››››››››››››››››
INSTITUTIONS DE DESIGN

Le Musée d'Art et d'Industrie, créé en 1889, réunit des produits de l'industrie et des Beaux-Arts. Fameux pour sa première collection française de cycles, de rubans et d'armes, ce musée a été rénové par Jean-Michel Wilmotte en 2001. ✕ Inauguré en 1987, le Musée d'Art Moderne abrite, après le Centre Pompidou, la plus grande collection de design et d'art moderne français. Il propose en outre un calendrier d'expositions inédites. ✕ Prochainement, le site Le Corbusier à Firminy, accueillera de manière permanente les collections de design du Musée d'Art Moderne. ✕ Enfin, la Cité du Design ouvrira en 2007.

›››››››››››››››››››››››››››››››››››››››

〉〉〉

ÉCOLES DE DESIGN

L'École Régionale des Beaux-Arts de Saint-Étienne a été créée en 1857 pour former des créateurs et répondre aux besoins des fabricants soucieux de la diversité décorative de la production. ✕ Municipale par son statut, l'École est un établissement d'enseignement supérieur, placé sous la tutelle pédagogique du Ministère de la Culture. Elle prépare sur la totalité du cursus de cinq années au D.N.S.E.P. Art, Communication et Design. C'est pour cette formation qu'elle a acquis une renommée internationale. ✕ Le département de Design se présente comme «design global» et développe un enseignement du projet. Il n'y a pas de sectorisation des disciplines. Des contrats de recherche sont établis avec des entreprises pour l'élaboration d'objets usuels ou de produits novateurs sur le plan technologique.

L'École Régionale des Beaux-Arts propose des formations de troisième cycle / post-diplôme :

〉 Postdiplôme Design et Recherche, créé en 1989. Les étudiants participent, dans le cadre de leur recherche, à la réalisation de la revue de design *AZIMUTS*.

〉 Master spécialisé «Dual Design», enseignement copiloté par l'École Régionale des Beaux-Arts de Saint-Étienne avec l'École Nationale d'Ingénieurs de Saint-Étienne (ÉNISE), créé en 2002.

〉 Master professionnel «Espace Public : design, architecture, pratiques», enseignement copiloté par l'Université Jean Monnet, l'École d'Architecture et l'École Régionale des Beaux-Arts, créé en 2004.

Des formations complémentaires ont été mises en place à l'Université Jean Monnet (master Territoire, Patrimoine, Environnement), à l'École des Mines (Développement durable), au CNAM (Design et innovation), à l'École de Commerce (Marketing). Un master doctorant en Design à l'Université Jean Monnet et en partenariat avec l'École Régionale des Beaux-Arts est en préparation.

〉〉

〉〉

STRATÉGIES DE DESIGN

La formidable dynamique qui se développe à Saint-Étienne autour du design illustre l'état d'esprit nécessaire à cette dimension de reconquête urbaine, culturelle et économique. ✕ Cette nouvelle identité de capitale française du design repose sur une légitimité naturelle liée à l'histoire de son agglomération et à son potentiel actuel, renforcée par un soutien politique et financier du gouvernement, qui cherche à doter la France de métropoles attractives de calibre européen.

〉〉

Portrait de Saint-Étienne
Renseignements colligés par

〉 L'École Régionale des Beaux-Arts de Saint-Étienne

〉 La Biennale Internationale Design Saint-Étienne

MICHEL THIOLLIÈRE

SÉNATEUR DE LA LOIRE
DEPUIS 2001
MAIRE DE SAINT-ÉTIENNE
DEPUIS 1995

CONSIDÉREZ-VOUS SAINT-ÉTIENNE COMME UNE NOUVELLE VILLE DE DESIGN?

En faisant se rencontrer, il y a plus de deux siècles, l'art et l'industrie, en inventant des objets fonctionnels, mais travaillés dans un souci artistique, Saint-Étienne a fait germer les racines du design français et, par ce statut de précurseur, a anticipé sur son avenir. ✕ Aujourd'hui, Saint-Étienne s'affirme parmi les capitales internationales du design grâce à la Biennale Internationale Design, créée en 1998, événement devenu incontournable dans le paysage du design international actuel. ✕ Par ailleurs, tout le monde s'accorde pour voir dans le projet de Cité du Design, au-delà d'un nouveau site de recherche, de formation et d'exposition, le symbole de cet état d'esprit stéphanois qui nous a permis de toujours rebondir et d'innover très souvent. Donc, Saint-Étienne, si elle a pu l'oublier, a toujours été une ville de design.

QUELLE A ÉTÉ VOTRE CONTRIBUTION PERSONNELLE AU DÉVELOPPEMENT DE CETTE NOUVELLE VILLE DE DESIGN?

Depuis 1995, Saint-Étienne mène un effort de renouvellement de son patrimoine urbain, traitant avec autant de soins des opérations d'envergure que des projets de quartier. ✕ Cette volonté de transformer la ville s'est accompagnée d'une nouvelle façon de travailler, avec des méthodes modernes expérimentées et qui s'affirment aujourd'hui dans chaque réalisation : projets concertés avec les usagers, modes d'élaboration de projets plus rapides, intervention accrue des créateurs par le design urbain. ✕ Lors de la première phase de transformation, nous avons créé des aménagements de qualité, chaleureux et créatifs. ✕ Le travail de l'Atelier Espace Public, conçu par Jean-Pierre Charbonneau, est l'un des éléments de cette réussite : cet atelier novateur fut la résultante d'une parfaite collaboration entre habitants, techniciens, conseillers et jeunes créatifs. Ainsi, ce qui se fait à Saint-Étienne ne se fait pas à Toulouse, Paris ou Lyon. ✕ J'ai voulu que nos jeunes architectes et designers (formés ici même à l'École Régionale des Beaux-Arts ou d'Architecture) puissent créer petit à petit notre environnement urbain avec l'écriture particulière, créative et chaleureuse stéphanoise, dans le respect des traditions de notre ville. ✕ Puis, en 1998, est née l'idée de la Biennale Internationale Design. Son succès dès sa première édition a donné un nouvel élan à notre ville et nous a prouvé que nous avions raison. Unique en France, cette manifestation est devenue essentielle pour les professionnels et passionnés. ✕ C'est donc avec Jacques Bonnaval, qui était patron de la Biennale Internationale Design et directeur de l'École Régionale des Beaux-Arts, que j'ai décidé de travailler à ce projet. ✕ Ce fut alors une longue aventure, un effort de tous les instants. Il a fallu convaincre nos partenaires, mais nous avons réussi. Le 26 mai 2003, le gouvernement français confirmait officiellement le bien-fondé de notre démarche par son soutien à la Cité du Design à Saint-Étienne. ✕ Il fallait encore donner envie aux meilleurs architectes du monde de venir y travailler. La talentueuse agence d'architecture LIN a été choisie. Cette société berlinoise fondée par Finn Geipel et Giulia Andi est à l'origine de réalisations prestigieuses : Galerie contemporaine de Rome, couverture des arènes de Nîmes, Zéniths de Tours et de Nantes, etc. ✕ POUR LA CITÉ DU DESIGN, L'ÉQUIPE A PROPOSÉ UNE ARCHITECTURE INTELLIGENTE ET FUTURISTE, ALLIANT TECHNICITÉ, CRÉATIVITÉ ET DÉVELOPPEMENT DURABLE. CE TRIO GAGNANT NOUS PERMETTAIT DE TRADUIRE NOTRE VOLONTÉ DE CONSTRUIRE UN AVENIR SACHANT CONJUGUER IDENTITÉ ET MODERNITÉ. ✕ En parallèle, le respecté Sir Norman Foster travaille actuellement à la conception du premier Zénith de la région Rhône-Alpes. ✕ Je suis heureux que les grands architectes du monde aient voulu participer à des projets comme le Zénith et la Cité du Design. Leur vif intérêt prouve indiscutablement que notre projet est égal, par son exigence, à ceux de villes telles Bilbao et Glasgow. ✕ Enfin, la réouverture du chantier de l'église de Firminy, ouvrage de Le Corbusier, associée aux deux grands projets de Finn Geipel et de Sir Norman Foster, nous permet de développer un nouvel axe touristique.

POURQUOI CROYEZ-VOUS IMPORTANT DE POSITIONNER SAINT-ÉTIENNE COMME UNE VILLE DE DESIGN?

Je lisais récemment un article détaillant quelles pourraient être les technologies développées par Sillicon Valley en 2010. Dans cette liste, arrivaient en bonne place les services créatifs et le design, au même titre que les biotechnologies et les nanotechnologies. L'étude précisait que le développement, la production, le marketing et la vente de produits technologiques entraînaient nécessairement des besoins en services créatifs. Le design deviendra un réel complément. Il enrichira la réflexion et multipliera les capacités de la technique dont il est le partenaire créatif. ✕ Il est un fait que le design est un vecteur de mutation industrielle. Pour preuve, sur l'agglomération stéphanoise, on compte 92 entreprises de design actives en environnement, packaging, design industriel, design interdisciplinaire, multimédia et l'identité visuelle. Notre territoire est marqué par le développement de ces PME/PMI innovantes.

D'AUTRES VILLES VOUS ONT-ELLES INSPIRÉ POUR LEUR STRATÉGIE DE PROMOTION? LESQUELLES ET DE QUELLES FAÇONS?

Montréal nous a inspirés. Au cours de la troisième Biennale Internationale Design Saint-Étienne, la Ville de Montréal a été invitée à présenter son concours Commerce Design Montréal lancé en 1995. L'enthousiasme né de cette rencontre a conduit à signer un partenariat dynamique et pluriel entre nos deux villes. Saint-Étienne, déjà «source du design français», devient alors la première ville d'Europe à faire sienne l'idée originale développée au Canada. ✕ Cette opération venait à point pour alimenter ce terreau déjà si fertile et pour confirmer notre volonté, déjà forte, d'inscrire le design comme élément fédérateur du développement de notre territoire. ✕ Mais nous avons déjà su créer un large réseau international à partir de la Biennale et nous sommes devenus une tête de réseau des villes internationales de design. Pour preuve, de plus en plus de villes nous sollicitent pour faire partie de ce réseau. Je pourrais citer Nagoya, Pasadena, Glasgow, Eindhoven et Courtrai, autant de partenaires avec lesquelles nous avons plaisir à échanger. ✕ Notre concept inspire aussi de nombreuses villes; certaines avec qui nous avons déjà créé des partenariats. D'autres, en Espagne, en Hongrie et même en Afrique du Sud, sont intéressées à reprendre le concept. On a aussi parlé de partager notre expertise avec Montréal pour la création d'une Biennale des Amériques.

QUEL EST LE RÔLE DU CITOYEN ET DU POLITICIEN DANS LE DÉVELOPPEMENT D'UNE VILLE DE DESIGN?

Si le Musée d'Art et d'Industrie, la Biennale Internationale Design, le projet de la Cité du Design existent à Saint-Étienne, c'est parce qu'il y a une réelle volonté politique. ✕ D'autres villes françaises ont des velléités autour du design, car c'est un phénomène à la mode. Mais à Saint-Étienne, les politiques ont su défendre ardemment ce projet parce qu'il était ancré profondément dans notre territoire. ✕ Il faut une forte conviction pour arriver à transmettre l'idée qu'un projet peut s'avérer important pour un territoire. Mais c'est le rôle du politique que d'être visionnaire pour sa ville, de savoir regarder au-delà d'un mandat, d'imaginer sa ville 10, 15 ans plus tard et donc, de préparer l'avenir de nos enfants. ✕ Le rôle du politique consiste à projeter à l'attention des concitoyens un champ des possibilités, de façon à ce que ceux-ci puissent comprendre et accepter le changement, puis que d'eux-mêmes, ils dessinent le futur visage de leur cité. ✕ Le design est aussi une politique d'image. Car pour faire parler de notre ville, pour prouver qu'elle avance, qu'elle vit, il faut attirer les visiteurs, leur démontrer qu'elle est entrée dans le XXIe siècle forte des épreuves et des leçons de son passé. ✕ Il faut des opérations d'envergure afin d'obtenir des retombées médiatiques, mais aussi pour fédérer les habitants, pour les faire vibrer et aimer leur ville. La Coupe du Monde de Football de 1998 représente un excellent exemple d'un événement déclencheur qui rassemble. De même, le sont quant à notre ville la Biennale Internationale Design, la Cité du Design, le Zénith, la Fête de la ville «les Transurbaines». ✕ Une ville est toujours un récit inachevé, une ville doit toujours être en mouvement. Saint-Étienne ne fait pas exception.

〉〉〉

01 Square Haubtmann, design : Stéphanie David, architecte 02 Parvis du Musée d'Art et d'Industrie, design : Sylvie Fillère, Christophe Chavanon, paysagiste 03 Biennale Internationale Design Saint-Étienne, 2002 04 Carrefour des 5 chemins, design : Christophe Massart, architecte

01

Visuels 3d de la future Cité du Design réalisés par l'agence LIN : 01 Vue de l'agora : passage public couvert

02 Vue depuis la Place d'Armes 03 Vue de l'ensemble

LA CITÉ DU DESIGN DE SAINT-ÉTIENNE

〉〉〉

En arrivant à Saint-Étienne, on ressent immédiatement combien cette ville est porteuse de l'histoire des XIXe et XXe siècles. ✕ Passementiers, armuriers, fabricants de cycles, chacun dans leur domaine ont contribué à l'évolution du design industriel et porté sa définition de la manière la plus noble qui soit grâce à leur travail d'artisans ingénieux, inventifs et créateurs. ✕ Initialement concentré sur les produits manufacturés, cet exercice de la « mise en forme d'une pensée » comme l'a dit le designer et architecte Sylvain Dubuisson, s'est ensuite porté sur la commercialisation des objets : Manufrance, pour la vente par catalogue (vente par correspondance), mais encore et surtout Casino, pour la grande distribution, qui prévoit ouvrir en 2007 un magasin concept et un nouveau siège social qui sera construit par le groupe Architecture Studio dans le nouveau quartier des affaires de la ville. ✕ Je veux parler ici de Manufrance, pour la vente par catalogue (vente par correspondance), mais encore et surtout de Casino, pour la grande distribution, qui prévoit ouvrir en 2007 un magasin concept et un nouveau siège social qui sera construit par le groupe Architecture Studio dans le nouveau quartier des affaires de la ville. ✕ De puissants relais ont étayé cette marche irréversible vers la modernité. Notamment, l'École Régionale des Beaux-Arts de Saint-Étienne est appelée dès 1857 à la demande des industriels à améliorer les produits de leur catalogue et à en inventer d'autres. ✕ Aujourd'hui, on compte nombre de lieux qui commémorent cet héritage industriel : le Musée d'Art et d'Industrie, le Musée de la Mine, le Musée d'Art Moderne détenteur d'une remarquable collection en design, mais aussi le patrimoine architectural de Le Corbusier, qui, à l'invitation du maire Eugène-Auguste Petit, a construit à Firminy une maison de la culture, un stade, une église et une unité d'habitation. ✕ Reste alors ce patrimoine, miroir de la construction d'une ville du XXe siècle.

〉〉〉

Depuis 1995, la Ville de Saint-Étienne mène un effort de renouvellement de son patrimoine urbain, avec le souci d'apporter autant d'attentions aux projets d'envergure qu'à ceux de quartiers. ✕ Ainsi, la rénovation des espaces de proximité est l'une des facettes de la politique urbaine de Saint-Étienne, lancée à l'initiative de Michel Thiollière, Sénateur-Maire. Elle a la double originalité de traiter tous les espaces du quotidien de la vie de la cité avec la même attention et de faire appel, pour concevoir les projets, à un atelier de jeunes créateurs stéphanois issus des écoles d'Architecture et des Beaux-Arts. ✕ Autre exemple, la deuxième ligne de tramway est en chantier, et le site de la gare de Chateaucreux en cours de réaménagement sous la baguette de Jean-Marie Duthilleul, architecte en chef de la SNCF. ✕ Autre grand chantier stéphanois : le Zénith, une salle de spectacles de 7000 places. À l'issue d'un concours international d'architecture auquel ont répondu les équipes les plus renommées, ce mandat a été confié à Sir Norman Foster. ✕ Pour répondre à tous ces projets, pour faire participer les Stéphanois, il fallait par ailleurs que la ville se dote d'institutions culturelles dynamiques, capables de réagir à cet élan de modernité.

L'École Régionale des Beaux-arts de Saint-Étienne répond à cette attente. Il s'agit d'un établissement d'enseignement supérieur dont la vocation est d'instituer un contexte favorable à la création et un lieu privilégié pour l'enseignement du design. ✕ Elle est aujourd'hui la première en France avec 500 étudiants. Elle va rejoindre la Cité du Design et en constituer le pôle de formation et de recherche. ✕ Son département de Design se présente comme «design global». Les étudiants y abordent toutes les disciplines du design. ✕ Elle propose : 〉 Un troisième cycle postdiplôme Design&Recherche 〉〉 Un Master spécialisé «Dual Design» copiloté avec l'École Nationale d'Ingénieurs de Saint-Étienne 〉〉〉 Un Master professionnel «Espace Public» copiloté par l'École d'Architecture de Saint-Étienne et l'Université Jean Monnet. ✕ Elle publie la revue de design *AZIMUTS*. ✕ L'École Régionale des Beaux-Arts s'est dotée d'un réseau international qui vise à faire échanger et circuler étudiants, expositions et ateliers, et qui a abouti à l'organisation, depuis 1998, de la Biennale Internationale Design Saint-Étienne.

La Biennale Internationale Design Saint-Étienne est une grande manifestation internationale ouverte à plus de 80 pays et réunissant 2 500 designers, 20 000 objets, 200 000 visiteurs en 2004 et 1 500 000 visiteurs sur le site Web en novembre dernier. ✕ La réussite éclatante de cette manifestation depuis sa création a permis d'imposer cet événement comme incontournable dans le paysage du design international, d'affirmer Saint-Étienne comme capitale du design et de pérenniser son projet : la Cité du Design. ✕ Celle-ci représente un enjeu stratégique d'aménagement du territoire, fédérateur de l'existant et catalyseur du devenir. Elle complétera un chantier de reconversion d'une cité emblématique de deux siècles de révolution industrielle. ✕ La formation, la création et la recherche en constituent les fondations. ✕ En 2007, au cœur de l'agglomération, la Cité du Design sera donc installée sur une friche industrielle de 18 hectares dans la Manufacture de Giat. Elle aura parmi ses objectifs de sensibiliser les entreprises à la culture du design et de les informer des tendances ainsi que de l'évolution des concepts et des matériaux. ✕ Cette action pourra se traduire par des aides à la conception, des mises en réseaux, des aides à la distribution afin de favoriser le lancement de produits et, enfin, des aides à la valorisation au moyen de salons et d'expositions. ✕ Globalement, la Cité du Design apportera aux entreprises à la fois des gestes de fond structurants et des actions ponctuelles d'événements marquants. Elle accueillera une trentaine de designers français et étrangers en résidence. ✕ L'opération architecturale, conduite par l'agence berlinoise LIN, de Finn Geipel et Giulia Andi, lauréats du Concours international d'architecture, sera un lieu contemporain, vivant, flexible et évolutif.

〉 Contemporain afin de véhiculer une image de modernité en accord
  avec le propos design et création ;

〉 Vivant pour attirer la population et contribuer à l'image dynamique de la ville.

〉 Flexible de manière à ce que les espaces satisfassent une programmation ;
  pluridisciplinaire : concerts, défilés de mode et événements divers ;

〉 Enfin, évolutif en prévision de son extension vers des commerces et activités tertiaires.

La Cité du Design présentera de grandes expositions culturelles et d'autres sur l'actualité du design. Elle proposera un centre de ressources et un centre de formation et de recherche en lien fort avec le monde industriel, le pôle universitaire et les écoles d'ingénieurs. ✕ Des formations postdiplômes seront offertes sur le design industriel. ✕ La Cité du Design sera fonctionnelle à l'échelle du monde puisque des accords de partenariats sont en négociation avec les grandes institutions de design à Montréal, mais aussi aux États-Unis, en Angleterre, au Danemark, en Italie, en Espagne, au Japon et en Chine. ✕ AVEC LA CITÉ DU DESIGN, IL S'AGIT D'AFFIRMER L'IMAGE D'UNE COMPÉTENCE SINGULIÈRE POSITIONNANT LA MÉTROPOLE STÉPHANOISE COMME ACTEUR PRIVILÉGIÉ DANS LE CONTEXTE DE LA COMPÉTITIVITÉ INTERNATIONALE. NOTRE BUT EST DE FAIRE DE SAINT-ÉTIENNE, LA CAPITALE DE L'EFFERVESCENCE INVENTIVE.

LA BIENNALE INTERNATIONALE DESIGN SAINT-ÉTIENNE — UN CONCEPT NOVATEUR

PAR JOSYANE FRANC
> **Responsable des relations publiques et internationales**
École Régionale des Beaux-Arts de Saint-Étienne, Biennale Internationale Design Saint-Étienne

〉〉〉

La singularité de la Biennale Internationale Design Saint-Étienne réside incontestablement dans le fait d'être imaginée et portée par une école d'art. ✕ Cette aventure est née de la rencontre de deux visionnaires : Jacques Bonnaval et Michel Thiollière. ✕ Jacques Bonnaval, alors directeur de l'École Régionale des Beaux-Arts de Saint-Étienne, a orienté dès 1989 le développement de son établissement autour des formations en design, des nouvelles technologies et des partenariats industriels, tout en ouvrant ses champs d'action vers l'international. ✕ Stéphanois d'adoption, il est fasciné par l'histoire de Saint-Étienne, liée à celle de la modernité industrielle, et, surtout, par le catalogue Manufrance, exemple le plus emblématique de l'avènement d'une culture des objets du quotidien. Il propose l'organisation d'une Biennale pour rendre pérenne la dynamique d'une cité où la culture transcendait l'ingéniosité. Michel Thiollière, Maire de Saint-Étienne, qui a déjà engagé le renouveau urbain de sa cité, est soucieux de dessiner et d'inventer la ville de demain, celle qui sera capable de répondre aux aspirations quotidiennes et à l'imaginaire des femmes et des hommes qui y vivent. Il soutient ce projet dont il rêvait et engage la ville pour relever ce défi. ✕ Dès sa première édition, en 1998, la Biennale Internationale Design Saint-Étienne s'inscrit d'emblée, non pas comme un salon professionnel où s'exposent les succès commerciaux du moment, mais comme une

École
d'Architecture
de Paris
Malaquais

01

02

plaque tournante, un forum international du design composé de rencontres et de débats autour de l'objet questionné dans ses résonances sociologiques et dans ses déclinaisons, toutes emblématiques des identités culturelles représentées ✕ Ici, se côtoient objets issus de savoir-faire traditionnels et articles à succès commerciaux, travaux d'étudiants et de designers professionnels, ceux des jeunes et des designers renommés, ceux nés dans des pays où le design est intégré à la culture et ceux issus de pays où il se trouve à l'état naissant. ✕ Même si cette manifestation apparaît souvent brouillonne pour le visiteur désireux de recettes, elle pose délibérément des questions afin de maintenir la pensée vivante.

〉〉

Ses objectifs sont multiples :
> Créer en France le seul événement permettant une confrontation de la création internationale Nord-Sud basée sur la mixité et l'échange
> S'interroger sur l'accélération des mutations technologiques, écologiques, architecturales et culturelles
> Montrer la dynamique d'une conquête industrielle internationale par le design
> Souligner la responsabilité des designers comme acteurs des enjeux économiques et culturels
> Mettre l'accent sur la recherche et l'imagination
> Convaincre les chefs d'entreprise de la diversité des enjeux du design
> Méditer sur la richesse des métissages culturels
> Révéler au public qu'il n'existe pas une attitude design, mais autant de points de vue que de pensées et de designers
> Susciter l'intérêt des professionnels, des entreprises, des étudiants et du grand public

L'École Régionale des Beaux-Arts de Saint-Étienne organise cet événement et crée ainsi un projet pédagogique pour ses étudiants. Par les ateliers, la rencontre de designers internationaux, la scénographie, la signalétique, le catalogue, le site Web, le montage et le démontage de l'exposition, s'ouvre un forum improvisé où designers, étudiants, industriels, stylistes, intellectuels débattent et nouent des liens lors des colloques, expositions, défilés de mode et moments partagés dans les bars et les festivités accompagnant l'événement. ✕ C'est aussi un événement fédérateur des acteurs politiques culturels, économiques et de l'enseignement supérieur de la métropole stéphanoise. La passion et l'enthousiasme de l'équipe des Beaux-Arts et de la Ville de Saint-Étienne ont contribué au succès de cette aventure humaine.

〉〉

03

〉〉
Laurent Grégori et Nadine Cahen
〉 Designers, Atelier Cahen & Gregori,
Saint-Étienne, France.
〉〉

Nadine Cahen, coloriste-plasticienne, née à
Saint-Étienne, et Laurent Grégori, designer
né à Genève, ont associé leurs spécificités
depuis 1998 avec une même envie :
concevoir des environnements dont les
surfaces sont porteuses de sens, d'émotions
et d'information. Par la couleur, la texture,
le motif, ils interrogent les sens, incitent au
toucher, recherchent la profondeur de la
surface. ✕ Champs d'intervention : direction
artistique, création de motifs et de chartes
de couleurs, scénographie, signalétique,
design d'environnement. ✕ Références :
Abet Laminati, Print-France, Groupe SEB,
Groupe Michelin, Grosfillex, RATP, Gaz de
France, Chaumont-sur-Loire, BHV Paris.
〉〉

Expositions
2002 〉 Festival des jardins de
Chaumont-sur-Loire
2003 〉 Designer's week — Tokyo
2003 〉 Habiter c'est vivre, Parc de la Villette,
Paris
2004 〉 Institut Français de Valence et Galerie
Papyrus, Espagne
2004 〉 Centre de design UQAM, Montréal
2005 〉 Cité du design, Triennale de Milan
2005 〉 Designers' week — Bangkok
〉〉

01 Découverte de la rue Ronsard (anciennement couverte par un stationnement), Saint-Étienne, 2005. Décors sur MEG, stratifié massif.

〉〉〉

QUELS ENDROITS PUBLICS DE SAINT-ÉTIENNE PRÉFÉREZ VOUS ?

Le quartier de la place Louis Comte, premier lieu de respiration au sud de l'Hyper-centre. Cet ensemble de petites places, entre la «rue du tram», le cinéma Mélies, les Halles et le Musée d'Art et d'Industrie, offre une des visions les plus harmonieuses de la ville : l'espace urbain est dégagé et permet d'apprécier la vraie qualité architecturale des bâtiments, qui, fait rare à Saint-Étienne, présentent une même identité de style. Cet espace n'a rien de marquant, ni de focalisant en soi, c'est peut-être ce qui en fait son intérêt. Ici, la ville présente un visage «naturellement beau», le propre de l'élégance. ✕ Le parc Montaud : à 1 kilomètre du centre, le plus grand parc de Saint-Étienne, ressemble plus à un bout de campagne qu'à un parc urbain. Et pourtant, il surplombe les quartiers les plus industriels. À l'opposé du premier lieu, il offre un télescopage de tous les visages de la ville, de ses histoires et de ses réalités parallèles. Une invitation à zoomer, cadrer, recomposer chaque fois une ville différente.

QUE VOUDRIEZ-VOUS VOIR CONSTRUIT OU AMÉLIORÉ DANS VOTRE VILLE ?

Nous ne souhaitons rien voir de construit de particulier, au sens architectural du terme. Beaucoup de biens d'équipement sont déjà construits ou sur le point de l'être, comme le Zénith ou la Cité du Design. ✕ Ce qu'il reste à construire — ou à améliorer par le design —, c'est un véritable «cœur de ville» : de par son étalement le long de la rue centrale, l'Hyper-centre n'a pas le dynamisme, la fluidité, la cohérence que l'on attend d'une ville moyenne. Surtout que la place de l'Hôtel de Ville, no man's land de banques et de cabinets d'assurances, coupe littéralement le tissu vivant en deux zones distinctes, au lieu d'être un point de convergence. Redéfinir le rôle de cet espace au cœur de la ville représente un enjeu de taille…

〉〉〉

MARINE LECOINTE

〉 Designer indépendante,
  Saint-Étienne, France

》》

〉〉

QUELS ENDROITS PUBLICS DE SAINT-ÉTIENNE PRÉFÉREZ VOUS?

La place Jules Guesde, pour la qualité de ses aménagements sur trois points :

〉 Adéquation esthétique et fonctionnelle avec l'esprit du lieu ;

〉 Qualité de la réalisation ;

〉 Très particulière ambiance qui en résulte.

La place Raspail, pour son incongruité. Îlot intimiste dans le quartier Beaubrun (centre-ville), ses possibilités d'usage répondent parfaitement aux besoins des habitants, qui les utilisent avec assiduité. Cependant, ce lieu aurait pu être encore plus réussi avec l'intervention d'un designer, car il est semblable aux aménagements désuets des banlieues difficiles et reste enclavé, donc isolé, au sein même de la ville.

QUELLES AMÉLIORATIONS POURRAIENT ÊTRE APPORTÉES DU POINT DE VUE DESIGN?

Les aménagements urbains nécessitent un engagement tripartite : politique, designer, population. Les ambitions des uns, souvent décalées par rapport à celles des autres, font souffrir les valeurs humanistes que portent les projets de design urbain. Une valorisation et un soutien du travail des designers ainsi qu'une communication juste avec (et j'insiste sur avec) la population permettrait sans doute une meilleure adéquation entre les ambitions des projets et leurs résultats. Il faut pour ça que le monde politique apprenne à travailler avec les designers et la population, et non à se servir des designers pour manipuler cette dernière.

QUE VOUDRIEZ-VOUS VOIR CONSTRUIT DANS VOTRE VILLE?

Des jardins (et non des espaces verts…). Les jardins sont toujours des images figuratives ou abstraites de la société. Nous vivons à une époque où les villes, à l'image de la communauté humaine (urbaine ou rurale), sont en pleine mutation. Les jardins, repères visibles et praticables, aident à la compréhension de ce que nous sommes et de là vers où nous allons. Ils sont territoires d'exemples, d'expressions, de propositions, de volontés du devenir humain et donc social. Or, à Saint-Étienne, ils font cruellement défaut.

〉〉

— LE DESIGN EST UNE RÉFLEXION SUR LA MODERNITÉ, QUI SUIT L'INVENTION. ON A MANIFESTEMENT DIGÉRÉ LA TECHNOLOGIE. ON A BESOIN AUJOURD'HUI DE SE L'APPROPRIER, DE L'UTILISER ET D'EN PROFITER DIFFÉREMMENT DANS UNE VILLE DITE DE DESIGN.

— SAINT-ÉTIENNE EST UNE VILLE AU PASSÉ INDUSTRIEL, RICHE EN TRADITION OUVRIÈRE. AUJOURD'HUI TOURNÉE VERS L'AVENIR, ELLE ACCORDE AU DESIGN URBAIN UNE PLACE IMPORTANTE. DE NOMBREUX TRAVAUX DE RÉNOVATION RENDENT SES PLACES PUBLIQUES, RUES ET BÂTIMENTS PLUS ATTRAYANTS, PLUS CONTEMPORAINS. LA VILLE EST AINSI PLUS LÉGÈRE; ON S'Y SENT BIEN.

Stéphane Laurier, propriétaire et chef du restaurant Nouvelle, Saint-Étienne.

STOC
HOLI

IRL

P

S

FIN

Stockholm

EST

RUS

Göteborg

LV

DK

LT

GB

—WE, AS A CITY, CANNOT LIVE OFF OUR HISTORY ONLY; WE MUST CONSTANTLY CREATE ANEW. DESIGN IS ABOUT CONSUMPTION AND COMPETITIVENESS AND THAT COMMERCIAL IMPETUS IS IMPORTANT TO THE GROWTH OF OUR BUSINESS AND INDUSTRY.
Annika Billström, Mayor of Stockholm

CZ

SK

UA

A

F

CH

H

RO

SLO

YU

I

BG

RO

01

DESIGN POR- TRAIT

POPULATION
The population of the city of Stockholm is 764,200 inhabitants, and the metropolitan area has a population of 1,870,800.

⟩⟩⟩⟩⟩⟩⟩⟩⟩⟩⟩⟩⟩⟩⟩⟩⟩⟩⟩⟩⟩⟩⟩⟩⟩⟩⟩⟩⟩⟩⟩⟩⟩⟩⟩⟩⟩⟩⟩

YEAR OF FOUNDATION
The city of Stockholm was founded in 1252.

⟩⟩⟩⟩⟩⟩⟩⟩⟩⟩⟩⟩⟩⟩⟩⟩⟩⟩⟩⟩⟩⟩⟩⟩⟩⟩⟩⟩⟩⟩⟩⟩⟩⟩⟩⟩⟩⟩⟩

⟩⟩⟩⟩⟩⟩⟩⟩⟩⟩⟩⟩⟩⟩⟩⟩⟩⟩⟩⟩⟩⟩⟩⟩⟩⟩⟩⟩⟩⟩⟩⟩⟩⟩⟩⟩⟩⟩⟩

STRENGTHS AND CHALLENGES
Over the last century Stockholm has gone from being a local crafts and industry town with 470,000 inhabitants to its present position as an international metropolitan area with a population of close to 2 million. Today, its industry is characterized by knowledge-based companies, in which 40 percent of the workforce has a post-secondary education. Approximately three-quarters of the city's jobs are in the private sector. Close to 200,000 private companies operate in Stockholm, and most are one-man operations, but the one hundred largest companies provide 40 percent of the jobs. ⤫ Stockholm's importance as a growth driver for the country as a whole has increased over the past few years, primarily because of developments in industries like finance, IT, media, bio-technology, biomedicine, environmental engineering, and tourism. In the past ten years, one-third of the economic growth—expressed by the GRP (Gross Regional Product)—has been created in this region. More than 40 percent of the employees in the IT industry work in Stockholm, the majority in Kista Science City, Stockholm's largest industrial estate, which comprises 28,000 employees and 750 companies, of which two-thirds specialize in IT/telecom. Many leading international companies have branches in Kista—Ericsson, for example. ⤫ Stockholm is also the headquarters for the top executive functions in the private sector. Over half of the privately owned Swedish companies with more than 250 employees have their head office in the region. Stockholm is an important centre for universities and R&D, and it has grown in importance as an international city; it now has 5,500 foreign-owned companies employing a total of 156,000 people.

⟩⟩⟩⟩⟩⟩⟩⟩⟩⟩⟩⟩⟩⟩⟩⟩⟩⟩⟩⟩⟩⟩⟩⟩⟩⟩⟩⟩⟩⟩⟩⟩⟩⟩⟩⟩⟩⟩⟩

SIGNIFICANT EVENTS

The Swedish Society of Arts and Craft was founded in 1845 and is the oldest design association in the world. The association organized Sweden's participation in international exhibitions, supported young artisans and designers through scholarships, and published free design and manufacturing flyers for artists, providing up-to-date examples of fashion and design. It also opened a museum, presenting objects stylistically displayed with an educational purpose in mind. The magazine *Form* was founded in 1905 and is still published today. In 1914, the association started a representation agency with the motto: "Artists for industry." In 1976, the association was renamed the Swedish Industrial Design Foundation (SVID). ✕ For the Home Exhibition at Liljevalchs in 1917, artisans and artists were commissioned to make better household goods for the poor and cramped homes of Sweden's working-class population. The exhibition displayed seventeen furnished rooms as well as modern, practical kitchens. ✕ The Stockholm Exhibition in 1930 was a manifesto and a breakthrough for functionalism. The ambition of the functionalists was to remove all "unnecessary" decoration. The exhibition emphasized a new and modern lifestyle and explored the themes of air, light, and greenery, which were thought to promote health and improve the quality of life. It also presented new functionalistic housing, school classrooms, restaurants, hospital wards, and so on. ✕ International appreciation of the work of Swedish artists became apparent at the Paris and New York World Fairs, in 1937 and 1939, respectively. Swedish Grace and Swedish Modern, with their simple, cool, and pleasant shapes, came into international prominence at the fairs. ✕ Stockholm was the European Capital of Culture in 1998, and design in various forms was a central element of the events and activities throughout the year. The city also played host to new, international design connections when the newly built Museum of Modern Art was opened in 1998. ✕ The year 2002 marked the 750th anniversary of the founding of Stockholm. Many of the celebratory activities throughout the year had a focus on both contemporary and historical design.

NUMBER OF DESIGNERS

It is difficult to get an accurate number of active designers in the city, given that there is no clear definition of what a designer is. In any case, close to 60 percent work on their own, and many are not registered members of design organizations. Several big design-driven companies employ designers, such as Hennes & Mauritz (H&M), which has 120 designers in Stockholm alone. The available statistics indicate that Stockholm has some 4,000 active designers. This figure includes industrial, graphic, textile, fashion, and interior designers. In addition, some 3,000 architects are active in Stockholm.

RENOWNED DESIGNERS WHO HAVE CONTRIBUTED TO STOCKHOLM AS A DESIGN CITY

Gunnar Asplund and Swedish Grace

In the twenties and thirties, neoclassicism in Stockholm evolved into the unique style known as Swedish Grace. While neoclassicism in other countries was imposing and ponderous, in its Stockholm variation it acquired an elegant lightness, reminiscent of late-eighteenth century ideals. The style is characterized by external rendering in warm colours with few decorative elements. One of the most characteristic buildings in Stockholm—the Stockholm City Library, by Gunnar Asplund—is built in the Swedish Grace style. Despite its location in the city centre, it sits in splendid solitude with its orange front, like a palatial mansion. Dark, slightly inclined stairs lead from the main entrance up to the abundantly lit rotunda where the books are stored. The stairs are reminiscent of a walkway to a temple, wherein the rotunda is the shrine itself and literature the object of worship.

Josef Frank, in defence of imagination

Josef Frank, together with Estrid Eriksson and the company Svenskt Tenn, was an important part of the school called Swedish Modern. Early in his career, Frank adhered to the modernist movement but he eventually broke with functionalism, which he found too dull and misanthropic. Frank emphasized imagination and individuality when creating new furniture and patterns. He designed close to 2,000 pieces of furniture, many of which are still in production; but it is mainly for his work as a textile designer that Josef Frank has been so loved in Sweden. Almost all of his patterns are strongly inspired by nature. With his exquisite drawings, glowing colours, and playful harmony, Frank stands out as the Botticelli of fabrics.

Wilhelm Kåge and the beautiful everyday object

At the beginning of the twentieth century, an appeal was heard around Europe: "Artists to industry!" In Sweden, it was quickly taken up by the Gustavsberg porcelain factory, which, in 1917, hired a young artist by the name of Wilhelm Kåge. The ambition of both Kåge and the factory was, among other things, to create well-designed utility goods for ordinary people. The practicalities were also important to Kåge; his Pyro set can be taken straight from the oven to the dinner table. Designed in the thirties, Pyro is still used in many Swedish homes. His best-known work includes the Argenta series: spherical vases and generous plates and bowls in green glazing with painted silver decor.

Peter Celsing and international modernism

In the mid-forties, plans were underway for redesigning Stockholm's city centre. That reconstruction took place from 1955 to 1965. Five, individually designed, eighteen-storey skyscrapers were built at the south end of Sveavägen. The transformation of the city centre continued with the construction of Sergels Plaza, the Stockholm Cultural Centre, Riksbanken, and an elliptical roundabout to manage the flow of traffic. Peter Celsing designed the buildings, and his Kulturhuset, with its open, horizontal front in glass and concrete, was seen as an ingenious approach to creating a cultural centre. The square linking the courtyard in front of Kulturhuset with the skyscrapers was given black-and-white paving, designed by Jörgen Kjeargaard, a pattern that has become a signature of Stockholm.

Jonas Bohlin and architecture moving indoors

In 1981, post-modernism arrived in Stockholm when interior design student Jonas Bohlin presented his Concrete Chair, a chair made of concrete and steel. Uncomfortable, heavy, and unusable in so many ways, it raised questions about the importance of furniture and provoked the Swedish furniture tradition, with its heavy focus on functionality. Swedish furniture would never be the same again. Jonas Bohlin introduced a more playful attitude to Stockholm interiors, an attitude which is readily apparent in restaurants and bars around the capital, the foremost representation being his Sturehof restaurant (1995). In designing its interior, Bohlin was inspired by the classical bistro environment, to which he added his own playful twist.

01 Arlanda VIP-Lounge, design: Jonas Bohlin 02 Josef Frank's furniture together with pewter goods by Estrid Ericsson

〉〉

ANNUAL DESIGN EVENTS

FutureDesignDays is an annual international design festival showcasing world-leading designers and architects. FutureDesignDays is a meeting place featuring a conference, seminars, and exhibitions for designers, architects, students, private enterprise, politicians, and other institutions. FutureDesignDays was named the world's best event at the 2004 EIBTM Awards. × Stockholm's annual Entrepreneur's Gala is Sweden's biggest meeting of established and experienced entrepreneurs and policy-makers in private enterprise and public administration. Among other activities, awards are given to entrepreneurs who suc-ceeded in bringing a product or a service to the market and who have generated economic growth and been role models in sectors where design usually plays an important role. × The city of Stockholm is a co-organizer of an annual Design Banquet to which selected individuals who work with design are invited. The purpose of this event is to create encounters between established and young designers and representatives of companies for which design is an important element of their operations. × Every year, the city of Stockholm awards a number of grants to inventors who have developed products or services with strong commercial potential. Design in various senses of the word is often a vital component of these inventions. × STREET is Stockholm's answer to the Camden Lock Market in London, where up-and-coming designers display their wares. STREET is an exciting market where hun-dreds of creative individuals meet con-sumers. Its Web portal enables designers, producers, and others to find partners and gain access to mail and export opportunities.

× A large number of trade fairs take place in Stockholm. Among those related to design are: Stockholm Furniture Fair and Northern Light Fair: the world's biggest venue for Nordic design—furniture, lighting, textiles, and interior design for private homes, offices, and contract markets. It is an annual event and takes place in February. × Focus Stockholm is the collective name for a new event involving a week full of activities, featuring fashion, shoes, design, and interior decorating. Some of the most important players in the industry hold presentations during one week in August or two weeks in February in Stockholm. Examples are:

〉 Nordic Shoe and Bag Fair: Scandinavia's leading trade fair for shoes, bags, and acces-sories. In February and August each year.
〉 Formex: Scandinavian's leading trade fair for design, home interiors, and giftware. It takes place biannually in January and August.
〉 Rookies: exhibitions and a forum for the fashion designers of tomorrow.
〉 Timeless Beauty: a jewellery, watch, and wedding fair.

Related websites
〉 www.futuredesigndays.com
〉 www.streetinstockholm.se
〉 www.stockholmfurniturefair.com
〉 www.stockholmsmassan.se
〉〉

DESIGN INSTITUTIONS
Design museums

Stockholm has a good one hundred muse-ums to visit, and many of them feature aspects of design. Here are just a few: The National Museum of Fine Arts (Nationalmuseum) houses Sweden´s largest collection of modern design, industrial design, and handicrafts. × The Swedish Museum of Architecture presents not only architecture, but also drawings and pictures of interiors and furni-ture. The title of its main exhibition is Architecture in Sweden—Function, Design and Aesthetics. × The Museum of Science and Technology deals with the history of technology, often involving objects with design qualities. The museum houses the history of Swedish industrial design, even if the focus is not always design per se. The museum has had a number of thematic exhi-bitions where design played a major role.

× The Nordic Museum collects objects from cultural history and presents them, for example, in the form of furnished rooms or as parts of environments from various eras. Design is an integral part of the museum's activities. × The Museum of Modern Art has a collection considered one of Europe's finest. × The well-known Liljevalchs' Art Gallery is dedicated to design during the 2005 Year of Design and has organized exhibitions under the title "Designable" featuring design, fashion, handicraft, woodwork, and other objects that shape our everyday lives. × The Gustavsberg Porcelain Museum displays the factory's products, renowned worldwide from 1827 to today. Gustavsberg has been an important contributor to twentieth century design, and several of its well-known designers had an impact on the concept of modernism.

Related websites

› The National Museum of Fine Arts
  www.nationalmuseum.se
› Swedish Museum of Architecture
  www.arkitekturmuseet.se
› Museum of Science and Technology
  www.tekniskamuseet.se
› Nordic Museum
  www.nordiskamuseet.se
› Museum of Modern Art
  www.modernamuseet.com
› Liljevalchs' Art Gallery
  www.liljevalchs.com

Stockholm is host to a number of other museums that are interesting from a design perspective, for example homes that have been converted into museums:

› www.hallwylskamuseet.se
› www.waldemarsudde.com
› www.millesgarden.se
› www.thielska-galleriet.se

Meeting places

The Stockholm Cultural Centre is a centre for photography, art, multimedia, fashion, music, dance, and theatre. The Centre is a cultural symbol of Stockholm and of the evolution of modernism in Sweden. Hundreds of people come here every day just to relax, read, or study and play chess, etc. It is a vibrant cultural place in the very heart of Stockholm. × Designforum is a place in Stockholm for everyone interested in design where you can look at design exhibitions, read magazines, participate in seminars, or have a cup of coffee. × Designtorget is a marketplace where newcomers and rising-star designers and craftspeople rent a space to sell their products. There are four such shops in Stockholm.

Related websites

› Stockholm Cultural Centre
  www.kulturhuset.se
› Designforum
  www.svenskform.se
› Designtorget
  www.designtorget.se

Design advocacy groups and associations

The Swedish Society of Crafts and Design (Svensk Form) is the world's oldest design association, founded in 1845. Today it forms public opinion and disseminates knowledge about design issues. It has been assigned by the government to promulgate Swedish design, both in Sweden and abroad. × The Swedish Industrial Design Foundation (SVID) aims to improve awareness within the private and public sectors of the importance of design as a competitive tool and to encourage the integration of design methodology into their activities. × Rookies is an organization for young fashion designers.

Related websites

› Swedish Society of Crafts and Design
  www.svenskform.se
› Swedish Industrial Design Foundation
  www.svid.se
› Rookies
  www.rookies.nu

››

01 Design: Martin Bergström 02 Design: Eva Leijon 02 Design: Gun Franzén

》》

DESIGN SCHOOLS

In Stockholm are found the most highly rated design schools in Scandinavia. We have both pure design academies—Konstfack and Beckmans, among others—as well as other schools that incorporate elements of design or where design is receiving increased attention. Around one hundred students annually pass their degrees at the pure design academies. × University College of Arts, Crafts and Design (Konstfack) is Sweden's oldest and largest arts university program, with courses ranging from free art to arts and crafts to design, for a total of nine different courses. The school offers courses in graphic design, industrial design, interior architecture, and furniture design, as well as in pottery, glass, metal, and textiles. It also has a comprehensive student exchange program with other schools across the globe. × Beckmans School of Design is a private school with partners like IKEA and H&M. Important programs include fashion, advertising, as well as product design and interior architecture. × The Carl Malmsten training program focuses on industrial furniture production, primarily in wood. The objective is to produce independent and creative furniture designers with extensive skills and awareness. Carl Malmsten was one of the leading personalities in the field of culture in twentieth-century Sweden; he had a huge impact on both public and private environments. × Bergs School of Communications works at the intersection of contemporary communications disciplines. It focuses on advertising, media, and public relations and integrates these three areas into a targeted concept of integrated communications. × Forsbergs is a private school for graphic design and fashion. × The Royal Institute of Technology has many courses that incorporate design: among others, the architectural program, innovation and design, structural engineering and design, and design and product development. × Upper secondary schools. The interest in design from private enterprise has grown and professional design has become increasingly popular among young people. This has led to the creation of special design programs in the upper secondary schools, as well as design courses for teachers.

Related websites
› University College of Arts, Crafts and Design
www.konstfack.se
› Beckmans School of Design
www.beckmans.se
› Bergs School of Communications
www.berghs.se
› Forsbergs
www.forsbergsskola.se
› Royal Institute of Technology
www.kth.se

》》

DESIGN STRATEGIES OR POLICIES

The Swedish government has proclaimed 2005 the Year of Design. The objective is to illustrate how design touches our everyday lives, our jobs, and our leisure time as well as to stimulate the use of design in society as a whole. The 2005 Year of Design is being promoted through a national campaign.

The city of Stockholm has arranged, for both employees and citizens, many design-related events aimed at making design a sustainable part of the city's activities. The Year of Design is a long-term project that will continue after the official events in 2005 are over. Stockholm has appointed a design coordinator, and a Design Centre is now being planned for the city. Design is one of the growth areas that will drive Stockholm's development in the future.

Related websites
› 2005 Year of Design
www.designaret.se
www.stockholmdesign2005.se

》》

Design portrait of Stockholm
Information provided by
GUNILLA RAASCHOU
› Project Manager
› Stockholm Economic Development Agency

ANNIKA BILLSTRÖM
MAYOR OF STOCKHOLM
SINCE 2002

DO YOU CONSIDER YOUR CITY TO BE A NEW DESIGN CITY?

Stockholm has a long tradition of various enterprises working in architecture and design. We were shaped by our vivid history in architecture and urban planning, which fostered our reputation internationally through innovation long before the concept of design existed. × Today, design is a growth segment that is carrying Stockholm's development at all levels—economic, social, and cultural. Swedes are skilful at adopting new materials, new technologies, and new values, and the results are intriguing products and good design visible in the offices of our companies, in public spaces, and in the wide array of sophisticated objects available in the market. All of the industry associations and advanced design education programs are found in Stockholm. The design departments of the country's major companies, such as Hennes and Mauritz (H&M) and Electrolux, are located here, and the majority of Sweden's most prominent designers are also based here.

**WHAT HAS BEEN YOUR PERSONAL CONTRIBUTION
IN FACILITATING THE EMERGENCE OF YOUR DESIGN CITY?**

I would like to believe that I have contributed on several levels. First and foremost, I have worked to put design on the agenda in the business community and within the city's administration: design as quality of life, as a crucial component of all urban planning, and as a developmental factor in working life. My vision of shaping a new development area for design and architecture just south of the city centre is on the way to becoming a reality. In the coming year we plan to create a design centre that will contribute to these fields and to Stockholm as a whole. It will be located at Telefonplan in the buildings of Ericsson´s former headquarters. Our top design college, University College of Arts, Crafts and Design, has already moved to the area, as have an exhibition space and several companies. In my work I also devote considerable time to visiting design exhibitions, meeting representatives of the design industry, and attending design expos and openings. I hope that my personal presence strengthens the understanding and importance of design in society.

**WHY DO YOU BELIEVE THAT POSITIONING YOUR CITY
THROUGH DESIGN IS IMPORTANT?**

We as a city cannot live off our history only. We must constantly create anew. Design is about consumption and competitiveness, and this commercial impetus is important to the growth of our business and industry. Design often has a young target group and it is vital that Stockholm attracts young, educated people to create a dynamic and modern city—whether they are tourists, residents, or employers. As odd as it may sound, this is an issue of supplying the competence structure of the city. Design is also linked to several other creative industries, and when all of this is combined with the effects of globalization, we bring Stockholm to the attention of entirely new target groups. If we can ensure that Stockholm is appealing as a design city for companies and individuals from an international perspective, we can attract more tourists, more new residents, and more new businesses.

**WHAT EXAMPLES OF DESIGN PROMOTION STRATEGIES DEVELOPED
IN OTHER CITIES INSPIRED YOU?**

There are so many! Older initiatives such as PS1 in New York, with regards to location as a way of reaching new target groups and liberating oneself from a physical or historical legacy, which a traditional location in the central parts of the city often entails. It is also a way to revitalize disadvantaged areas. The Design Museum in London has similar qualities and characteristics that I find intriguing. More recent sources of inspiration naturally include the new Norwegian Design Centre in Oslo and the Danish Design Centre in Copenhagen, each of which brings a national perspective that entails creating accessibility and vitality while enriching the central areas in the city. That is a difficult balance to achieve, and as a capital city we have to consider this multiplicity of interests.

**WHAT SHOULD BE THE ROLES OF THE CITIZEN, THE DESIGNER, AND
THE POLITICIAN IN THE DEVELOPMENT OF A DESIGN CITY?**

Politicians must set the overall tone and be actively involved in developing the city in line with the needs of citizens and the business community. ╳ As politicians, we have to practise what we preach. In other words, we also have to be role models in the design area. ╳ We all have different tools and instruments, of course, but the catalyst is the will to create an interesting city in which to live, visit, and do business. Because we traditionally work in different fields, we must focus on co-operating in order to achieve maximum impact. In that respect, those of us who work in government agencies have an important role as brokers and enablers. City planning is one example where politicians can contribute to creating a city that functions for everybody—not forgetting children, elderly, and disabled persons. I also believe it is our responsibility to spotlight the issues or industries that are either neglected or that we have assessed as strategically important to the city's development and growth, and the design and other creative industries definitely belong to that category. ╳ With consistent and well thought out concentration on design during the 2005 Year of Design, we are creating even better conditions for Stockholm's economic, social, and cultural development. Internationally, we can be a model for other cities in the creation of public spaces. This can generate publicity and increase tourism, as well as enhance the well-being and attraction to the city of Stockholmers. ╳ Viewed from a larger perspective, there is every indication that design is a growing area which, along with IT, telecom, and biomedicine/biotechnology, will be the bulwark of Stockholm's development in the coming years. ╳ Design is a large and comprehensive area that is part of our everyday lives and affects us all. Design constitutes both quality of life and a developmental factor in working life.

〉〉

STOCKHOLM NEW AND THE NEW STOCKHOLM

BY CLAES BRITTON

› Editor-in-chief, Stockholm New and CEO Britton & Britton, Stockholm

››

Though Sweden is an old nation, it's a young civilization. As recently as a century ago, Sweden was still a poor and backwards agrarian outpost with a great and terrible martial history. Then, in the late 1800s, when northern Sweden's enormous resources of wood and iron became accessible because of the new railroads, an extremely rapid industrial revolution started. In just fifty years this revolution transformed Sweden from one of Europe's poorest and most primitive countries to one of the world's richest, most developed, and sophisticated societies. × This extreme period is known as "Sweden's economic miracle," and is sometimes compared to Japan's economic miracle of some decades later. Although a total disaster for most of Europe, the two world wars were in fact the main engines in the rapid development of industrial Sweden, which was spared from war damage. × The place where this extraordinary economic success was manifested first and foremost was the Royal Capital of Stockholm, a city that just a hundred years earlier had been a provincial town with a small, medieval city centre and rural outskirts. Historically, Stockholm resembles in some ways the older North American cities, including Montreal: apart from its historic centre, all of central Stockholm was built over the past century. × Parallel to this economic evolution, Sweden was developing a distinct aesthetic culture, style, and philosophy, after having cast off the influence of powerful foreign cultures, in particular, France. Stockholm's architecture reflects this aesthetic evolution, from the imposing architecture style of the bourgeois stone city of the early 1900s, to neoclassicism, modernism, and its special Scandinavian version, functionalism, until the so-called late functionalism of the mid-sixties. × Throughout this long period—the late 1800s to the mid-sixties—Sweden was a world leader not only in architecture and urban planning, but also in design and crafts, and in heavy industry. Even the most humble and seemingly insignificant object was meticulously designed for practical as well as aesthetic purposes. This was the thorough, ambitious, and farsighted design strategy that became the hallmark of Swedish industry. In Sweden, this program was labelled "More beautiful everyday products," wherein form follows function in the very finest sense of the expression. × But a dramatic shift occurred in the mid-sixties when bold entrepreneurship turned into blatant hubris, and modernism mutated into brutalism: from quality to quantity. Although this phenomenon took place throughout the Western world, in Sweden it assumed an extreme form. The nation's political and economic leaders—who were still of the pre-war generation—wanted to do away, once and for all, with the old agrarian Sweden that reminded them of their own humble origins, to create a utopian futuristic welfare state. What's worse: they had the means to do it. In just ten years (1965–75) as a result of this political initiative, 1 million new homes were built in Sweden, a country that had less than 8 million inhabitants at the time. During this period large parts of the historic city centre of Stockholm and several other Swedish cities were eradicated to make way for "modern society." In a parallel process, Sweden's traditional and internationally admired design and craft industry was also severely crippled, replaced by mass production. The natural ties between the country's economic and aesthetic cultures were thus abruptly cut. × There is another fascinating story about Sweden's amazingly successful production of designs for the masses. It's probably enough to mention that IKEA and H&M, two of the world's most recognizable budget design multinationals in home and fashion, respectively—and virtual identical twins in terms of business concepts and strategies—were both founded in close proximity to each other in southern Sweden by typical Swedish entrepreneurs and, what's more, in the same year, 1947. × History was quick to sober up and condemn the "crimes" committed in the name of social engineering during this short period, referred to in Sweden as the "record years." It's a sad fact that the record years resulted in a national trauma that for twenty-five years has made the Swedish political and economic establishment wary of all modernistic, not to mention futuristic, expressions in general. Out of fear of re-igniting the public outrage that still lingers after the record years, Swedish builders and politicians have regressed to building in a populist manner and to mimicking older, safer aesthetic eras such as classicism and early modernism, but with lower quality standards than those of the original models. Respect for aesthetics in general has deteriorated alarmingly among the political establishment and in industry, where aesthetic concerns were for decades actually kept out of the production process. × The two decades between 1965 and 1985

—OFFICIAL SWEDEN HAS REALIZED THE HUGE POTENTIAL OF STOCKHOLM'S AND SWEDEN'S NEW IMAGE —LET'S GIVE IT CREDIT FOR THIS—BUT IT HAS YET TO FIGURE OUT HOW TO CAPITALIZE ON THAT TRADEMARK. WE HAVE YET TO BUILD AN EFFECTIVE BRIDGE BETWEEN THE ESTABLISHMENT AND THE CUTTING EDGE.

01 02

01 McDonald's cafe, design: Ytterborn Fuentes 02 Nordic Light Hotel, design: Jan Söder and Lars Pihl

appear to be a blank in Swedish design history. Then, in the late eighties, a new generation of designers, along with a new group of creative entrepreneurs in related fields—baby boomers, for the most part—started a movement in Stockholm. Some of them attracted micro-global attention at design trade fairs, particularly in Milan and Cologne. By the early nineties, a whole new creative culture was brewing in Stockholm—although still on a small scale—in design, fashion, music, restaurants and clubs, media, and so on. In many ways it fed on the tradition established in the pre-war years. We in Sweden called the phenomenon the "Björn Borg effect," after our national star tennis player who, only a couple of years after his retirement, had no fewer than five Swedish successors in the top-ten ranking internationally. × I was personally very much a part of this scene; at the time (late eighties) I was working on Sweden's first fashion magazines of international standards. My colleagues and I began to sense a certain curiosity about Stockholm and Sweden in the big international fashion metropolises— Paris, London, Milan, and New York. We sensed that Stockholm and Sweden were trademarks with very positive, but also very diffuse, values. × And that is how, in 1991, we came up with the crazy idea of creating a new, international, English-language fashion, design, and lifestyle magazine showcasing the new, creative Stockholm to the world. How we did it is much too long a story to tell here, but our success exceeded all expectations. *Stockholm New* became a new kind of magazine, with an editorial mix based on the very best of contemporary Swedish creativity, particularly fashion, design, and gastronomy. However, from the outset we knew that this alone wouldn't be good or interesting enough, so we featured cutting-edge contemporary material alongside items on Sweden's traditional aesthetic culture and, not least, our magnificent nature. This truly original mix was even able to cut through the buzz of the global fashion, design, and media industries. *Stockholm New* became an international

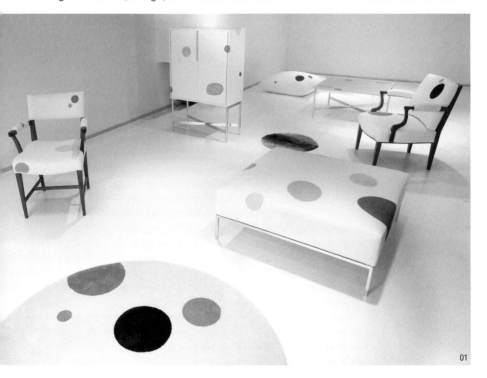

01

01 Exhibition at Svenskt Tenn, design: Thomas Sandell

forum for an emerging creative scene. ✕ Together with our friends and colleagues in other creative industries, we also created a new kind of international lifestyle event featuring a mix of design, fashion, music, and excessive amounts of food, drink, and partying—in many ways a kind of three-dimensional version of our magazine. We staged the events in Milan, Tokyo, New York, and, on a smaller scale, in London and Paris, attracting global attention. ✕ A few years into this process our dear Canadian friend, Tyler Brûlé and his London-based *Wallpaper* magazine, founded in 1996, caught on to it, and he made Stockholm his and the magazine's second home. The snowball was rolling and, by the early 2000s, the new "hot" Stockholm had been hyped in the media all around the globe. As we all know, that's the way it works with global trends and branding: it's a challenge to capture the attention of a small number of influential global trendsetters and opinion leaders, but once you do, the dynamics involved are tremendous. ✕ This entire development process occurred organically in a small group of enthusiasts and entrepreneurs of Sweden's contemporary creative culture who received marginal or no official support. The process had taken on a life of its own. The international hype for Stockholm, Sweden, and Swedish design, in turn, boosted the domestic Swedish hype for design and aesthetic creativity in general. With time, official Sweden (politicians and industry moguls, alike) learned to rediscover the international marketing potential of design and national branding. Today 25 percent of international advertising and publicity about Stockholm is related to or uses design. A veritable design boom has taken place in the wake of the burst IT bubble in Sweden. The changes have been very dramatic. From being a matter of no concern, design is now right at the top of Swedish politicians' agendas, with 2005 proclaimed the Year of Design. Even more importantly, Swedish industry—not only in furniture, fashion, and textiles, but also in the traditional and future industries—has once again started to work consciously and strategically with designers. ✕ The direct and positive consequences of the international Swedish design boom are many. Official Sweden has again become a buyer of contemporary Swedish design and creativity, and now markets it internationally in every way possible. Swedish industry in general has radically updated its design policy, making itself more contemporary and competitive. We have also seen the emergence of a new kind of tourism—design and lifestyle tourism, led by the affluent, international urban consumers who come to Stockholm to indulge in the city's contemporary creative scene. Stockholm has actually become a stop on the same circuit as London, Paris, Milan, New York, and Tokyo—but, needless to say, at a smaller scale. A whole new spectrum of international creative and commercial connections has opened up. As I often say, in the past ten years Stockholm has turned from a big small town into a small big city. ✕ We now find ourselves at a critical junction. The original entrepreneurs, ourselves included, have faded into the background due to economic and other kinds of exhaustion, and official Sweden has taken over the responsibility of marketing the new "hot" Stockholm and Sweden. This has been problematic, since the cultural gaps between political society and cutting-edge creativity remain considerable. In other words, combining the politically correct with the avant-garde is no easy thing to do. Worse, the authorities still lack understanding of the economic and dynamic forces at work in modern international commercial culture and global image-building. ✕ Official Sweden has realized the huge potential of Stockholm's and Sweden's new image— let's give it credit for this—but it has yet to figure out how to capitalize on that trademark. We have yet to build an effective bridge between the establishment and the cutting-edge. ✕ Fifteen years of work with *Stockholm New* and other related projects has given me ideas about how this bridge can be built, but I have little time to go into this here. I can, however, say that it's a matter of entrusting professionals with the artistic (re)presentation, and with keeping politically correct fingers out of the pot. This also means taking political risks. Politicians and administrators must select artistic professionals and trust them 100 percent, then be prepared to face the political consequences in case of mishaps and even failure— which are preferable to the anonymous and non descript.

>>>

›››

CECILIA HERTZ
› Industrial designer
› Director of umbilical design

›››

Cecilia Hertz is an industrial designer who works in the fields of outer space and extreme environment design. She is currently designing an interior for a parabolic plane for Xero AB (a Swedish company planning to fly tourists in "weightlessness"). "I call it 'space tourism light,'" comments Hertz.

›››

WHAT ARE YOUR FAVOURITE PUBLIC SPACES IN STOCKHOLM?

Since Stockholm is a town situated by the sea, my favourite place is the archipelago of islands that comprise Stockholm. Lovely to visit by boat for a weekend or just a day, they can rightfully be considered public places. On some islands you find hotels and restaurants, while others are totally undeveloped.

WHAT WOULD YOU LIKE TO SEE IMPROVED DESIGN-WISE?

There are many things when it comes to urban development that would benefit from a totally new design approach. As our cities grow bigger we have to find new ways of structuring complex environments while keeping the human being in mind. Because of my professional background, I believe there's a lot to gain from the transfer of outer space materials/technologies/solutions to our everyday life on Earth. It would be a real challenge to try and adapt products for zero-gravity environments. I call it "weightless thinking," which is about integrating the 0g factor in the design process. One example would be to apply the idea of volume management with the objective to create an integrated "waterline" + city zone (it's been proven that people feel better when they live close to water), wherein cubic metres are a complement to square metres. It would be exciting to invite designers to think: How to design a building on Earth where all the surfaces are equally important?

WHAT WOULD YOU LIKE TO SEE BUILT IN YOUR CITY?

I'd like to see our cities improve and integrate environmental issues in their agendas, to create buildings truly based on sustainable concepts. The environment on Mars has a lot in common with the extreme environments on Earth; for example, the lack of water. By integrating the water-recycling systems from the Advanced Life Support Systems developed for living on Mars, we could generate improved solutions for developing countries as well as new ecological systems for growing city structures.

01 Stockholm suburb 02 Moodlight system developped for Xero AB's weightless flights

>>>

JOHAN HULDT
> Designer
> Co-founder of Innovator
> Professor of industrial design at the
  University College of Boras, Sweden.
>>>

Johan Huldt is the co-founder of Innovator Ltd., a breakthrough Swedish design studio founded in the nineteen seventies that exports furniture to twenty-two countries and has licensed manufacturing in Japan and Brazil. Johan Huldt is a professor of industrial design at the University College of Boras and was the managing director of Svensk Form, the Swedish Design Council, from 1997 to 2002.

>>>

WHAT ARE YOUR FAVOURITE PUBLIC PLACES IN STOCKHOLM?
The library in the Skogaholm Mansion of the Skansen outdoor museum, a fantastically well-designed library from the eighteenth century, and the Stockholm City Library, by Gunnar Asplund. Both places are worth visiting, both for their architectural qualities and their wonderful design details.

WHAT WOULD YOU LIKE TO SEE IMPROVED DESIGN-WISE?
I would like to see the exterior colour scheme of Stockholm Public Transportation revised—the trams, buses, and subway.

WHAT WOULD YOU LIKE TO SEE BUILT IN YOUR CITY?
A wonderful design museum in the city designed for its purpose.

>>>

TIME
SQUA

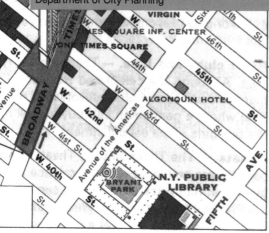

— THIS IS A CITY OF PASSIONATE PEOPLE, FOR WHOM MEDIOCRE DESIGN SIMPLY
WILL NOT DO. AND THE CITY HAS MADE GREAT STRIDES IN ENSURING THAT FORM
AND FUNCTION ARE CONSIDERED HAND-IN-HAND.
Amanda M. Burden, Chair, New York City Planning Commission and Director, New York City
Department of City Planning

S

ARE

01

02

01 McHale's Restaurant 02 Paramount Building 03 Times Square

— THE DESIGN
OF THE CITY IS A
REFLECTION OF
THIS: AS A CITY
OF NEIGHBOUR-
HOODS, REPRE-
SENTED BY
COUNTLESS
NATIONALITIES,
DESIGN IS A
COMMONALITY
THAT CAN UNIFY
AN OTHERWISE
FRAGMENTED
POPULATION.

Amanda M. Burden, Chair, New York City Planning Commission and Director, New York City
Department of City Planning

01 Roy Lichtenstein, Times Square Mural, 1994. Porcelain enamel on steel: 6 feet x 53 feet.
Subway station at 42nd and Broadway, New York City (Installed in 2002).

AMANDA M. BURDEN

CHAIR, NEW YORK CITY
PLANNING COMMISSION
AND DIRECTOR, NEW YORK CITY
DEPARTMENT OF CITY PLANNING

WHY DO YOU CONSIDER YOUR CITY TO BE A NEW DESIGN CITY?

New York has a varied and fascinating design legacy, and this history is always and forever inflected in the future growth of our city. Largely a city of industry in the earlier part of the last century, New York has employed innovative land use and design techniques to remain current with the needs of businesses and residents. In many respects, the universal validation of multi-use, high-density design around the globe has its roots in New York City. Housing units atop street-level retail, recently embraced by new urbanists, have been de *rigueur* in New York for decades. ✕ Design's most important and relevant by-product for New York is its economic impact. Well-designed buildings, plazas, parks, and sidewalks are essential components of the city's economic development plans, encouraging businesses to headquarter here and inviting close to 38 million people to visit in 2003. ✕ I think that New York is always seen as an innovator in all aspects of design, from fashion to finance, from consumer products to architecture. Residents of New York have a true appreciation for arts and culture, which allows great works by architects such as Cass Gilbert and Mies Van der Rohe to beautifully co-exist with buildings by today's internationally renowned architects. This is a city of passionate people, for whom mediocre design simply will not do. And the city has made great strides in ensuring that form and function are considered hand-in-hand. This sort of development has a significant impact on sustainability—it is interesting to note that, because of the density of the city and its fantastic access to public transportation, New York has been called the "greenest" city in the world. ✕ It is not just the design of iconic buildings and public works that is important to the image of New York as the epicentre of arts, culture, and business. At its heart, New York is a city of neighbourhoods, all woven together with a functional and beautiful system of public parks and pedestrian throughways that provide the perhaps unheralded foundation for its better-known business districts and landmarks.

WHAT HAS BEEN YOUR PERSONAL CONTRIBUTION IN FACILITATING THE EMERGENCE OF YOUR DESIGN CITY?

I like to believe that I have introduced the concept of design as not merely the domain of architects, artists, and urban planners, but of anyone involved in walking the streets and taking in the majesty of New York's built environment. ✕ I am compelled to promote excellence in design in the public realm because I believe it elevates the individual's experience of city living in both a spiritual sense and a practical sense. ✕ I strongly believe that the creation of great places—spaces that draw the visitor in and generate excitement—is paramount to the embodiment of great design. The vitality of the street life is a critical component in creating a great place. A breathtaking building is made all the more intriguing when coupled with even the most simple of elements such as benches, street trees, and sidewalk cafes. These additions invite the passerby to stop a moment, observe these places, and take in their surroundings— a true sign of the city's success. Beginning at the street level and working one's way up is, I believe, a necessary component of holistic, vibrant, and successful design. ✕ In previous administrations, the City Planning Commission operated with a stricter interpretation of its duties as an arbiter of land-use issues in the city. In my time as chair of the Commission, I am proud to foster the inclusion of design principles in our evaluation of land-use applications.

WHY DO YOU BELIEVE POSITIONING YOUR CITY THROUGH DESIGN IS IMPORTANT?
When you ask people what New York means to them, an image of the Empire State Building, Central Park, or the Brooklyn Bridge will come to mind. All are icons of design that have been reinterpreted around the world. It is these images of New York, these tactile experiences, which have brought people to the city for generations and continue to do so in record numbers. The design of the city is a reflection of this: as a city of neighbourhoods, represented by countless nationalities, design is a commonality that can unify an otherwise fragmented population. New York is Central Park, New York is Flushing Meadows, New York is 42nd Street. Each embraces its own very unique take on design, but all are equally relevant for the people who visit them. ✕ The importance of design as a barometer of the economic health of New York City has reached new heights during the Bloomberg administration. Design has emerged as a catalyst to growth that supersedes market fluctuation. New York has long been the city that never sleeps, and we must maintain this youthful vitality by increasing our immigrant population, attracting new businesses, and sustaining our strong tourism industries. Ensuring that the city is safe, accessible, and, above all, innovative, will keep New York where it has always been—ahead of the curve.

02

**WHAT EXAMPLES OF DESIGN PROMOTION STRATEGIES DEVELOPED
IN OTHER CITIES INSPIRE YOU?**

There are several cities that inspire me, particularly with their ability to introduce new, bold architectural and urban design alongside their most treasured historic structures. These cities include Barcelona, London, Paris, and Amsterdam. These are places that were at the forefront of design centuries ago and continue to welcome and cultivate gifted and talented designers who interpret these vibrant environments in ways that are wholly modern and yet true to the essence of the urban settlement. Barcelona merits special mention for its astonishing innovation and investment in the public realm.

**WHAT SHOULD BE THE ROLE OF THE CITIZEN, THE DESIGNER, AND THE POLITICIAN
IN THE DEVELOPMENT OF A DESIGN CITY?**

For great urban design to occur in a dense urban setting, it is essential that every stakeholder participate fully to balance the private agenda with the public good, the short-term goals with the long-term vision. Citizens must offer their critical wisdom on the fine grain texture of their neighbourhoods. Designers must acknowledge and embrace the neighbourhood and city scale of their work, not just the narrow confines of their site boundaries. Politicians and public servants must show leadership to cultivate design as an essential ingredient of a healthy metropolis and make the difficult decisions to adhere to this commitment, when other considerations can threaten to make design expendable. ✕ Although it emerged from such profound tragedy, the overwhelming interest in the future design of the World Trade Center site really changed the notion of public participation in the design process. There was a sense of entitlement, and rightfully so, of New Yorkers to be involved in the future of so sacred and important a site. The mechanisms for community planning and design that emerged from these series of events should be reviewed by anyone involved in planning, as they reveal a level of sophistication and transparency that comes from such discourse which, to date, is unparalleled. ✕ I am particularly pleased with the public interface that has occurred with the concept plan and design for the High Line in West Chelsea. When completed, this neglected former elevated train track will provide a unique open space for New Yorkers, offering a new vantage point from which to experience the city. Our department has sponsored wonderfully transparent community design sessions, where New Yorkers are invited to regularly scheduled sessions to contribute their ideas to a final product that will best serve the neighbourhood as well as the city as a whole. This project has created a new paradigm for the public-planning process, with an active community creating the best-laid plans for the city.

〉〉

01 Toys "R" Us 02 Conde Nast Building, Architect: Fox & Fowle 03 INew Amsterdam Theater, design: Herts & Tallant, 1903 restored in 1995 by Hardy Holzman Pfeiffer Associates and Disney Imagineering

CREATIVITY, ENERGY, AND EDGE: USING DESIGN TO NURTURE AN AUTHENTIC AND DYNAMIC TIMES SQUARE

BY TIM TOMPKINS
President, Times Square Alliance, New York

〉〉

One look and Times Square can seem too dynamic for good design: does the world's cross-roads of commerce and culture—selling and sizzling as fast as it can—really have time for design's order and nuance? Then, upon second glance, one finds a century's worth of formi-dable design intelligence. There's inspiration where you least expect it: the authenticity in a good fake, the subtlety in a flashing sign, and the success of a restaurant that has made it through the district's toughest times. In the end, understanding where design inspiration comes from, and what a crossroads can offer it, leads one to appreciate the design talent and tenaciousness that has made Times Square what it is.

Ray Gastil, Design Times Square juror

Manhattan director, New York City Department of City Planning.

In 1904 Longacre Square was named Times Square after its newest resident, The New York Times. A star was born—and new ways of entertaining Americans, as well. By 1928, some 264 shows were produced in 76 theatres in Times Square, the world's most condensed theatre district. In lieu of old-world traditions, Times Square theatres showcased America's emerging variegated popular culture—vaudeville, musicals, jazz, and film. And yet Times Square blossomed in the first third of the twentieth century only to slide into notorious decay in the face of the post-war world of television, suburbs, and racial strife. A slow but inexorable decline followed, and by the sixties and seventies the neighbourhood had witnessed a descent from the carnival and cotton candy frivolity of flea circuses and human oddities to live nude shows, erotic bookstores, and X-rated movies. By 1975, many viewed the area as a dysfunctional danger zone of soaring crime rates and urban decay. × In the eighties, serious city and state efforts were established to reverse the direction Broadway was headed. Beginning in the early nineties, The Times Square Business Improvement District (now the Times Square Alliance) was formed to help restore and revitalize the neighbourhood along with the New York City Police Department, the 42nd Street Development Project Inc., The New 42nd Street, and Common Ground. Abandoned and decaying theatres were reopened. Families and businesses returned to the district. Over the past two decades a different Times Square has emerged from the ashes, and the crowds that first made the place what it became have also returned (it hosted more than 20 million visitors in 2004). Times Square, though not America at its best or worst, is America at its most, vitalized by its constant evolution. × Today, Times Square is home to 27,000 residents and more than 10,000 people working in various design and creative fields, including graphic design, architecture, publishing, television, and performing arts.

TIMES SQUARE ALLIANCE DESIGN MISSION

Ultimately, we at the Alliance envision Times Square as a vibrant centre for creative and cutting-edge expression, through better private and public architecture and small-scale, temporary public art and performance programs, along with a continued emphasis on the performing arts and live entertainment that have always energized the area. × Across all of our initiatives and programs we are using design to nurture the unique mix of creativity and commerce, energy and edge that have made Times Square a local and international icon. Ultimately, we want Times Square to engage New Yorkers as much as it engages the rest of the world, and to represent the diversity and dynamism that have always characterized the best of New York.

01 John's Pizzeria, once the Gospel Taberbacle Chruch, originally built in 1888, redesigned 100 years later by Adrew Tesoro. Mural by Douglas Cooper 02 Hershey's Store

DESIGN STRATEGIES
The "Problems and Possibilities" dossier

Although many recognize Times Square's success, the district still faces challenges. What can be done to address these issues and what are the tools that can be used to nurture life, energy, and creativity in the neighbourhood? This is what the Alliance has been tackling through various initiatives. ✕ Design Times Square (2004), a derivative of the Commerce Design Montréal program, has triggered a redefinition of the district's identity, yet more needs to be done at a deeper, structural level. On the occasion of Times Square's centennial, the Times Square Alliance partnered with the Design Trust for Public Space to undertake a series of workshops with New York creatives, professionals, and thinkers who share an affinity for the area. The group, which convened during the summer of 2003, worked to identify what is unique and thrilling about the world's best-known public space, as well as specific "problems and possibilities." Ultimately, they sought how to celebrate and preserve the spirit of a place where creation rather than preservation is the norm. ✕ Below are the challenges and recommendations that participants helped identify for a better Times Square:

⟩ Balance different elements. Times Square must carefully balance tensions that also contribute to its personality. Be careful not to upset the balance of all these elements in a way that could diminish the area's distinctiveness. Strive to balance:
  ⟩⟩ traffic and pedestrians
  ⟩⟩ the vertical and the horizontal
  ⟩⟩ the fixed and the changing
  ⟩⟩ the historic and the new
  ⟩⟩ its function as static plaza and fluid intersection
  ⟩⟩ regulation and spontaneity
  ⟩⟩ choreography and chaos
  ⟩⟩ observers and doers
⟩ Recognize and encourage the diversity of people and activities. There are spectators and performers, tourists and locals; all the diversity of the city, the country, and the world is spontaneously interacting in one locale. Times Square must accommodate multiple uses, allow the mixing of the grand scale and the human scale, and encourage both the planned and the spontaneous. Explore ways to have restaurants and retail engage the street in new ways. Be aware of the layers in Times Square: above, below, the vertical, the horizontal—think of how they relate to each other. Think of layers of history as well. Create connections between streetscapes and subways and underground passages. Explore the utilization of balconies, terraces, and platforms on buildings, as well as idiosyncratic signage and billboards.
⟩ Create places where people can meet, where one can stop to observe—along the centre, along the periphery, in the interstitial spaces, up above the ground plane. Times Square is one of the most visually dense and compelling places in the world, yet there are so few places where one can stop to observe it. Allow people to see and be seen. A new, expanded Duffy Square is critical, and the need for increased pedestrian spaces remains crucial.
⟩ Make Times Square a destination not only for visitors but for New Yorkers as well. If Times Square is not authentic, creative, and spontaneous, New Yorkers will not want to come. Encourage distinctive design, public art, and small-scale performances, allowing maximum design innovations to articulate Times Square's status as the "Crossroads of desires," where art, life, and commerce coincide while individuals and the rest of the world watch.

> Look for opportunities to reinforce what is authentic and recognize what is historic. Allow for the expression of the individual and unique as well the mass-produced, the commercial, and the common (which are also elements of Times Square's identity). The density and the congestion are part of what is authentic. Times Square will always be full of people and movement, but in addressing the issues related to its clutter and chaos don't lose what is authentic.

> Re-think the relationship between pedestrian and vehicular spaces. Explore new ways to regulate both pedestrian and vehicular traffic. Look at signal timing and consider closing parts of streets at certain times, making more flexible the boundaries between vehicular and pedestrian space. Use pedestrian engineering to choreograph the chaos: keep pedestrians and vehicles moving without necessarily lessening the density.

〉〉〉

ANALYZING THE TIMES SQUARE "BRAND"

In 2003–04 Ogilvy & Mather, a world-renown advertising agency based in Times Square, worked with the Times Square Alliance to conduct a brand analysis of both the district itself and the organization. A new vibrant logo—inspired by iconic neon light—and a brand identity serving both the organization and the district were launched in early 2004. One of the concerns of the Alliance was to preserve the unique qualities that established the Square as an anomaly, a place different from any other, with respect to its New York-ness and edge. The design/brand identity brief to Ogilvy & Mather emphasized a number of important criteria: Times Square as a cauldron of creative activity, including first-rate art and public performances, a forum for public opinion, a venue for historic events, and a place distinguished by its architecture. ✕ Ogilvy & Mather's design/branding solution highlighted the different "consumers" of Times Square, who can be categorized as both visitors and creators, and the necessity for the Alliance to cater to both. They also concluded the following:

> Throughout all of the change that shaped the landscape of Times Square, the destination has endured. Its image as America's "main street," an inclusive place where all different types of people and activity come together, has become deeply ingrained in popular culture.

> Times Square derives its meaning from its experiential content, which is constantly evolving and changing.

> Times Square's historic and cultural significance has come to shape how people perceive New York City as a whole. For many, New York is synonymous with Times Square.

> More than just the central place on a map of New York City, Times Square is a brand with which people have an emotional connection. The potent sense of energy, movement, innovation, optimism, and opportunity that characterizes the physical space also reflects the mentality of those drawn to it.

> Once the historical, consumer, and geographic audit was analyzed, attributes that best capture the essence of the Times Square brand were identified. These values inspired and informed the final design solutions:

〉〉 Timeless—enduring

〉〉 Iconic—epicentre of New York City

〉〉 Extraordinary—one of a kind

〉〉 Exhilarating—energetic, magnetic, kinetic

〉〉 Connector—creator of popular culture and in touch with it

01

DESIGN TIMES SQUARE

Times Square, at its best, is a place where creativity is always being expressed in a wide variety of forms, styles, and media. By nurturing creative expression through design, architecture, public art, and public performance, Times Square can maintain its unique and edgy character. Inspired by the Commerce Design Montréal program, the Alliance adapted it to the specificity of the area while respecting its core objectives. Design Times Square hopes to celebrate quality design in Times Square, encourage businesses to invest in good design, and demonstrate that good design is good for business. It focuses on quality architecture, commercial signage, publicly accessible interiors, public spaces, and public art. The first Design Times Square, in honour of Times Square's centennial, recognized a broad sampling of both new and old noteworthy designs, as well as designers, architects, and artists, including Sol Lewitt, Roy Lichtenstein, Jacob Lawrence, Arquitectonica, Kohn Pedersen Fox, Rem Koolhas, Richard Gluckman, Hugh Hardy, Fox and Fowle, and Yabu Pushelberg. × Hand in hand with this program are some significant efforts to improve the pedestrian experience by improving the streetscape through better architecture and design. The Alliance is spearheading a project to build the winning design from a worldwide competition for a new theatre discount booth and plaza. Prior to the Ground Zero competition, this was the largest architectural competition held in New York City—with over 680 submissions. In addition, the Alliance is working with the city to improve the streetscape through a major sidewalk improvement project. × Also in the works are projects to bring more public art to Times Square (often in the face of enormous regulatory obstacles). In collaboration with a variety of arts-based curatorial groups the Alliance is promoting temporary public art projects that can enrich the pedestrian experience.

02

01 Blue Fin restaurant, design: Rockwell Group 02 W Hotel, design: Yabu Pulshelberg

〉〉〉

BRIAN COLLINS
〉 Executive creative director of BIG
(Brand Integration Group)
at Ogilvy & Mather Worldwide,
Times Square, New York.
〉〉〉

Brian Collins is executive creative director
of BIG (the Brand Integration Group) at
Ogilvy & Mather Worldwide, the global
advertising agency that preaches the
integration of design at all steps of branding
efforts. Bluechip clients include Coca-Cola,
Motorola, IBM, Kodak, and Hershey's
(Collins's Chocolate Factory on Times Square
was a controversial experience/retail branding
and design project).
〉〉〉

〉〉

WHAT ARE YOUR FAVOURITE PUBLIC SPACES IN NYC'S TIMES SQUARE?
Standing in the middle of Times Square's bowtie, that spot is the most exhilarating of all, although I would not want to live there. Seeing all the brands of the world trying to seduce and delight me, and on my right a tourist from Beijing, on my left another from Osaka, Berlin, or LaPaz… Everyone seems happy congregated there in this narrow triangle, taking pictures. It's the antithesis of nature: entirely man-made, it's an unapologetically exuberant celebration of brands, technology, and commerce, and also a capsule of the rest of Times Square.

WHAT WOULD YOU LIKE TO SEE IMPROVED DESIGN-WISE?
The boulevards need to be safer, the circulation and the traffic crossing are just maddening, but of course this would need to be done without losing the hustle and bustle. Don't get me wrong: I love the democratic, even populist character of the district. But there is also a need for places to just rest and watch. I'm always participating in the parade here, so I literally have to pay and enter a restaurant, most likely an expensive one, to stop for a second. There is no public "seating on the steps" area that could potentially amplify and also complement the invigorating experience of being in Times Square. ✕ Finally, there is no sense of place where I can easily go in and out, no access points that engage the passerby. The Swatch Store, Toys"R"Us, and the Hershey's store—with its entrance on the corner—are a few of the only inviting thresholds at street level. Look at London's Piccadilly Circus for instance: there are many big, easy-access storefronts and inspiring entrance points from the great boulevards that surround it.

WHAT WOULD YOU LIKE TO SEE BUILT IN YOUR CITY?
Architects too often think of "improving" as a janitorial, cleaning-up process of the bantering, the cacophony, the messiness—all the noise that makes cities delightful. Today, we still suffer from the result of soulless, modernist urban planning—empty, cold, concrete plazas that people run through but never stay or congregate in to enjoy themselves. Plazas for cyborgs. So in our city I'd challenge architects to propose even more messiness, umbrellas, carts, fountains, trees, street bazaars, tents, hotdog vendors—things that are people-scaled, lively, and inspire spontaneous human contact. Look at the Rigoletta shopping area of Buenos Aires (my favourite public space in the world). It is unparalleled in its human scale, a great urban design with intersecting streets of small shops selling crafts, art, clothing, books—but with no famous brands anywhere. It's an alternative universe. ✕ The Hershey store we designed replaced a shuttered and nasty Cosmestics Plus store from the late nineties. So I don't think we lost anything really interesting there. But I really don't want to see anything else built in Times Square if it means destroying the few forty- to fifty-year old spots still in place. Sure, change is part of the constant here, but if Howard Johnson's were to be closed, the Square would become just a big outdoor Mall of America. These odd places are the soul of the Square, and I believe their loss will move us even closer into Times SquareLand. I hope it's not too late to find a way to keep these places alive.

〉〉

〉〉〉

HUGH HARDY

〉 FAIA, architect, H3 Hardy Collaboration
  Architecture, New York.

〉〉〉

Hugh Hardy is the founder of H3 Hardy
Collaboration Architecture, known for the
design of new buildings, restoration of historic structures, and planning projects for the
public realm. His most celebrated projects
are the new New York Botanical Garden
Visitor Center (Bronx, NY); the Baseball Hall
of Fame (Cooperstown, NY); the Brooklyn
Academy of Music's restored façade
(Brooklyn, NY); a U.S. Federal Courthouse
(Jackson, MS); Packer Collegiate Institute
(Brooklyn, NY), a new school in a nineteenth-
century James Renwick church; restoration
of Radio City Music Hall (New York, NY); the
U.S. Customs and Immigration Center at
Rainbow Bridge (Niagara Falls, NY); and
Bryant Park (New York, NY).

〉〉〉

Hardy's latest national awards include the
2001 Placemark Award from the Design
History Foundation and the 2000
Commissioner's Award for Excellence in
Public Architecture from the U.S. General
Services Administration.

〉〉〉

Hardy established Hardy Holzman Pfeiffer
Associates in 1967 and Hugh Hardy &
Associates in 1962. Earlier, he worked with
Eero Saarinen and Jo Mielziner on the con-
struction of the Vivian Beaumont Theater at
Lincoln Center and served with the Army
Corps of Engineers. He earned his bache-
lor's and master's degrees in architecture
from Princeton University, where he was a
D'Amato Prizeman.

〉〉〉

01

〉〉

WHAT ARE YOUR FAVOURITE PUBLIC SPACES IN NYC'S TIMES SQUARE?
Other than the remarkable intersection of Broadway and 7th Avenue, where everything comes together, my favourite place in Times Square is the restaurant in the Renaissance Hotel. At the mezzanine level you can sit and enjoy the live theatre of the streets, blinking and blapping away. It is the most spectacular elevated view looking south on Broadway and toward the north end of the Bowtie.

WHAT WOULD YOU LIKE TO SEE IMPROVED DESIGN-WISE?
Times Square has become too uniform, with the same LED technology used all over the place. The business of moving images is okay, but the signs are too similarly kinetic. We need something like giant letters or fixed pictures as a counterpoint to all of this movement. ✕ It would be a fantastic idea to get the advertisers in the square, who spend a fortune on those giant billboards, to sponsor a program where the whole area would be advertising-free for one night and given over to artists to program. It would be a dazzling effect if you let artists transform the place for just one night. And it would be of course an extraordinary publicity campaign for the city!

WHAT WOULD YOU LIKE TO SEE BUILT IN YOUR CITY?
I wish there were more fantasy entertainment places like those that once were part of Times Square. These would not be just for eating or entertainment, but fantastic locations that mixed video, live performance, and music all together. At the Earl Carol and the Folies Bergères theatres, both now demolished, people had dinner and watched a show. But now, in addition to food and dancing, we could delight in magical electronic illusions. In the dazzling tradition of the district, we could have experiences that are out of the ordinary.

〉〉

—THERE IS NOT ENOUGH GREEN SPACE FOR PEOPLE TO SIT AND STOP, UNLIKE IN PARIS, MILAN, ROME, BARCELONA, WHERE PUBLIC PLANNING ALLOWS FOR THESE UNEXPECTED ENCLAVES OF REST. WE NEED A MOMENT TO BLINK, TAKE A BIG BREATH— THE CITY WOULD GAIN SO MUCH MORE ENERGY.

〉〉

GARY VAN DIS

〉 A Midwesterner from Saugatuck, MI, with a "point of passion," Van Dis graduated from the
Institute of Design at the Chicago Institute of Technology. Gary Van Dis is VP, corporate creative
director at Condé Nast Publications (a Times Square-based giant media company).

〉〉

WHAT'S YOUR FAVOURITE PUBLIC PLACE IN NEW YORK/TIMES SQUARE?

Bryant Park, which is out of the official district. It's fascinating to see how they managed to
reconfigure the everyday use of this place, essentially through the planning of seasonal
foliage. You can sit there and you feel comfortable entering and exiting at all times; you see
completely across from all four corners. It's hard to imagine, but twenty years ago it was full of
rats, bums, and drug dealers. Public programs such as the outdoor summer movie festival
have also helped bring different users at various times of the day.

WHAT WOULD YOU LIKE TO SEE IMPROVED DESIGN-WISE?

Times Square is already a theme park, and although it probably seems successful to the real
estate brokers that own it, there's nothing special, nothing pure in that experience. If Times
Square is an entertainment place, then really make it entertainment. Look at Tokyo: it's so
exhilarating. On the sidewalks, at street level, on mid-level building surfaces, the visual con-
gestion of ever-changing entertainment and information becomes a true pleasure. Here we
took it part way; we have not reached out far enough. If it's going to be a hub, then really push
it 150 percent more—over the top! If we are moving towards a wi-fi society and if bigger-than-
life plasmas are going to be the new urban fabric, then make it interactive, let me play in that
cartoon world, let me get something out of it that can enrich my life (humour, statistics, sensations, etc.), let me be part of the process. Every inch of real estate should be a blank palette
open for extreme creativity. Even twenty-five years ago, it was purer in its degraded condition.
Sure, you cannot long for that time, but it was so complete in its state of aesthetics, with its
sinister neon signs and prostitutes.

WHAT WOULD YOU LIKE TO SEE BUILT IN YOUR CITY?

New York never decided to be a city of architectural integrity, as only a few examples of this
remain; it's a city in which to make money and it does that well. But there's no historical
integrity of a particular type of architecture that is understood to be an anchor for the city;
unlike Chicago, for example, where good master urban geographers and architects thought
about the city with proper planning (the new addition to the Millennium Park is a brilliant creation). Times Square is not really part of the plan of New York City, anyway. ✕ I wish more
responsibilities were taken by the city: a real estate developer should be accountable for giving back public and green spaces and creating community integration. One can be so
enriched by the experience of a public space (take the Lever House, which brings up another
level of public architecture when you walk underneath it). There is not enough green space for
people to sit and stop, unlike in Paris, Milan, Rome, Barcelona, where public planning allows
for these unexpected enclaves of rest. We need a moment to blink, take a big breath—the city
would gain so much more energy.

〉〉

VIVRE LA VILLE, DU VOISINAGE AU TERRITOIRE

PAR FRANÇOIS BARRÉ

> **Conseiller en projets urbains et culturels, Paris**

〉〉

Qu'est-ce qu'une ville de design face à la complexité de la ville ? Il est certes des villes de design, comme il y a des villes du charbon, des banques, des filatures ou du chocolat! Mais elles sont d'abord des villes d'architecture, de passions, de production, de conflits, d'art et d'histoire, de relations et d'échanges, d'urbanité, de fêtes et de rituels, de cultures et de communautés. La part du design y est toute relative.

Les théories des designers industriels sur la ville sont souvent de pures pétitions de principe. Reprenant le vieux rêve de l'œuvre d'art totale, Gio Ponti veut tout maîtriser *de la petite cuillère à la ville*. Plus tard, Archizoom et, surtout, Superstudio font preuve d'une juste conscience (surtout graphique) de la dimension territoriale de la ville. Dans *Nouvelles de la métropole froide*, puis avec ses projets *Non-stop city*, *Agronica* et son master-plan pour Philips à Eindhoven, Andrea Branzi désire annuler la distinction entre monde métropolitain et monde domestique, intérieur — propre au design — et extérieur. Invoquant Walter Benjamin ou Louis Kahn, il considère la ville comme un intérieur qu'il s'agit de meubler. Un monde d'objets entre en opposition avec l'architecture dont Branzi appelle la liquidation. «*Il se dessine à présent*, écrit-il, *une métropole de l'objet sans extérieur ; elle envahit tout l'univers matériel, tout le territoire de l'homme.*»

Il m'importe personnellement d'habiter la ville plutôt que de la meubler. Une *ville d'ameublement* répondrait-elle à la *musique d'ameublement* dont parlait Satie ? Triste perspective. Les villes de design sont les villes de design urbain où le design produit de la ville et non l'inverse. Je me référerai donc à un processus de conception et de réalisation d'aménagements physiques permettant de définir un écosystème de relation et de maîtriser par la permanence et les changements, l'organisation formelle de la croissance urbaine. En cela, je privilégierai un urbanisme culturaliste, tel qu'enseigné à l'École d'architecture de l'Université Laval sous l'appellation Forme urbaine et pratiques culturelles. Et je m'intéresserai à l'action conjointe des urbanistes, architectes, designers, paysagistes, artistes, nul ne sachant enfermer la ville en une discipline. La ville est indisciplinaire.

Mon souci de mettre en avant culture, récit, émotion et plaisir plutôt qu'économie et fonction n'est pas oubli du présent, mais attachement à une culture du projet. Quel projet ?

Agir pour transformer. Être au monde et de quelque part. Concevoir des villes d'aujourd'hui sans renier le déjà là ni se prolonger en un mimétisme historiciste ou une uniformisation généralisée. Sommes-nous condamnés à vivre dans la ville-monde cent fois reproduite ou saurons-nous être de notre temps et de notre lieu? Les villes qui émergent, celles de plus de 10 millions d'habitants, les villes génériques pour habitants génériques et sociétés génériques exercent une fascination du nombre et de la quantité; rarement de la qualité. Anciennes ou neuves, elles sont souvent inhabitables. Souvenons-nous de Gaetano Pesce, qui salue la production en série et fait de chaque objet produit un objet différent. Apprenons le projet d'habiter la ville dans ses singularités.

LE DESIGN DE LA VILLE : SA FORME ET SES TERRITOIRES.

Selon Yves Chalas[1], les figures de la mobilité, du territoire, de la nature, du polycentrisme, du choix, du vide et du temps continu remplacent les figures des villes d'hier : harmonie classique, unité formelle, minéralité, densité, fixité, centralité unique, contour défini, séparation de la nature, et créent de nouveaux espaces. Les oppositions binaires centre/périphérie, continuité/discontinuité, mixité/ségrégation, homogénéité/hétérogénéité, plein/vide cèdent le pas à la ville paradoxale du tout à la fois dans un monde partagé entre le global et le local. Mais entre lieux et temps multiples, entre ubiquité et simultanéité, se pose alors la question du tout à la fois et son possible délitement en un rien du tout, ou tout égalant tout, le sens serait réduit à néant. La réalité est-elle ce qu'on subit ou ce qu'on construit? Serait-ce la fin du projet? La forme et la nature des villes ne résultent jamais exclusivement du destin ou du projet. Mais en toutes choses, le projet me semble préférable au destin. Peut-on dire encore la forme d'une ville?

En 1914, à l'occasion de l'exposition du Deutscher Werkbund, qu'ils ont fondé, la querelle de Cologne oppose les architectes et designers Hermann Muthesius et Henry van de Velde. Le premier prône la standardisation et l'emporte contre le second, qui en appelle à la variation. Ce débat célèbre marque l'essor du rationalisme et du fonctionnalisme liés au développement industriel et prônant la diffusion universelle d'un modèle scientifique. Peut-on appliquer ces notions à la ville et à sa forme? Comment habiter et ordonner une forme urbaine? Par la norme, affirme Ildefonso Cerda, en 1859, avec son projet d'extension de Barcelone. Par la composition urbaine ou l'art urbain, répond Camillo Sitte, en 1889, dans *L'art de bâtir les villes*. Vingt ans après, Raymond Unwin continue le combat avec un langage qui nous touche : «*Il manque à nos villes l'esprit vivifiant de l'art qui les eût complétées et en eût décuplé la valeur, il y manque quelque effort dans la conception des compositions urbaines... L'absence de beauté, c'est-à-dire de ce qui, plus que tout, agrémente la vie, nous oblige à dire que l'œuvre de la construction des villes au cours du siècle passé a été imparfaite. Aussi réelles qu'avaient été les améliorations apportées, les pauvres eux-mêmes qui en ont bénéficié ont constaté, comme tout le monde, qu'elles ne visaient que les conditions matérielles de la vie urbaine; sensibles eux aussi à la beauté, ils ont eu la sensation que quelque chose leur manquait : l'Art.*»[2] Aldo Rossi avec L'architectura della citta, en 1966, puis Carlo Aymonino, en 1975, nourrissent la problématique de la morphologie urbaine et de la typologie du bâti. Contre les tenants d'un modèle exportable qui s'imposerait à tous, Rossi avance l'idée d'une autonomie de la forme urbaine qui, tel un fleuve souterrain, continuerait de sourdre et de traverser les époques.

Qu'en est-il aujourd'hui à l'heure de la mondialisation et du passage d'une ville des stocks à une ville des flux? Nos villes, autrefois savamment balancées entre pleins et vides, s'étendent souvent aléatoirement en fonction du prix du foncier et de la recherche d'un habitat individuel dont l'éloignement est relativisé par les facilités de déplacement. Une ville diffuse la *citta diffusa*, étudiée par l'urbaniste italien Bernardo Secchi se répand sans limite. Elle n'est ni la ville-centre, la ville constituée ni même la banlieue et les périphéries, mais un au-delà qui les englobe sans les entourer vraiment : un territoire informe et plein de vides. Les vides y sont les pleins, et, plus que ceux-ci, en constituent la véritable structure. La moitié de la population européenne vit dans la ville diffuse. Ses habitants ne sont ni des urbains ni des ruraux, mais, dit Secchi, des urbains dispersés jaloux de leur repli individuel.

C'est ainsi que la ville devient informe et fragmentaire, s'étalant sans réponse à un projet. Voilà la vraie question du design.

Donner à la ville une forme que chacun puisse lire est démocratique, selon Secchi. *«J'arrive, dit-il, à pratiquer une ville si j'arrive à la lire […], à comprendre où sont les choses, à comprendre la forme de la ville.»* Mais comment dessiner l'espace ouvert, l'espace informe des grands vides qui sont des trous dans le tissu de la ville et la rendent illisible? En se tournant vers des réalités non urbaines, le paysage ou l'art. Secchi propose d'étudier *«ce que l'agriculture a dessiné dans nos paysages, car on y voit des dessins formidables.»* Peter Cook s'est pareillement exercé à relever dans la nature des tracés informes dont il a fait des projets. L'exemple d'Emscher Park recomposant un paysage-réseau de villes avec les villes de la Ruhr nous permet d'espérer[3]. L'art peut également donner des réponses : collage, découpage, montage, sérialité, arrachage, mixage, cadrage, morphing, sampling ont engendré des formes improbables et remarquables. Si nous savons, avec Giulo Carlos Argan, qu'en matière de villes, *«la forme est le résultat d'un processus dont le point de départ n'est pas la forme elle-même»*, il faut en retrouver le cheminement. La recherche et l'expérimentation sont nécessaires pour recoudre cette ville diffuse et donner à sa territorialité vaste des éléments de dignité et d'urbanité. La couverture territoriale du paysage a déjà été expérimentée par des artistes qui ont rendu intelligible la forme d'un territoire. Ainsi, firent Christo[4] par l'enveloppement, Felice Varini par le soulignement et Llorenc Barber par la spatialisation du son. Même l'informe peut être un projet. Cy Twombly l'a démontré avec éclat.

LA VILLE EST UN RÉCIT. IL S'ÉCRIT AVEC LE TEMPS.
Le temps des récits. Il était une fois…

La ville se construit sur elle-même. Elle est livre et flèche. Il faut en lire les traces pour en énoncer le futur. L'ordre de la ville obéissait autrefois aux nécessités de la défense et à la mise en perspective du pouvoir. L'espace public et les grandes pièces urbaines célébraient la ville-miroir, et un vivre ensemble, fait de domination, d'ostentation et de familiarité. Les tout premiers, l'agora et le forum, ont permis l'échange, l'expression fondatrice de la cité (la *polis*) et du politique.

Aujourd'hui, nul n'ose assigner à l'espace et aux monuments la représentation des valeurs du contrat social : justice, patrie, éducation, administration, surveiller/punir. Aurions-nous perdu la vision politique qui nous faisait citoyens pour n'être plus que des consommateurs, habitant le marché et le spectacle, plutôt que la cité et ses espaces collectifs? Et si des valeurs nouvelles sont apparues, il faut alors leur donner une existence urbaine.

Le récit, était-ce le sens de l'histoire dont Francis Fukuyama annonce la fin? Les idéologies d'un monde séparé? Leur disparition a, selon Jean-François Lyotard, ouvert une ère de postmodernité propice à l'anamnèse et à la citation. Le temps de la ville nous outrepasse. Elle nous précède et nous survit. Mais sa longue temporalité semble menacée. Fernand Braudel distinguait trois temps : le temps long de l'histoire, le temps moyen de la conjoncture et le temps court de l'actualité. Cette belle trilogie a bougé. Nous sommes dans un temps de la chronique et vivons ce dont nous nous souvenons. Quand le futur manque, les souvenirs affluent; la mémoire devient le projet. C'est ce que François Hartog appelle le présentisme[5]. La ville conjuguait autrefois un temps long et un espace, une histoire et une géographie, lisibles et mémorables. Il faut maintenant inventer des récits plus courts et plus rapides. L'architecte doit oublier l'éternité (Rem Koolhaas a raison de dire que l'urbanisme consiste à gérer les incertitudes) et nous tous la conviction des identités immuables. Paul Ricœur perçoit cela et met en doute la pérennité de l'identité collective, qui se renforce actuellement sous l'effet de l'intimidation et de l'insécurité. Il en appelle au récit et à ses variations : «*Je voudrais opposer à cette idée d'une identité immuable l'idée d'identité narrative : les collectivités vivantes ont une histoire qui peut être racontée, et je ferai du récit l'un des chemins [..] du rayonnement croisé des cultures.*

Je voudrais introduire l'idée de variations d'horizon : à l'intérieur même d'une culture donnée, les horizons de valeur varient en rythme, ils n'avancent pas ou ne reculent pas de toutes pièces, mais sont échelonnés.

Je prendrai la métaphore du paysage vu d'un train en mouvement : il y a des horizons courts, qui se déplacent rapidement, des horizons moyens, qui évoluent plus lentement et, enfin, l'horizon ultime du paysage, quasi immuable. Donc nous ne sommes pas face à une alternative entre l'immuable et le mouvant : l'idée d'horizon suggère l'idée de variation des horizons en rythme d'évolution.»[6] Symboliques et rythmes nouveaux marquent le temps et le récit des villes. À la célébration du pouvoir par le monument se substituent des valeurs liées à la puissance économique, à la culture et aux événements.

La culture raccorde les fragments du réel et donne aux récits de la vitesse et de la production la profondeur de champ qui leur fait défaut. Enfin, le faudrait-il! Les figures de proue des projets urbains d'aujourd'hui sont des équipements culturels. C'est vrai à Sydney, avec l'opéra d'Utzon, à Paris, avec le Centre Pompidou de Piano et Rogers, à Bilbao, avec le musée Guggenheim de Gehry, à l'île Seguin à Boulogne-Billancourt, avec Ando et la Fondation Pinault, bientôt à Saint-Étienne, avec le Zénith de Foster et la Cité du Design de Finn Geipel, à Pékin, avec l'opéra de Paul Andreu.

Au-delà de cette célébration, proche du statut dévolu au sacré, apparaît une variante liée aux rythmes nouveaux : l'événement. La ville présentique est programmatique avant d'être historique. L'architecte Bernard Reichen a analysé ce qu'il appelle une société du prétexte. «*L'événement*, dit-il, *est devenu composante essentielle de la ville et répond à une attente de la population.*» L'individualisation valorise le présent et un urbanisme du flux.

Cette idée du prétexte — il y a un avant et un après Bilbao — prend des tours variés. Prenons l'exemple de l'événement des événements : les Jeux olympiques. L'opéra de Sydney fut construit pour les Jeux de Melbourne en 1956. Pour ceux de 1976, Montréal se dota de nombreux équipements dont le Parc olympique, le Stade et sa tour penchée et le vélodrome. Mais Barcelone, à l'occasion des Jeux de 1992, s'est restructurée de la façon la plus specta-culaire. De grands architectes ont été conviés et de nouveaux quartiers créés.

Athènes s'est profondément transformée en 2004 avec notamment la voûte «papillon» de Santiago Calatrava. Et Pékin convoque le gotha de l'architecture pour transformer la ville jusqu'en 2008. Figurer dans le dernier carré des villes candidates est devenu un déclencheur en soi. Les deux plus grands projets urbains parisiens d'aujourd'hui, le Nord-Est et les Batignolles, ont été lancés alors même que rien ne garantissait que Paris serait finalement choisie.

Les expositions universelles provoquent des effets semblables. Tout a commencé avec le Crystal Palace, en 1851, à Londres. À Montréal, en 1967, sur les îles Notre-Dame, Sainte-Hélène et dans la Cité du Havre, une mue importante s'opérait. On en retient encore le dôme géodésique de Fuller, Habitat 67 de Safdie est une très belle construction, mais c'est une architecture de papier, la Montréal Tower d'Archigram.

La généralisation de fêtes, telles les nuits blanches à Paris, Montréal, Rome ou Bruxelles, engendre des formes nouvelles d'usage et d'urbanité. Le défilé de la danse et la fête des lumières à Lyon, le Festival Montréal en lumière, la Biennale Internationale Design et la Biennale de la ville/les Transurbaines à Saint-Étienne mettent les villes en mouvement et en média.

PUBLIC/COLLECTIF/PRIVÉ

Établissement humain multiculturel, la ville accueille et protège des intimités et des indivi-dualités, qui ne peuvent à elles seules révéler son identité globale. Mixité, hybridation, plura-lisme expriment un lien commun/lieu commun fait de diversité solidaire et d'usage collectif d'espaces appartenant à tous. On doit donc récuser les tentatives de réduction de cette nature chorale : les privatisations et leurs *gated communities*, forme exclusive de ghetto volontaire et de refus de l'autre, autant que la folklorisation des espaces consacrés aux seules déambula-tions touristiques. À l'est de Paris, une ville nouvelle, Marne la Vallée Val d'Europe, a été conçue par les responsables américains de Disney. L'architecture et l'urbanisme y obéissent à des règles strictes visant à créer une ville conforme à l'idée que peuvent s'en faire des visiteurs dont l'information de pointe les fait imaginer Paris comme un subtil composé de Toulouse-Lautrec, du Moulin Rouge, de communistes, de petites femmes et de restaurants où déguster des baguettes de bon pain et des cuisses de grenouille. Le site Internet de Val d'Europe livre les clés de cette féerie : «*Une architecture conviviale de fonte et de verre à visage humain, inspirée par Baltard, Eiffel et Haussmann*», et des quartiers placés sous le signe «*du bien-être, de la liberté et du plaisir… le quartier traditionnel Serris village, évoquant le charme authentique des fermes briardes*». Où que ce soit dans le monde, le tourisme inter-national, nécessaire et bénéfique, peut à la longue vitrifier les villes et travestir leurs habitants.

L'espace public des villes est à la fois matériel et virtuel, et constitue deux versants de l'échange et du débat. L'un des premiers, Richard Sennett, a dit les dangers encourus par des espaces publics dont la conception et l'usage ne reposeraient plus sur un socle collectif : «*La société reste dominée […] par l'effondrement de la res publica. Nous estimons que les valeurs sociales sont produites par les individus. Cette croyance a semé la confusion dans deux domaines de la vie sociale : je veux parler du pouvoir et de la ville […]. L'idolâtrie intimiste nous empêche d'utiliser notre compréhension des phénomènes du pouvoir comme une arme politique. La ville est l'instrument de la vie impersonnelle, le creuset dans lequel la diversité des intérêts, des goûts, des désirs humains se transforme en expérience sociale. Or, la peur de l'impersonnalité tend à détruire cette expérience.*»[7] Cette analyse prône un espace matériel laïc dévolu à l'accueil de tous pour y célébrer les ressemblances, et non les différences. L'espace public est aussi un espace immatériel de paroles et de pensées connectant des personnes privées que réunit l'intérêt général. Dans cette acception, il est, selon Jürgen Habermas, une conquête de l'esprit critique s'exerçant contre le secret de l'État[8]. La presse et les médias y jouent un rôle essentiel pour y garantir la liberté de l'échange. Les risques de confiscation et de commercialisation de cet espace seraient réels si la publicité n'était définitivement plus la capacité de rendre public, mais la seule imposition d'un imaginaire de la marchandise. Quand Paul Virilio écrit que «*l'image publique devient l'espace public*», il exprime la même crainte. La ville se dématérialise, se privatise et se marchandise. Rem Koolhaas appelle *junkspace* ce continuum d'espaces intérieurs et le plus souvent commerciaux «*où il n'y a plus de murs, mais des cloisons. C'est là, dit-il, que le public fusionne avec le privé et que parce que ça coûte de l'argent, l'espace conditionné devient conditionnel.*»[9] Ce conditionnel privatif peut oublier l'hospitalité.

Si l'analyse radicale de Sennett ne correspond plus à une réalité où privé et public s'interpénètrent, il convient de distinguer un usage familier de l'espace public donnant à celui-ci une forme d'intimité sociale (manifeste en Méditerranée, par exemple) et une privatisation stricte qui, au nom de l'hygiène et de la sécurité, conduit souvent à ne plus garantir à tous un libre accès. Agora, la Biennale 2004 de Montréal, s'est consacrée à l'étude de l'espace public. Le texte de présentation met en lumière les questions d'aujourd'hui : «*Le Quartier international, les quartiers universitaires et le projet de Quartier des spectacles de Montréal répondent à notre désir d'espaces aisément accessibles à l'échelle de la ville. La ville se partage graduellement en morceaux thématiques cherchant chacun à séduire les clients par des bannières et un mobilier de rue à l'avenant. Ce nouveau design d'espace public tend cependant à fermer ses frontières aux promeneurs, aux vendeurs et aux artistes de la rue — éléments qui pourraient troubler les environs soigneusement régis. L'obsession de la sécurité écarte ces éléments indésirables des vieux espaces et parcs publics dans l'embellissement desquels la ville a investi.*» Voilà bien le risque de l'accès conditionnel.

L'espace public doit être préalable et dessiné, répondre à un projet et n'être pas un reste. Gratuit et accueillant comme un intérieur ville — une chambre urbaine aurait dit Louis Kahn —, il doit s'ouvrir à tous, notamment aux plus démunis. Mais il ne peut rester fixé sur un modèle hérité pour une large part de la ville européenne ancienne. Le *shopping*, le loisir, la culture, le goût du déplacement, l'ubiquité procurée par Internet modifient nos modes et espaces de vie. Les stades, centres commerciaux, aéroports, gares, moyens de transport et leurs stations, centres de congrès, halls d'exposition, musées, galeries marchandes, salles de concert, festivals et fêtes, panneaux d'affichage, mobilier urbain, façades, média buildings, le mobilier urbain constituent l'espace public au même titre que les places, rues, mails, parcs. Le design de la ville doit maîtriser leur conception et leur implantation. De nouveaux centres se développent ainsi dans la ville polycentrique. Ils sont nécessaires pour éviter un engorgement des vieux centres et un délaissement de l'espace majoritaire. Cette nécessaire attention au cadre de vie majoritaire oblige à prendre en compte les éléments d'une ville et d'une histoire ordinaire.

ORDINAIRE/EXTRAORDINAIRE/SINGULARITÉ/SIMILITUDE

Le patrimoine nous renvoie à l'histoire de quelques-uns, presque jamais à l'histoire de tous et encore moins d'aujourd'hui. Les monuments et grandes pièces urbaines édifient au double sens du terme : construire et instruire, porter à la vertu. «*Ce que peut la vertu d'un homme ne doit pas se mesurer par ses efforts, mais par son ordinaire*», pensait Pascal.

Dans la ville, l'ordinaire s'estompe devant l'apparat et les effets de la puissance. Mémoire sélective, éradicatrice. Cet oubli institutionnel minore la part majoritaire du passé et confisque l'espace de célébration en ignorant le quotidien et les créations d'aujourd'hui, les espaces de socialité, les métiers, les usages partagés. Pierre Nora, dans *Les lieux de mémoire*[10], établit pour la France un inventaire de ces mémoires et de ces lieux en allés. Le temps est venu de donner sens à de nouveaux parcours et de percevoir, hors des beautés monumentales, les instances du quotidien.

Il n'existe pas de petits projets. Si le monument et les pièces urbaines doivent jalonner l'espace et lui donner ses repères, l'espace séculier est tout aussi important. Les petites formes urbaines, ainsi que les appelle l'urbaniste Jean-Pierre Charbonneau, sont les éclats nécessaires d'une considération et d'un usage partagé de la ville. Il est plus facile de construire un arc de triomphe ou une tour que d'ordonner une rue ou un quartier. L'architecture doit échapper au double danger du monument expiatoire (tout est laid, mais nos monuments nous sauvent) et de l'architecture de promoteurs, l'*easy-architecture*. Entre les deux, le chemin est étroit vers une architecture aimable et confortable de vie quotidienne locale, globale, contemporaine et ordinaire.

Peut-on être tout cela à la fois : d'ici, du monde et d'aujourd'hui ? Peut-on être universel sans renier ses racines; inventif sans s'éloigner de l'ordinaire, d'aujourd'hui sans oublier hier ? C'est la mission que Kenneth Frampton[11] assignait aux architectes dans ses propositions pour une architecture de résistance instituant un régionalisme critique. Si, comme l'écrit Miguel Torga, «*le global, c'est le local sans les murs*», il s'agit bien de garder les murs tout en s'ouvrant vers le grand large. L'architecture de la ville doit exprimer ces vérités indissociables. On en précisera le contenu identitaire en ne confinant pas l'histoire à un lointain passé, mais en y inscrivant les évolutions plus récentes et en y intégrant la pluralité culturelle des habitants. Le régionalisme critique doit donc s'amplifier d'apports exogènes devenus éléments constitutifs du corps hybride de la ville. Tout cela est complexe. Mais rien ne serait pire que le délestage de toutes les ambitions au profit du marché, au marché du profit. Encore une fois, il faut réinventer des récits, des horizons narratifs, du politique. C'est aussi cela le design de la ville. Ce serait aussi une architecture ordinaire qui, retrouvant des symboles et des significations autres que la poésie de l'angle droit, les magies de la peau ou les infatuations de la taille, ne considérerait plus le style, l'ornement, le corps comme les signes d'une dégénérescence passéiste.

LE CORPS DE LA VILLE/LA VILLE DES CORPS/LA RELATION

Avec la proxémie, Edward T. Hall montre que chacun d'entre nous dispose d'une sorte de bulle variant selon les cultures, les usages et les lieux[12]. Il explicite ainsi des organisations d'espaces en fonction de traditions différentes et permet de projeter des espaces nouveaux, intégrant cette dimension cachée des esprits et des corps. Si l'architecture est d'abord de lumière, nous vivons aussi dans un paysage sonore que Murray Schaefer, le premier, a saisi et analysé dans ses ouvrages, dans son enseignement à l'Université Simon Fraser[13] et dans le développement depuis la fin des années 60 de son *World soundscape project*. Il a fait école, et le travail sur le son est progressivement apparu comme inhérent à la connaissance et à la pratique de la ville. Beaucoup reste à faire cependant pour que les villes intègrent ces analyses dans leur aménagement. Plus encore si l'on poursuit l'inventaire de notre sensorialité. L'espace urbain est un espace que pratiquent nos corps, sensibles à la température, à l'air, à l'ombre, aux déplacements et bruissements, aux couleurs et… aux autres corps. Il faudrait porter une attention active à l'aspect physique de la ville, à la manière dont ses parcours, ses architectures, ses flux, sa topographie, ses matériaux interagissent avec notre corps, nous pénètrent et créent inconsciemment un capital d'affects et de percepts,[14] fondateurs d'un plaisir et d'une richesse de l'espace. La ville aux savoirs et aux saveurs accumulés se situe entre le sens et le sensible. La raison n'est pas son seul empire et l'espace ne s'y décrète pas. «*L'espace est une poésie qui se sent au lieu de se mesurer*», déclarait Antoine Pevsner. Résistons au nom du sensible et introduisons dans le design de la ville ce riche composé de nos sensations, cette ressource subtile et, pour l'essentiel, inutilisée. Maîtrisons pour cela la relation entre les éléments d'ambiance, de lumière, de son, de chaleur, d'odeur (*smellscape*), de tactilité et de kinesthésie. Conjuguons l'objectif et le subjectif, ce que Jean-François Augoyard appelle l'unité paradoxale, afin de créer une esthétique fondée sur l'organisation contextualisée des sensations.

La création de la ville comme univers sensible passe par la relation au corps. La ville est tissu; les relations s'y nouent: entre les corps, entre les espaces, entre le plein et le vide. «*Oublions les choses, ne considérons que les rapports*», recommandait Georges Braque. Dans la ville fragmentée plus encore que dans la ville constituée, il importe de tisser le lien et de donner lieu. Ce liant de cohérence et de sens qui rend la ville intelligible et habitable, c'est à la fois de la forme et du fond, une écologie urbaine, un design de relations.

Le design doit prendre en compte la demande et la parole du commanditaire pour en apprécier la nature, déterminer la part du désir et celle du besoin, relier l'enracinement et la projection, concevoir et réaliser un projet. Qui est donc le commanditaire de la ville et n'y a-t-il pas place pour une nouvelle maîtrise, non plus seulement celle d'ouvrage et celle d'œuvre, mais la maîtrise d'usage? Ainsi, mêlerait-on aux voix du pouvoir et de la conception celle de l'habitant. Cette voix-là, cette parole de faible énergie dont parle l'architecte-urbaniste belge Lucien Kroll, portée par des groupes divers, est sans doute le socle d'un projet local qui ne subirait plus les conséquences de la mondialisation, mais y répondrait sans l'ignorer ni la nier. «*Le projet local*, dit Alberto Magnaghi,[15] est une mondialisation par le bas, une gestion dynamique des conflits et la mise en réseau de villes en réponse à leur dessaisissement.

Le design de la ville, c'est l'organisation de sa gouvernance et le subtil équilibre de la représentation politique et de la vie associative. Nous sommes, selon François Ascher, écartelés entre des axiomatiques différentes et peut-être opposées: celle de la performance pour l'économie, celle de la justice pour le social et celle de l'éthique pour l'environnement. Il serait navrant que la perte d'un récit et d'un projet collectif conduisent à une division de la gouvernance entre des expertises spécialisées. Le politique, comme la ville, traverse et abolit les sectorisations, affirme le caractère généraliste de nos vies et de leur cadre spatial et symbolique. La politique doit réinventer la *polis*; la cité doit devenir notre horizon. Aussi, serait-il essentiel de donner aux villes davantage de pouvoir et une représentativité plus réelle dans les instances internationales, économiques, sociales et culturelles.

Les villes sont différentes. Entre hors limite et perte d'identité, entre autonomie réductrice et dépendance amnésique, elles désignent un monde de relation et d'interdépendance consentie.

Elles nous font semblables et fraternels en énonçant les récits possibles d'un avenir et d'un projet qui nous enrichiraient de nos diversités.

〉〉

1. Yves Chalas. *Villes contemporaines*. Cercle d'art. Paris 2001 ✖ 2. Raymond Unwin. *L'étude pratique des Plans de villes. Introduction à l'art de dessiner les plans d'aménagement et d'extension*. Trad. de l'anglais. Paris, L'Équerre, 1981. Publié en 1909 à Londres, cet ouvrage constitue un des tout premiers manuels de la «science des villes». ✖ 3. L'«exposition urbaine» *Internationale Bauausstellung* (IBA) de la Ruhr (IBA) comprend sur 803 km^2 17 villes qui ont connu la crise sidérurgique et minière. En 1990, ont été décidés 76 projets sur les thèmes suivants : parc paysager de l'Emscher à partir du paysage d'origine; restructuration écologique du canal de l'Emscher; utilisation du canal Rhin-Herne en espace de loisirs; aménagement d'espaces industriels et tertiaires dans des friches industrielles sur le thème du travail dans le parc (500 hectares de zones d'activités intégrant 17 centres technologiques); restauration et reconversion de monuments industriels comme supports culturels; construction de lotissements et réhabilitation des cités ouvrières. ✖ 4. *The umbrellas*, Japon-É.-U.; *The Wrapped Coast* en Australie; *The Valley Curtain of Colorado; Surrounded Islands* au large de Miami. ✖ 5. François Hartog. *Des régimes d'historicité — présentisme et expérience du temps — Du seuil*. Paris 2003 ✖ 6. Paul Ricœur. *Cultures, du deuil à la traduction*. in *Le Monde*, 25 mai 2004. ✖ 7. Richard Sennett. *Fall of Public Man. On The Social Psychology of Capitalism*. New York 1977. Vintage books, New York. En français : *Les tyrannies de l'intimité*. Du seuil, 1979, Paris. ✖ 8. Jürgen Habermas. *L'espace public, Archéologie de la publicité comme dimension constitutive de la société bourgeoise*. Payot. Paris 1978. L'édition originale allemande est parue en 1962. ✖ 9. Rem Koolhaas. *Mutations* Actar, Arc en rêve, centre d'architecture, 2000. ✖ 10. Pierre Nora. *Les lieux de mémoire*. Ouvrage collectif, Gallimard, trois volumes , 1984-1992. ✖ 11. Kenneth Frampton. *Pour un régionalisme critique et une architecture de résistance*. Critique : *L'objet architecture*. N°s 476-477. ✖ 12. Edward T. Hall. *The Hidden Dimension*. Garden City NY Doubleday. 1966. En français : *La dimension cachée*. Du Seuil, Paris, 1971. Voir également *The Silent Language*. Garden City, NY Anchor Press/Doubleday, 1959. En français : *Le langage silencieux*. Du Seuil, Paris, 1984. ✖ 13. R. Murray Schaefer. *Paysage sonore*. Édition française Jean-Claude Lattès, 1979. ✖ 14. «*Les personnages ne peuvent exister, et l'auteur ne peut les créer que parce qu'ils ne les perçoivent pas, mais sont passés dans le paysage et font eux-mêmes partie du composé de sensations […]. Les affects sont précisément ces devenirs non humains de l'homme, comme les percepts* (y compris la ville) *sont les paysages non humains de la nature.*» Gilles Deleuze et Félix Guattari, *Qu'est-ce que la philosophie?* De Minuit, 1991. ✖ 15. Alberto Magnaghi. *Le projet local*. Mardaga, 2003. Première édition en italien : 2000.

〉〉

GLOBALIZATION AND UNSETTLEMENT: WHITHER DESIGN?

BY SASKIA SASSEN

> Professor of Sociology, University of Chicago
> Visiting Professor, London School of Economics

》》

Today is a time of massive structures, massive markets, and massive capabilities deployed by businesses and military powers. We might wonder about the options that even the most creative designers are left with to express their interests and ideas. The issue here is not so much the few either exceptional or lucky designers who gain a global stage in their particular field or with a general audience. Nor am I concerned here with questions of successful marketing of ideas and innovations. My concerns are rather a more diffuse urban landscape of opportunities for creative work and, further, the opportunities for different kinds of creative work to enter domains dominated by massive actors (e.g., global firms) or systems (e.g., large infrastructures). The objective, then, is not to describe design but rather to examine the larger political economy of design in cities confronting globalization, acceleration, and unsettlement. I want to tease out the landscape within which design functions.

GLOBALIZATION AS UNSETTLEMENT: HOW TO NARRATE THE OLD AND THE NEW

Globalization and digitization are two marking features of the current period. One effect is the growing importance of process and flows over final product. This is partly a function of the velocity through which a "product" can move through different phases, so the experience is more of flow than thing, even though there is a lot of thingness around. One of my concerns in researching globalization and digitization has been to recover the materialities underlying much of global and digital experiences and the representations that everything is becoming flow and digital.

What I want to emphasize here is that for the digital domain to exist it takes much material and, further, that much of the meaning of digitized images and representations comes from the non-digital world. Second, the globalizing of activities and the growing importance of global flows are in good part dependent on a vast international network of places, mostly global cities, full of fixed (as well as mobile) resources. In brief, things and materiality are critical for digitization, and places are critical for global flows.[1]

One critical politico-economic question we can ask is to what extent the logic of global corporate actors penetrates what design bridges into. In this case design is the bridge that allows corporate actors to enter the heart and minds, homes and pocketbooks, of individuals. It is of course a fact that people have needs that they want met, so it is to some extent a partnership, not simply voracious corporate machinery that penetrates all domains.

But how about looking at the bridging as a kind of frontier zone, an in-between space that is in principle under-specified, ambiguous, under-narrated. Design, including corporate design, could do some interesting work here. How to tell the story, how to narrate that under-specified in-between space. Provocative or evocative advertising or architecture can have this effect. And that takes me to the designer as narrator.

First, I want to examine the conditions in our political economy that have led to the growing importance of design as a type of value-adding creative work, which also has the effect of repositioning creative work in circuits that are now central to the globalized economy. Second, I want to identify domains that can escape com-mercialized design practice and bring art and artists into spaces now increasingly taken over by exclusively commercial uses. To do this I propose to conceive of design as a type of mediation and narration that blurs the bridge between art-making and the work of profit-making, and to conceive of art-making as disruptive interventions.

The focus is on the practices involved; that is to say, although unlikely, the same per-son might engage in all these types of work, but the subjectivity engaged by each of these types of practice will be distinct, often sharply different.

THE ASCENDANCE OF PROCESS AND FLOW: A GREATER NEED FOR INTERMEDIARIES

In addressing these issues I distinguish three conditions in today's political economy within which it might be helpful to situate design as the blurring between artistic and profit-making work; that is, design as a mediation that effectively obscures that distinction. The first condi-tion is the importance placed on process, flow, and networks rather than the final product per se. Such "diversion" also advances the significance of intermediary actors and typologies of intervention. It is in this context that I regard designers as intermediaries. A second condition arises out of the fact that globalization displaces existing arrangements and boundaries, and does so with great velocity. This in turn raises the need to narrate that unsettlement. Here designers assume the role of narrators. Third, displacement and the push continuously to innovate lead to a sharp proliferation of new products, systems, and configurations. Such overabundance and saturation demand the correlative endowing of these "novelties" with ever-newer shapes and forms. This is the designer as designer in the general sense of the term. Clearly all three conditions can come together in a particular work of design.

Design functions as an intervention that bridges the virtual and material world. It tra-verses global corporate growth strategies and place-bound local consumer needs through branding. It joins the human body and the world of clothing through fashion. And it connects individuals and public space through architecture and urban design.

Such continuous and omnipresent mediations suggest that within a context of globalization, acceleration, and unsettlement, creative work is becoming an important quality for more and more economic sectors. When creative work negotiates in this way it becomes, at best, applied art and, at its poorest, branding. Design as applied art can have very commercial objectives (how to sell a product by capturing the imagination) or it can aim at enhancing the public good (great public architecture).

NARRATING UNSETTLEMENT

Globalization today, and its bearings on these types of issues, can be thought of as a mix of dynamics—economic, political, cultural, imaginary—that destabilize existing formalized arrangements and configurations. In some ways, the world of design is continuously engaged in shaking up existing meanings, shapes, iconographies. We often call this fashion or style. What concerns me here is a set of deeper, structural changes that can be quite ambiguous or diffuse, and also difficult to grasp.

We see prominent trends both toward specialization and toward the blurring of traditional boundaries. This often calls for particular forms describing or capturing or representing what is actually going on. Design has become crucial partly because of such explanatory narrative strategies. In fact, interventions in nondescript, *under*-specified situations are often expressed as design—thereby expanding the category of conventional design. The whole notion of a risk society further adds to this experience of unsettlement. Obviously, the actual design practice does not remain unaffected: work in small firms with highly creative, open environments is often far better attuned to capturing these perturbations in the larger social world than is work in large corporate firms. Similarly, complex cities, especially global cities, are highly imaginative *milieux*, partly because they contain both the most advanced and the most desperate conditions.

But how about looking at the gaps and blurrings bridged through design as a kind of frontier zone, an in-between space that is, in principle, ambiguous and under-narrated? Artists can and are doing some interesting work here.

To tell the story, to narrate that indefinite, intermediate space, is a type of work that might be political, although not necessarily in the narrow sense of the word as would be the case with explicit critiques of specific political events or actors. Rather, I mean political here as the possibility of "making present," of giving speech. This would stand in sharp contrast to design that is meant to endow extra utility, which today increasingly means added profit.

Let me illustrate some of these issues with two concrete cases that capture, on the one hand, massive transitions, and on the other, political interventions. By political interventions I mean narrative strategies that do not consolidate links with the world of commerce but are rather borne out of and act upon a larger political field. One case is that of urban design in today's large complex cities, and the second is the new media artists and Internet-based or aided activism.

INTERVENTIONS: RESISTING PERMANENCE AND UTILITY LOGICS

The meanings and roles of architecture and urban design centred in the older traditions of permanence are irrevocably destabilized in complex cities—that is, cities marked by digital networks, acceleration, massive infrastructures for connectivity, and growing estrangement. Those older meanings do not disappear, they remain crucial.

But they cannot comfortably address the newer meanings, which include the growing importance of such networks, interconnections, energy flows, subjective cartographies. Architects need to confront the enormity of the urban experience, the overwhelming presence of massive architectures and dense infrastructures in today's cities, and the irresistible logic of utility that organizes much of the investment in cities.

There are, clearly, multiple ways of positing the challenges facing architecture and planning as practice and as theory. In emphasizing the crucial place of cities for architecture, I construct a problematic that is not only positioned but is also, perhaps inevitably, partial. It is different from the problematic of neo-traditionalist architects who are also concerned about the present urban condition. And it is distinct from the problematic focused on how current conditions are changing the profession and its opportunities, or one that centres its critical stance on questions of the growing distance between the winners and the losers. What is often seen as the most judicious stance is largely internal to the specific problems of the architecture profession, and it fails to extend to the social field in which it operates.

At the same time, these cities are full of under-used spaces that are often characterized more by memory than current meaning. These spaces are part of the interiority of a city, yet they lie outside of its organizing utility-driven logics and spatial frames. They are terrains vagues that allow many residents to connect to the rapidly transforming cities in which they live, and to bypass subjectively the massive infrastructures that have come to dominate more and more spaces in their cities. Jumping upon these *terrains vagues* in order to maximize real estate development would be a mistake from this perspective. Keeping some of this openness, might make sense in terms of factoring future options at a time when utility logics change so quickly and often violently—the excess of high-rise office buildings being one of the great examples.

This opens up the salient dilemma of the current urban condition in ways that take it beyond the notions of high-tech architecture, virtual spaces, simulacra, theme parks. All of the latter matter, but they are fragments of an incomplete puzzle. In addition to all the other forms of work they represent, architecture and urban design can also function as critical artistic practices that allow us to capture something more elusive than what is represented by notions such as theme-parking. There is a type of urban condition that dwells between the reality of massive structures and the reality of semi-abandoned places. I think it is central to the experience of the urban, and it makes legible the transitions and unsettlements of specific spatio-temporal configurations.

The work of capturing the elusive quality that cities produce and make legible is not easy. Utility logics won't do it. I can't help but think that artists are part of the answer—whether by ephemeral public performances and installations or more lasting types of public sculpture; whether by site-specific/community-based art or nomadic sculptures that circulate among localities.

And it would take architects able to navigate several forms of knowledge to introduce the possibility of an architectural practice located in spaces—such as the intersections of multiple transport and communication networks—where the naked eye or the engineer's imagination sees no shape, no possibility of a form, only pure infrastructure and utility. On the other hand,

there is the work of detecting the possible architectures and forms of spaces that architectural
practices centred in permanence consider as merely empty silences, non-existences.

MICROENVIRONMENTS WITH GLOBAL SPAN

It will not be long before many urban residents begin to experience the local as a type of microenvironment with global span. Much of what we keep representing and experiencing as something local—a building, an urban place, a household, an activist organization right in our neighbourhood—is actually located not only in the concrete places where we can see them, but also on digital networks that span the globe. They are connected with other such localized buildings, organizations, households—possibly on the other side of the world. They may indeed be more oriented to those other areas than to their immediate surrounding. Think of the financial centre in a global city, or the human rights or environmental activists' home or office; their orientation is not towards what surrounds them but to a global process. I think of these local entities as microenvironments with global span.

Three issues are of interest here. One is what it means for "the city" to contain a proliferation of globally oriented yet very localized offices, households, and organizations. In this context the city becomes a strategic amalgamation of multiple global circuits that loop through it. As cities and urban regions become increasingly traversed by non-local, notably global circuits, much of what we experience is the local because the locally sited is actually a transformed condition in that it is imbricated with non-local dynamics or is a localization of global processes. One way of thinking about this is in terms of the spatialization of various projects: economic, political, cultural. This produces a specific set of interactions in a city's relation to its topography. The new urban spatiality this produces is partial in a double sense: it accounts for only part of what happens in cities and what cities are about, and it inhabits only part of what we might think of as the space of the city, whether this be understood in terms of a city's administrative boundaries or in the sense of the multiple public imaginaries that may be present in different sectors of a city's people. If we consider urban space as productive, as enabling new configurations, then these developments signal multiple possibilities.

A second issue, one coming out of the proliferation of digital networks traversing cities, concerns the future of cities in an increasingly digitized and globalized world. Here the bundle of conditions and dynamics that marks the model of the global city might be a helpful way of distilling the ongoing centrality of urban space in complex cities. Just to single out one key dynamic: the more globalized and digitalized the operations of firms and markets, the more their central management and co-ordination functions (and the requisite material structures) become strategic. It is precisely because of digitalization that the simultaneous worldwide dispersal of operations (whether factories, offices, or service outlets) and system integration can be achieved. And it is precisely this combination that raises the importance of central functions. Global cities are strategic sites for the combining of the resources necessary for the production of these central functions.[2] Thus, much of what is liquefied, circulates in digital networks, and is marked by hypermobility actually remains physical—hence, possibly urban—in some of its components. At the same time, however, that which remains physical has been transformed by the fact that it is represented by highly liquid instruments that can circulate in global markets. It may look the same, it may involve the same bricks and mortar, it may be new or old, but it is a transformed entity. Take, for example, the case of real estate. Financial services firms have invented instruments that liquefy real estate, thereby facilitating investment and the circulation of these instruments in global markets. Still, part of what constitutes real estate remains very physical, but the building represented by financial instruments circulating globally is not the same building as one that is not.

We have difficulty capturing this multi-valence of the new digital technologies through our conventional categories: if it is physical, it *is* physical; and if it is liquid, it *is* liquid. In fact, the partial representation of real estate through liquid financial instruments produces a complex imbrications of the material and the de-materialized moments of what we continue to call real estate. And the need of global financial markets for multiple material conditions in very grounded financial centres produces yet another type of complex imbrication which reveals that precisely those sectors that are most globalized and digitized continue to have a very strong and strategic urban dimension.

Hypermobility and de-materialization are usually seen as mere functions of the new technologies. This understanding subverts the fact that it takes multiple material conditions to achieve this outcome. Once we recognize that the hypermobility of the instrument, or the de-materialization of the actual piece of real estate, had to be produced, we introduce the imbrication of the material and the non-material. It takes capital fixity to produce capital mobility, that is, state-of-the-art built environments, conventional infrastructure—from highways, to airports and railways—and well-housed talent. These are, at least partly, place-bound conditions, even though the nature of their place-boundedness is going to be different from what it was a century ago, when place-boundedness might have been marked by immobility. Today it is a place-boundedness that is inflected, inscribed, by the hypermobility of some of its components/products/outcomes. Both capital fixity and mobility are located in a temporal frame where speed is ascendant and consequential. This type of capital fixity cannot be fully captured in a description of its material and locational features, for example, in a topographical reading. Conceptualizing digitization and globalization along these lines creates operational and rhetorical openings for recognizing the ongoing importance of the material world, even in the case of some of the most de-materialized activities.

The third issue concerns the typically urban interventions that can also be part of the exploding world of new media artists and new media activists, both of which are deeply urban-based and growing groups. That is the subject of the next section.

INTERVENTION: DIGITAL MEDIA AND THE MAKING OF PRESENCE

A very different type of instance is that of new media artists using computer-centred network technologies to represent and/or enact political as well as artistic projects. What I want to capture here is a very specific feature: the possibility of constructing forms of globality that are neither part of global corporate media or consumer firms, nor part of elite universalisms or "high culture," but rather that represent the possibility of giving presence to multiple local actors, projects, and imaginaries in ways that may constitute these forms of counter-globality. One of the outcomes of these interventions is the different uses of technology—ranging from the political to the ludic—that subvert corporate globalization. We are seeing the formation of alternative networks, projects, and spaces. It is perhaps emblematic that the metaphor of "hacking" has been dislodged from its specialized technical discourse and become part of everyday life. In the face of the predatory regimes of intellectual property rights we see the ongoing influence of the free software movement.[3] Indymedia gains terrain even as global media conglomerates dominate just about all mainstream media.[4]

The new geographies of power that bring together the elites from the global south and north find their obverse in the work of such collectives as the Raqs Media Collective, which are destabilizing the centre/periphery divide.[5]

Such outcomes must be distinguished from the common assumption that if "it" is global it is cosmopolitan. The global forms I'm concerned with here are what I like to refer to, partly as a provocation, as non-cosmopolitan forms of globality. Through the Internet (or, more generally, internetworking) local initiatives and projects can become part of a global network without losing their focus on the specifics of the local. This enables a new type of cross-border work, one centred in multiple localities yet intensely connected digitally. For instance, groups or individuals concerned with a variety of environmental questions—from solar energy design to appropriate-materials-architecture—can develop networks for circulating not only information but also political work and strategies.

In an effort to synthesize the diversity of subversive interventions into the space of global capitalism, I use the notion of counter-geographies of globalization: these interventions are deeply imbricated with some of the major dynamics that make up corporate globalization, yet they are not part of the formal apparatus or the objectives of this apparatus (such as the formation of global markets and global firms). These counter-geographies thrive on the intensifying of transnational and translocal networks, the development of communication technologies which easily escape conventional surveillance practices, and so on. Further, the strengthening and, in some cases, the formation of new global circuits are ironically embedded or made possible by the existence of that same global economic system that they contest. These counter-geographies are dynamic and changing in their locational features.[6]

The narrating, giving shape, and making present involved in digitized environments assumes very particular meanings when mobilized to represent/enact local specificities in a global context. Beyond the kinds of on-the-ground work involved in these struggles, new media artists and activists—the latter often artists—have been key actors in these developments, whether it is through tactical media, indymedia, or such entities as the original incarnation of Digital City Amsterdam[7] and the Berlin-based Transmediale.[8] But new media artists have also focused on issues other than the world of technology. Not surprisingly perhaps, a key focus has been the increasingly restrictive regime for migrants and refugees in a global world where capital gets to flow wherever it wants. Organizations such as Nobody is Illegal,[9] the Mongrel Web Project,[10] Mute Magazine,[11] the Manchester-based Futuresonic,[12] and the Bonn/Cologne-based Theater der Welt,[13] have all done projects focused on immigration.

In conclusion, the work of both design and making art can narrate the unspecified at a time of increasing velocities, the ascendance of process and flow over objects and permanence, the creation of massive structures not on a human scale, and the growth of branding as the basic mediation between individuals and markets. The work of design produces narratives that add to the value of existing contexts, and in the narrowest reading, to the utility logics of the corporate world. But there is also a kind of art-making work that can produce disruptive narratives. The artist narrates unsettlement and inserts the local and the silenced, making it legible, giving it presence. The same individual can, in principle, engage in both types of work, but the subjectivity of each type of work is distinct. Both types of work play a strategic role in today's cities.

〉〉

1. Elsewhere, I have detailed the complex imbrications of the digital and the material, of flows and places. See Saskia Sassen, "Towards a Sociology of Information Technology." *Current Sociology. Special Issue: Sociology and Technology* 50 May 2002): 365–88. ✕ 2. Other dimensions of the global city are discussed in Saskia Sassen, *The Global City*, 2d ed. (Princeton, NJ: Princeton University Press, 2001). ✕ 3. See <http://www.gnu.org> for more information. ✕ 4. Indymedia is "a network of collectively run media outlets for the creation of radical, accurate, and passionate tellings of the truth." See <http://www.indymedia.org>. ✕ 5. See their contribution to this volume, pp. 62-78. ✕ 6. They are also multivalent; i.e., some are "good" and some are "bad." I use the term as an analytic category to designate a whole range of dynamics and initiatives that are centred in the new capabilities for global operation coming out of the corporate global economy but that are used for purposes other than their original design: examples range from alter-globalization political struggles to informal global economic circuits, and, at the extreme, global terrorist networks. ✕ 7. The Digital City Amsterdam (DDS) was an experiment facilitated by De Balie, Amsterdam's cultural centre. Subsidized by the city of Amsterdam and the Ministry of Economic Affairs, it allowed people to access the digital city host computer to retrieve council minutes and official policy papers as well as to visit digital cafes and train stations. See <http://reinder.rustema.nl/dds/> for documentation; see also the chapter by Geert Lovink and Patrice Riemens in *Global Networks, Linked Cities*, ed. Saskia Sassen (New York and London: Routledge, 2002) for the full evolution of DDS. ✕ 8. An international media arts festival; see <http://www.transmediale.de>. ✕ 9. A campaign led by autonomous groups, religious initiatives, trade unions, and individuals in support of refugees; see <http://www.contrast.org/borders/> for more information. ✕ 10. London-based media activists and artists; see <http://www.mongrelx.org>. ✕ 11. See <http://www.metamute.com>. ✕ 12. A festival exploring wireless and mobile media; see <http://www.futuresonic.com>. ✕ 13. A theatre festival; see <http://www.theaterderwelt.de>.

〉〉

BIO OF ARTIST FOR IMAGES: Hilary Koob-Sassen holds a B.A. from Yale University. He won Yale's top prize for the arts (Suttler Prize 1997). He was a finalist for the ZKM prize. He has shown his sculpture at Lombard Fried and at Exit Art, both in New York, and at Workspace in London . The New Yorker has said about his sculpture "uglier than the ugliest Louise Bourgeois" and The New York Times "…complex… visionary…". He has shown his films at ZKM (Karlsruhe, Germany 2002), Goldsmith College (London 2003), among others, and has been selected for the Transmediale 05 (Berlin). He is currently Artist-in-Residence at ZKM. His sculpture studio is in Sommerset, England.

01–02–03 Video stills from "The Paraculture" by Hilary Koob-Sassen, under production at ZKM (Germany, 2003-2004)

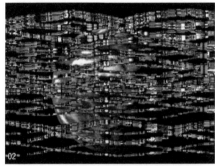

CREATIVITY AND THE CITY

A CONVERSATION WITH JOHN THACKARA
> Director of Doors of Perception.[1]
BY CAROL COLETTA
> Director of the U.S. public radio program *Smart City*.[2]

〉〉〉

"We now design *messages*, not interactions. … We are in a transition to a post-spectacular, post-massified culture. A sustainable city has to be a city of encounter and interaction, not a city for the passive participation in entertainment," explains John Thackara, founding director of the Doors of Perception conference—a design futures network founded in 1993 that connects a worldwide network of visionary designers, thinkers, and grassroots innovators. For the city of the future Thackara believes in the concepts of connectivity, in human interaction vs. technology-driven networks, as well as in bottom-up, collaborative innovation inspired from archaic yet imaginative models of survival and community services for daily life.

CC › You gave a lecture at The Creativity and The City conference held in Amsterdam a few months back. I wish I had been there to listen to you and to see the sparks fly after you spoke. Now, I get to ask you the questions I wanted to ask when I read the conference transcripts. Your lecture was entitled "The Post Spectacular City." In it you skewer the so-called creative class for the "catatonic spaces that despoil our physical and perceptual landscape." In fact, you state that the legacy left by the creative class is meaningless, narcissistic cities. You obviously don't think much of the creative class. Why?

JT › The problem dates back to the extraordinary success of Richard Florida who wrote a book called *The Rise of the Creative Class* in 2003 (and a follow-up *The Flight of the Creative Class* in 2005). The success of Florida's book did two things that have skewered, I think, the way people think about their cities. First, he provided lots of data about the existence of people who he deemed to be members of the creative class and how much money they bring in the form of jobs or new business to a place. His data gave authority and respectability to the idea that the presence of creative people is, per se, good for cities.

But the second thing that happened was that, all over the world, planners got the wrong end of the stick. I've been in cities throughout Europe and in Asia where people hold Richard Florida's book in their hands as if it's a kind of guidebook to making a place special. What bugs me is that these people tend to perceive "creatives" as a breed apart—the kind of people who go to smart restaurants and wear Prada shoes. The word "creative" gets interpreted as a form of consumerism or creating products and services for consumerism, rather than a condition of being genuinely creative and different.

CC › You run a worldwide network of visionary designers, thinkers, and grass-roots innovators, as you call them. They are surely creative people. You don't seem to consider them as part of the movement described in Richard Florida's best-selling book.

JT › To be honest I probably am, as are you, a member of the creative class. We appear in the lists of professions in Richard's book when he measures how many of us there are. And it's a lot: 30 percent of the U.S. workforce, by his estimation. What I find objectionable is the conclusion or implication that only members of the creative class do creative things. When that understanding is used to plan cities, you end up with a ghetto filled with creative people in one bit of town. Some planners and developers I've met think that because there are creatives in a particular area, property values will go up, chic restaurants will come in, and so on. Now in Florida's second book, he tries to remedy that problem by talking about the 70 percent of citizens who are not designers or PR consultants. He is clearly a social progressive, and I suspect he was disturbed by the ways his first book was misunderstood in some quarters. But I don't think he can have it both ways: a "class" is not a class if it contains 100 percent of the population!

But for me, the most exciting cities are those where unexpected things happen in unexpected places on the edge of town in unglamorous locations. That's how cities in the past have become interesting places. The danger is that the creative class idea will achieve the opposite of what people set out to do.

CC › Which do think are the most exciting cities today, John?

JT › I am stimulated by a variety of strange places. I'll give you a couple of examples—one big, one small. The city of Calcutta in India is a remarkable city because it's one of the most intensively walked cities in the world, despite being rather large, with its 15 to 16 million residents. Like all Indian cities, and many Asian cities, it has a tremendous density of activity. But what's special about it is the city manages to work despite most people agreeing that it's a planning nightmare, the traffic systems don't work properly, the trams are ancient and clanking. Everything is apparently disorderly, but the sheer vibrancy and excitement of being there and just wandering around is fantastic. For me, Calcutta is the antithesis of the top-down creativity you encounter in many European cities.

The other places I find interesting and stimulating are small, unglamorous towns all over Europe. In the United States as well, hundreds of towns are fighting to reinvent themselves because traditional industries and livelihoods have disappeared. I was in an obscure small place called Nexo, on an island called Bonholm (it's Danish, but located near Poland), which is one of many hundreds of fishing ports in Europe. The fish have gone, but the people have a deeply rooted culture of fishing. They are trying to figure out, "What do we do with our lives?" Here is a place where people are up against it and really have no choice but to be creative just to survive. So, the people in this small place have come up with lots of very interesting ideas.

CC › But would you want to live in Calcutta?

JT › I could live in Calcutta. I'm not limitlessly adventurous, so I would probably look for a quiet place with less racket and noise than you find on the main drags! In Delhi, for example, I stayed in a place called Defence Colony, which was physically central but amazingly quiet, like an inner-city suburb. Quiet except for human and animal noises: dogs fighting, monkeys monkeying, birds that meow like cats while swooping overhead, loud insects shouting at each other, people sweeping leaves off their drive, pedestrians saying "sshhhh" to cows so they will move out of the way! I spent ages just listening to the cries of street traders on a variety of bikes: the man with eggs; the man with the pink and red fruit; the knife sharpener; and a man with brightly coloured brushes and feather dusters who looked like a huge electrocuted parrot as he moved with his wares up the street.

CC › You've said that our buildings, museums, science and convention centres, and sports stadia are now about one-way communication delivering pre-cooked experiences to passive crowds. I want to challenge you on that statement. When I'm sitting in an arena as a basket-ball fan or a convention attendee, I don't feel like part of a passive crowd. We're screaming; we're talking to each other; we're bumping into old friends, meeting new people. Why do you call us passive?

JT › That's a very fair criticism of what I said. It was patronizing of me to suggest that people are dumb and accept at face value the things they encounter in, for example, museums. Several people have said to me, "When you look at an object, it triggers you to reflect about deep things in ways that aren't necessarily obvious when you look at them in a museum." The problem is that many of the people who build museums, and the people who provide the money for them, are motivated by a business model in which tourists pay good dollars to have a pre-designed experience once in their life.

CC › Everyone says that they are designing interactive experiences. It's something you call for when you use this idea, which I love, of "deliberately choosing a life of action over a life of observation." Can designers encourage that choice?

JT › This is one of the many questions that intrigue me and for which I don't have an answer. Our dilemma, as designers and as citizens, is that anything that is designed by one person, for somebody else, is in some sense controlling the experience of that other person. If you design a building in a particular way, it determines by its physical shape and orientation how other people will use it. What happens, then, it's true, is people appropriate buildings and do things to them and in them that the designers or the architects didn't anticipate. That's the positive aspect of the interaction between people who design things and people who use them.

 The problem is that people in the museum business or theme parks or retail have become over-excited by new technologies and the potential of what they call hybrid space. They see a new gadget or special effect and say, "Wow, we must have that in our place!" This tech boom will peter out once investors realize that the average amount of time that a visitor spends in a so-called interactive exhibit is less than a minute—46 seconds, or so. Interactive rooms and exhibits may stimulate us to press buttons and jump up and down, but they don't cause you to think more deeply than the non-interactive exhibit.

CC › But you see great potential with technology, particularly in terms of networked commu-nication. You imagine that networked communication will assist in living a life of action and having more vivid relationships between people. What are those possibilities?

JT › The more I look at the inflated promises made for technology, and experience the reality of its operations, the more I come to the conclusion that the simple, unmediated person-to-person experiences are what we find most valuable—indeed, are most valuable. Technology has helped bring more of those about since the telegraph and the telephone. "Let's Meet" is the number one killer application of communication technology. It's time we chilled out and had far more modest ambitions for technology. We need to think about tech like we think about water or electricity, which is: not very much. It does things for us. It provides a means to communicate. It provides a stimulus for us to meet.

CC › You often talk about technology or networked communications as giving one access to people one would not otherwise meet. You even proposed a new definition of the creative city…

JT › For me a creative city is one in which the innovation is done by regular citizens of all walks of life in ways that we designers and experts don't always anticipate. A creative city is one when you are surprised by the way people get things done in their daily lives. This is why India is always very fascinating to me as a Westerner. Every ten yards one encounters somebody doing something in a remarkable way that they don't consider being a design action or an innovation move. But they say, "I need to eat. I need to get my kids looked after. I want somebody to wash my clothes." In Bombay, they have this famous system for distributing lunch where runners take steel pots of food from the house to working family members somewhere else in the city. It's an incredible distribution system of pots of freshly made food without any computers or mobile phones or anything high tech at all. It's a handmade logistics marvel in a city where people felt it important to have that connection of somebody making the food for the partner. It's a social obligation, so people find a way to do it.

CC › You talk about India. Your series of Doors events in India suggests that India is becoming a centre of design. It seems that there's a certain conceit in the American idea that we'll only send to India those jobs that are at the bottom of the value chain. Tell me what's really happening in Bangalore, in particular, in terms of design and the kind of thinking that you and your network are doing.

JT › I try to avoid generalizing about countries where I go as a visitor. But let me give you one example of something that has a direct U.S. connection. General Electric has a campus in Bangalore with 3,000 or more researchers on it who do very high-level applied chemistry, with polymers, plastics, new materials. Here you have a huge concentration of post-graduates, PhDs—scientists from Indian universities, principally. And I was told there that teams of scientists on this campus can achieve polymer development in one-fifth the time and at much lower cost simply because of their innate cultural innovativeness of getting things done. This was not just about people sitting in call centres reading off scripts on computer screens. India is a culturally rich and complex country with a 5,000-year-old history, and it has the diversity and the cultural complexity that biologists tell us is one of the keys to evolutionary success.

Now, GE hired all those people and it's a pretty top-down, command and control company, to put it mildly. But that's a U.S.-style campus on the edge of town. The true creativity in Asia's cities is much messier. A majority of the population in many Asian cities lives in shantytowns. These make urban planners anxious and are perceived as problem areas by bureaucrats. But these areas are also sites of intense social and business innovation. They play a crucial role in keeping the city and its economy running. Indian users of technology-based devices cannot rely on formal networks of distribution, support, and maintenance. These are often incomplete, unimaginative, or unrealistically priced. They therefore turn to the temporary fixes, or "jugaads," carried out by Indian street technicians. An army of pavement-based engineers keeps engines, television tubes, compressors, and other devices working. Outside our office in Delhi, for example, hundreds of tiny workshops, plus sole traders sitting on the street, sell (and fix) the countless hardware peripherals that keep office life running. Everything from toner cartridges to USB sticks is available, and bustling basements contain an amazing array of ancient monitors, terminals, and motherboards awaiting repair. The irony is this: many bureaucrats (and property profiteers) in Asia want to get rid of these so-called suitcase entrepreneurs. But in the North, proponents of "creative cities" are desperate to foster a comparable level of small-scale industries and street-level productivity.

This takes us back to our conversation earlier about what makes a place creative. What makes a place creative is a high degree of diverse cultures with things going on that have unexpected results. The dilemma for designers and city managers and planners is that by trying to make a place creative "by design," you may end achieving the opposite! This is one reason why in Europe today *un*-designed urban areas are now understood to be sites of social innovation. Urban planners are talking about the protection of "design-free zones"—a bit like wildflower gardens, only meant to attract wild humans!

This is a terribly sensitive subject in India, too. Half or more of the inhabitants of major South Asian cities like Delhi are "illegal," for example, but they are economically active, too. (Robert Neuwirth has written a book on the subject called *Shadow City*; he also has an excellent blog on squatters and squatter cities around the world: http://squattercity.blogspot.com/).

Laurent Gutierrez and Valerie Portefaix, who founded MapOffice in Hong Kong, have published a stunning new book, *HK Lab 2*, which contains photography, maps, and writings about the Special Administrative Region and China's Pearl River Delta. When not working in the informal economy, a floating population of more than 15 million migrant workers sleeps in dormitories so small that there is no room to accumulate consumer goods. As a result, new patterns of living, consuming, and play have emerged. These challenge traditional notions.

In Europe, interest is also growing in so-called "free zones" as breeding grounds for creativity. A report from Urban Unlimited, a radical urban-planning group based in Rotterdam, also called "The Shadow City," compares free zones in Rotterdam and Brussels with other examples in Berlin, Helsinki, Vienna, and Naples. Their report promotes the idea that some areas should be left deliberately unplanned—protected, even, from the predations of politicians, social reformers, and developers. Now there's a thought: saving cities from design in the name of creativity!

CC › How does the design conversation in Bangalore differ from the conversation about design in Amsterdam or even the U.S.?

JT › What's interesting about it is that you have people who combine lifestyles that are probably 2,000 years old together with the very latest technology and network thinking. That's what's exciting.

CC › In your lecture, you say that most businesses operate in a highly localized geography. You emphasize that local conditions and trading patterns, networks, skills, culture are critical success factors. Do you think that it will continue to be the case in our networked world?

JT › This is a fascinating question. It was in a book called *Telecosm* by George Gilder, that I first read about something called "The Law of Locality." When people are deciding how much capacity to put in a telephone or a communication network they assume, based on historical patterns, that 70 to 80 percent of all traffic is local in the sense it's between one or more people within a 50-kilometre area. This does not mean that globalization or global communication flows are going to stop. But we need to keep a sense of geographical and cultural perspective. Globality is a bit like the jet stream in the weather: it's the weather that is global, big currents of air or water and climate change happen at a macro level. Don't get me wrong: the big financial flows of the global economy are real. But 97 percent of the global economy is speculation—money being played with like a game. In contrast, the great majority, I think 95 percent, of companies by number, if not by value, operate in a small local area with a limited number of clients and don't even grow very much. We're taught to believe that all healthy businesses are growing, spreading around the world, and changing all the time. But that simply doesn't accord to the reality of normal life in many places.

CC › The conference New Design Cities in Montreal asks a couple of questions such as, What is a design metropolis? How does a city become one? How do you answer those questions?

JT › By saying, I'm going to change the question! I'm not at all sure, if I were a city, that I would want to be a "design metropolis." That idea suggests an arid monoculture that contains only designers, architects, artists, and public relations consultants. I'd hate to live in or even visit such a place. Or you might end up with the problems of somewhere like Venice, a 700-year-old design city in which everything is beautiful, there are fantastic buildings, there's a fantastic level of detail in the urban environment, but the city is being literally killed by tourists. If you make your city fantastically well-designed with beautiful objects and beautiful restaurants and beautiful people everywhere, either it's going to be the same as all the other ones, in which case, it will be boring, or it will be overrun by coach loads of people coming to look at the design, in which case, you suffer that way, too. I know it's a perverse argument, and I don't argue that cities should be badly designed and unpleasant to visit, but I do think we have to be careful about this business of turning them all into perfect little places.

CC › If you were mayor of a city or civic leader and you aspired to have a creative city in the way you describe it, what would be on your "to do" list?

JT › I would ask designers to help me organize collaboration workshops about alternative futures for my town. Or maybe just have lunch on a regular basis with my fellow citizens. At this lunch, I would say, "What do we find valuable about our town that is different from the other towns that we know?" I'd focus really hard on just that simple question, "What is special about our place?" I've run such events (including lunches!) and they often deliver unexpected answers. People tell you things you didn't realize were there, or didn't necessarily appreciate. For example, I recently invited a group of cultural innovators to Breda, a medium-sized Dutch town, to discuss the topic: "What would it mean to design for fast *and* slow speeds in a High Speed Train environment?" High Speed Train travel is an advanced form of mobility, but we needed to think how we might add social and cultural value to the places we reach by High Speed Trains, which are spreading all over Europe. Our workshop touched on such topics as high-speed movement and slow encounter, mapping local knowledge, or living memory. The idea was to develop a series of specific proposals for new services that could be commissioned by local entrepreneurs and citizens. What brought the exercise to life was the participation of local people on an equal basis with the design experts.

Breda was not unique in its aspirations. Lots of cities in high-speed Europe share similar ambitions: to be the centre of a network, to be culture-based, to have a knowledge economy. What cheers me tremendously is meeting so many people who are determined to help their town develop from unimaginative transit spots to surprising places with emotional impact and economic benefits.

Creativity does not just exist among a specialized creative class or in special activities. Creativity is better thought of as an aspect of the ordinary activities of daily life, from preparing food to navigating around the city. Another example is those fishing towns I mentioned earlier. Places where people have been fishing for 150 years. That's all they know—except it's not all they know. Once you start talking, it emerges that what they know is about the sea. They know about boats. They know about building boats. They know about weather. They know about all sorts of stuff over and above just catching fish. These communities have a fantastic amount of knowledge and interesting stories to tell you. What's beginning to happen is that these towns that thought they were finished are realizing that because they are by the sea, because they have this knowledge, and because they have this culture, actually they have a rather interesting future.

I'd also ask myself: Is my city as diverse as it could be? Mixed societies seem to innovate more than homogeneous ones because new ideas and innovations emerge when people of diverse cultures interact. Some friends of mine at Comedia, a city-planning group in the UK, have launched an 18-month project called www.interculturalcity.com across cities in several countries to find out how interactions between cultures might be formed into new products, services, and styles, and how these then spread. The idea is to provide policy-makers in city development with evidence and a toolkit of techniques with which to encourage greater intercultural innovation.

By way of summarizing our discussion, let me read you a mini-manifesto I wrote as part of this debate about creative cities:

1. Creativity is not planned. It emerges. Think about planning free zones!
2. Treat us as actors, not as tenants or taxpayers.
3. Don't build edifices. Enable events.
4. Content is something you do, not something you look at, or buy.
5. All citizens are actors. All these actors can be creative.
6. Don't think "city centre." Think "network." *Combine* Landscape + Cityscape
   + Trainscape + Mediascape.
7. Don't just think "new." Re-combine that which exists.

〉〉〉

1. Blog: http://doors8delhi.doorsofperception.com/ — His new book: www.thackara.com/inthebubble/index.html ✕ 2. www.smartcityradio.com

AUTHORS
AUTEURS

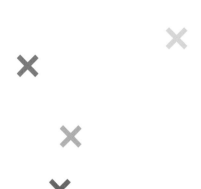

>>

FRANÇOIS BARRÉ › En 1969, François Barré fonde à Paris avec François Mathey le Centre de Création Industrielle (CCI), qu'il dirige jusqu'en 1976. Il devient ensuite rédacteur en chef de la revue *Architecture d'Aujourd'hui* et est nommé, durant cette période, conseiller du président du constructeur automobile Renault pour la politique architecturale. De 1981 à 1990, il assume les fonctions de directeur du parc de la Villette, puis celles de président de la Grande Halle de la Villette. De 1993 à 2000, François Barré a successivement été président du Centre national d'art et de culture Georges Pompidou, de l'Institut Français d'Architecture (IFA) et de la Caisse Nationale des Monuments Historiques et des Sites. De 1996 à 2000, il fut aussi délégué aux arts plastiques, puis directeur de l'architecture et du patrimoine au ministère de la Culture. Aujourd'hui, François Barré joue auprès d'élus un rôle de conseiller et d'expert pour des projets urbains et culturels. Membre de différentes associations culturelles, il est, entre autres, président des Rencontres Internationales de la Photographie d'Arles.

>>

CLAES BRITTON › Claes Britton, en partenariat avec sa conjointe Christina Sollenberg Britton, est le fondateur et éditeur du magazine international de design et de style de vie *Stockholm New*. Publié pour la première fois en 1992, pour 12 numéros à ce jour, *Stockholm New* est considéré comme l'un des magazines les plus originaux et influents des années 90 et début 2000. Il a contribué à faire de la capitale suédoise une incontournable en matière de créativité urbaine contemporaine. Claes Britton dirige aussi l'agence de publicité Britton & Britton, spécialisée en mode et en design. Experte du marketing de la Suède à l'échelle internationale, l'entreprise a notamment été responsable de la récente refonte de l'image de marque du pays. On lui doit, entre autres, la conception du microsite Sweden & Swedes, attaché au portail officiel de la Suède, Suede.se, lancé en 2002. Claes Britton est l'auteur de l'essai *Turn of the Century in Stockholm* publié en 2004.

› www.stockholmnew.com
› www.sweden.se

>>

MARC H. CHOKO › Marc H. Choko est professeur titulaire à l'École de design de l'Université du Québec à Montréal (UQAM), où il enseigne depuis 1977, et directeur de recherche à l'Institut national de la recherche scientifique (INRS), Urbanisation, culture et société, depuis 1985. Depuis 1999, il dirige aussi le Centre de design de l'UQAM, seul véritable lieu de diffusion au Canada voué à la création et à la présentation d'expositions en design industriel, design graphique, mode et architecture. Il est l'auteur de nombreux rapports, articles et ouvrages sur le développement urbain et les questions de logement, sur les scènes nationale et internationale – notamment en Chine, où il a été consultant et professeur associé de 1991 à 2000. Passionné par l'affiche, Marc H. Choko a créé plusieurs expositions, dont *L'affiche contemporaine au Québec* et *L'affiche chinoise, 1921-2001*, qui ont fait l'objet de tournées internationales. Il est également l'auteur de livres sur le design graphique, dont *L'affiche au Québec. Des origines à nos jours* (Éditions de l'Homme, 2001) et *Le design au Québec*, en collaboration avec Paul Bourassa et Gérald Baril (Éditions de l'Homme, 2003).

› www.unites.uqam.ca/design
› www.centrededesign.uqam.ca

>>

FRANÇOIS BARRÉ > In 1969, François Barré and François Mathey founded in Paris the Centre de Création Industrielle (CCI), which Barré directed until 1976. He went on to become editor-in-chief of the magazine *Architecture d'Aujourd'hui* and, during the same period, was appointed advisor on architectural policy to the president of Renault. From 1981 to 1990, he was director of Villette Park and, subsequently, president of the Grande Halle de la Villette. He was appointed a delegate for the arts in 1990 and president of the Centre national d'art et de culture Georges Pompidou in 1993. He served as president of the Institut Français d'Architecture (IFA) from 1996 to 1998 and of the Caisse Nationale des Monuments Historiques et des Sites from 1997 to 2000. He also served as director of architecture and heritage with the French Ministry of Culture from 1996 to 2000. Today, Mr. Barré works as a consultant and expert on urban and cultural issues. A member of various cultural associations, he is currently the president of the international photography exhibition of Arles.

CLAES BRITTON > Claes Britton is the founding editor-in-chief/publisher of the award-winning international fashion, design, and lifestyle magazine *Stockholm New*, in partnership with his wife Christina Sollenberg Britton. First published in 1992, the magazine has published twelve issues to date, becoming one of the most original and influential image magazines of the 1990s and early 2000s. It is also acknowledged as a key contributor to the innovative and successful unofficial marketing of Stockholm and Sweden as one of the most dynamic international scenes for contemporary urban creativity. Claes Britton also operates the advertising and media agency Britton & Britton, specializing in commercial and non-commercial commissions for Swedish and international fashion and design clients, as well as in the international marketing and imaging of official Stockholm and Sweden. Britton & Britton has been the leading creative team behind the recent "re-branding" of Sweden in a number of campaigns, including the theme-site "Sweden & Swedes" under Sweden's official web-portal Sweden.se, launched in 2002. Britton is also an author; he published his first major book in 2004, *Turn of the Century in Stockholm*, a non-fiction novel.

> **www.stockholmnew.com**

> **www.sweden.se**

MARC H. CHOKO > Marc H. Choko is a full professor with the School of Design at the Université du Québec à Montréal, where he has been teaching since 1977, and director of research into urbanization, culture, and society at the Institut national de la recherche scientifique (INRS), since 1985. He has directed the Design Centre of the Université du Québec à Montréal since 1989. The centre, founded in 1981, is the only one of its kind in Canada devoted to producing and hosting exhibitions on industrial and graphic design, fashion and architecture. He has numerous reports, articles, and studies on urban development and housing to his credit looking at both the national and international scene – particularly in China, where he worked as a consultant and associate professor from 1991 to 2000. He is a great fan of poster art, and has put together a number of exhibitions, including one on posters in contemporary Quebec and another on posters in China from 1921 to 2001, both of which toured internationally. He has written several books on graphic design, the most recent ones being *L'affiche au Québec. Des origines à nos jours* (Éditions de l'Homme, 2001) and *Le design au Québec*, in collaboration with Paul Bourassa and Gérald Baril (Éditions de l'Homme, 2003).

> **www.unites.uqam.ca/design**

> **www.centrededesign.uqam.ca**

CAROL COLETTA › Animatrice et productrice de l'émission *Smart City* diffusée sur la chaîne nationale américaine de radio publique, Carol Coletta met à profit son expérience en développement urbain pour débattre avec les plus grands experts de la ville. *Smart City* constitue une source d'information intarissable qui aide élus, promoteurs, chercheurs, urbanistes et citoyens à repenser leur ville. Carol Coletta contribue depuis plus de 30 ans à la croissance des villes au moyen de stratégies novatrices. Elle est notamment chef de la direction de CEOs for Cities, un regroupement américain non partisan dont la mission est de soutenir les villes dans leur développement économique et urbain.
› **www.smartcityradio.com**

JOSYANE FRANC › Josyane Franc est chargée des relations publiques et internationales de l'École Régionale des Beaux-arts de Saint-Étienne depuis 1989. Elle s'investit dans la promotion de l'École par l'organisation d'expositions et de séminaires internationaux, la coordination de projets européens, le développement de relations avec les entreprises et la diffusion de la revue de design *Azimuts*. Elle est aussi responsable de la mise en place d'un réseau international d'échanges étudiants avec 40 établissements dans le monde. Depuis la création en 1998 de la Biennale Internationale Design Saint-Étienne, Josyane Franc, membre de l'équipe fondatrice, participe à son organisation en tant que responsable des communications, des relations de presse et du suivi international. Elle fait également partie de l'équipe qui a mis sur pied le projet Commerce Design Saint-Étienne en partenariat avec la Ville de Montréal.
› **www.artschool-st-etienne.com**

MARIE-JOSÉE LACROIX › Commissaire au design au Service de la mise en valeur du territoire et du patrimoine de la Ville de Montréal, Marie-Josée Lacroix est diplômée en design de l'environnement de l'Université du Québec à Montréal et détient une maîtrise en sciences de l'information, spécialisée en design et en architecture, des universités McGill (Montréal) et Columbia (New York). Depuis son entrée en fonction en 1991, on lui doit plusieurs initiatives de promotion du design, dont le concours Commerce Design Montréal. Créé pour inciter les commerçants à investir dans la qualité de l'aménagement de leur établissement avec l'aide d'un designer ou d'un architecte qualifié, ce concept inédit est aujourd'hui repris par d'autres villes européennes et nord-américaines. Protagoniste de la commande publique en design, Marie-Josée Lacroix agit aussi comme conseillère auprès de divers ministères et institutions sur les scènes canadienne et québécoise afin de stimuler l'innovation en design dans le cadre des projets d'équipement public et privé. Elle a collaboré bénévolement, de 1998 à 2003, au Festival international de Jardins de Métis, dont elle est cofondatrice. Elle est la principale instigatrice du colloque Nouvelles villes de design.
› **www.commercedesignmontreal.com**
› **www.ville.montreal.qc.ca**

DENIS LEMIEUX › Formé en tant qu'architecte, Denis Lemieux est aujourd'hui responsable du dossier de l'architecture au Ministère de la Culture et des Communications du Québec, où il opère depuis 1988. Il a contribué au développement de concours d'architecture et a participé à des réflexions et à des activités d'intérêt public dans les domaines de l'architecture, du design et du paysage (colloques, missions, expositions). Il a été co-fondateur et directeur du Festival international de jardins de Métis qui a connu, dès sa première édition, un succès public et médiatique exceptionnel, s'est mérité de nombreux prix d'excellence et a contribué de manière significative à l'avancement de la création contemporaine en architecture, design et paysage.

〉〉〉

CAROL COLETTA 〉 Carol Coletta has been pioneering innovative strategies to improve cities for thirty years. As host and producer of the award-winning U.S. public radio program *Smart City*, Carol draws on her extensive experience in city-building to engage in provocative conversations with the world's smartest thinkers on urban life. *Smart City* provides a wealth of knowledge about trends and standard-setting programs that help citizens, planners, elected officials, developers, and researchers to change their cities. As president and CEO of CEOs for Cities, Carol heads a national, non-partisan alliance of cross-sector urban leaders who work to strengthen the abilities of cities to compete in the global economy.

〉 www.smartcityradio.com

〉〉〉

JOSYANE FRANC 〉 Josyane Franc has served as co-ordinator of public and international relations at the École des Beaux-Arts de Saint-Étienne since 1989. She promotes this school of fine arts by organizing international exhibitions and seminars, co-ordinating European projects, developing contacts and relationships with the private sector, and publishing the design magazine *Azimuts*. She is also responsible for setting up an international network that arranges student exchanges among forty institutions around the world. Since helping to found the Biennale Internationale Design Saint-Étienne in 1998, Josyane Franc has handled communications, press relations, and international follow-up for the event. She is also part of the team that established the Commerce Design Saint-Étienne contest in partnership with the city of Montreal.

〉 www.artschool-st-etienne.com

〉〉〉

MARIE-JOSÉE LACROIX 〉 Marie-Josée Lacroix, design commissioner with the Business Development Branch of the city of Montreal, holds a degree in environmental design from the Université du Québec à Montréal (UQÀM) and a master's in information science, specializing in design and architecture, from McGill University (Montreal) and Columbia University (New York). After taking up her position with the city of Montreal in 1991, she initiated the Commerce Design Montréal contest that was adopted in 2003 by the city of Saint-Étienne, in France, and the Times Square District of New York. Marie-Josée Lacroix works to encourage public commissions of design work, and also advises a number of federal and provincial government departments and institutions on ways to foster innovative design in major public projects. From 1998 to 2003, on a volunteer basis, she helped organize the International Garden Festival at the Reford Gardens, of which she was also a co-founder. In 2004, UQÀM presented her with its Prix Reconnaissance de la Famille des Arts.

〉 www.commercedesignmontreal.com
〉 www.ville.montreal.qc.ca

〉〉〉

DENIS LEMIEUX 〉 Trained as an architect Denis Lemieux is now responsible for architecture at the Quebec Department of Culture and Communications, where he works since 1988. He has contributed to the promotion of architecture competitions and has taken part in analyses and public-interest activities in the fields of architecture, design and landscaping (seminars, special missions, exhibitions, etc.). He was the co-founder and director of the Métis International Garden Festival, which has enjoyed exceptional public and media success right from the start, and over the years has won many awards for excellence and made a significant contribution to the development of contemporary creativity in architecture, design and landscaping.

〉〉〉

〉〉〉

DR STUART MACDONALD 〉 Stuart MacDonald est directeur du Lighthouse, le centre national d'architecture et de design d'Écosse. Cette institution organise chaque année un grand nombre d'événements, expositions, projets éducatifs, conférences et activités interentreprises, occupant ainsi une position centrale dans la promotion des politiques architecturales écossaises et un rôle de précurseur en design. Après des études en beaux-arts à la Gray's School of Art et un Ph. D. à l'École d'architecture de l'Université de Liverpool, Stuart MacDonald a été professeur, puis conseiller en éducation de la région économique de Glasgow. Il a ensuite fait partie de l'organisation du Glasgow's 1996 International Festival of Design et du Glasgow 1999 UK City of Architecture and Design Festival. Ancien observateur externe à l'Université de Wales à Cardiff et à la Glasgow School of Art, il est aujourd'hui observateur externe à l'Université de Dundee. Stuart MacDonald participe à de nombreux comités et groupes de travail sur l'art, l'architecture, le design, l'éducation et le patrimoine. Il a récemment été nommé Honorary Fellow par le Royal Institute of British Architects.
〉 **www.thelighthouse.co.uk**

〉〉〉

AUGUSTA REGINA MOURA GUEDES 〉 Augusta Regina Moura Guedes est présidente d'Experimenta, un centre culturel de Lisbonne voué à la promotion du design, qu'elle a créé en 1998. Elle est également cofondatrice de la biennale ExperimentaDesign de Lisbonne, qu'elle dirige depuis 2002. Augusta Regina Moura Guedes est diplômée en architecture de l'Université Técnica de Lisbonne. Elle a amorcé sa carrière de designer en 1992 en lançant le studio Elementos Combinados. Depuis, elle a dessiné, développé et produit plusieurs lignes de meubles et contribué à de nombreux projets en design d'intérieur. Elle est membre du conseil d'administration de la collection Francisco Capelo, propriété de l'Hôtel de ville de Lisbonne, depuis 2003, et administratrice de la Fondation du Centre culturel de Belém depuis 2004. Le gouvernement français lui a attribué le titre honorifique de Chevalier de l'Ordre des Arts et des Lettres en 2005.
〉 **www.experimentadesign.pt**

〉〉〉

SASKIA SASSEN 〉 Saskia Sassen est professeur de sociologie à l'Université de Chicago et professeur invité de sciences économiques à la London School of Economics. Elle a terminé pour l'UNESCO une étude de cinq ans sur les solutions humaines durables pour laquelle elle était entourée de chercheurs et d'activistes d'une trentaine de pays. Ses propos ont été publiés dans le *Herald Tribune*, le *Die Zeit*, *Le e Monde Diplomatique*, le *Vanguardia*, le *Guardian* et le *New York Times*. Elle est l'auteure de plusieurs livres dont *Global Networks, Linked Cities* (Routledge, 2002), *Digital Formations: IT and New Architectures in The Global Realm*, *The Global City* et *Denationalization : Territory, Authority and Rights in a Global Digital Age* (tous chez Princeton University Press). Aux États-Unis, Saskia Sassen est membre du Council on Foreign Relations, de la National Academy of Sciences Panel on Cities et de la Chair of the Information Technology and International Cooperation Committee of the Social Science Research Council.

〉〉〉

DR. STUART MACDONALD › Stuart MacDonald studied fine art at Gray's School of Art and later completed a PhD at the Architecture School of the University of Liverpool. After an early career as a teacher, he worked for Strathclyde, Glasgow's economic region as a senior education adviser, before becoming involved in Glasgow's 1996 International Festival of Design and the Glasgow 1999 UK City of Architecture and Design Festival. He joined The Lighthouse, Scotland's National Centre for Architecture, Design and the City, as its first director in 1998 prior to its opening in 1999. The Lighthouse is central to the promotion of Scotland's architecture policy and is the country's lead body on design. Under Stuart MacDonald's leadership, it operates a wide-ranging program of exhibitions, events, educational projects, conferences, and business to business activities targeted on a very broad audience. Stuart MacDonald has served on numerous national and international bodies, committees, and working groups concerned with art, architecture, design, education, and heritage. He is currently an external examiner at the University of Dundee and has been an external examiner at the Glasgow School of Art and De Montfort University and The University of Wales in Cardiff. He was recently made an Honourary Fellow of the Royal Institute of British Architects.

› www.thelighthouse.co.uk

AUGUSTA REGINA MOURA GUEDES › Augusta Regina Moura Guedes started working as a designer in 1992, when she founded Elementos Combinados design studio. She has since designed, developed, and produced several lines of furniture, as well as working in interior design. Founder of Experimenta – Lisbon's cultural association aimed at promoting design, created in 1998 – she is also co-responsible and co-author of the ExperimentaDesign Lisbon Biennale, which she has been engaged in developing, managing, programming, and directing. She works as well as a curator in the design field. As Experimenta chairman, she is responsible for all the activities of the association, and she has been the director of the biennale ExperimentaDesign since 2002. She is also a member of the administration board of Francisco Capelo's Design Collection, owned by Lisbon City Hall, since 2003. She was appointed by the Portuguese government to the position of administrator of the Centro Cultural de Belém Foundation in November of 2004. She was distinguished in 2005 by the French government with the honorific title of Chevalier de l'Ordre des Arts et des Lettres.

› www.experimentadesign.pt

SASKIA SASSEN › Saskia Sassen is the Ralph Lewis Professor of Sociology at the University of Chicago, and Centennial Visiting Professor at the London School of Economics. She has also just completed for UNESCO a five-year project on sustainable human settlement for which she set up a network of researchers and activists in over thirty countries. Her comments have appeared in the International *Herald Tribune*, *Die Zeit*, *Le Monde Diplomatique*, *Vanguardia*, *The Guardian*, *The New York Times*, among others. Her books include *Global Networks, Linked Cities* (Routledge, 2002), the co-edited *Digital Formations: IT and New Architectures in the Global Realm*, *The Global City* and the forthcoming *Denationalization: Territory, Authority and Rights in a Global Digital Age* (all Princeton University Press). Saskia Sassen is a member of the Council on Foreign Relations, a member of the National Academy of Sciences Panel on Cities, and chair of the Information Technology and International Cooperation Committee of the Social Science Research Council (USA).

〉〉

JOHN THACKARA 〉 John Thackara est directeur de Doors of Perception, une communauté de savoir qui se consacre aux questions de processus d'innovation et de design située à Amsterdam et à Bangalore. Simple colloque en 1993, l'événement est aujourd'hui un réseau international qui met en communication des designers visionnaires et des penseurs des quatre coins de la planète. En plus d'organiser des conférences et de proposer un site Web, Doors élabore, par une approche collaborative, des solutions en technologies de la communication adaptées à des clients variés : hôpitaux, universités, aéroports, etc.. Ancien journaliste et ex-éditeur, John Thackara a été le premier directeur du Netherlands Design Institute (1993-1999). Il est membre de Virtual Platform, un comité qui conseille le gouvernement néerlandais en matière de politiques culturelles et d'innovation ; il est membre du comité scientifique de l'Interactive Institute de Suède ; il fait partie de plusieurs groupes d'experts qui conseillent la Commission européenne sur les questions liées à l'innovation ; et il a été membre du comité de pilotage de l'Interaction Design Institute Ivrea, en Italie (un centre de recherche commandité par Telecom Italia et le groupe Olivetti), et membre du comité de coordination du projet Vision building de Convivio, le réseau européen consacré au «social computing».
〉 **www.thackara.com**
〉 **www.doorsofperception.com**

〉〉

TIM TOMPKINS 〉 Depuis 2002, Tim Tompkins est président du Times Square Alliance (anciennement Times Square Business Improvement District). Il a fondé et dirigé l'association Partnerships for Parks, un partenariat privé-public travaillant à embellir les parcs de New York. L'association a reçu, en 2000, un prix Innovations in American Government de la fondation Ford et de la JFK School of Government. Il a aussi cofondé et codirigé Parks 2001, une campagne de financement pour les parcs de New York. À la fin des années 80, Tim Tompkins a travaillé pour la Charter Revision Commission de New York en tant qu'adjoint particulier du directeur général de la commission, alors présidée par Frederick A. O. Shwarz Jr. Il a été rédacteur en chef du *Mexico City News* et directeur du 42nd Street Project à la corporation du développement économique de la ville de New York. Tim Tompkins détient un diplôme de troisième cycle de l'Université Yale et un MBA de la Wharton School de l'Université de Pennsylvanie.
〉 **www.timessquarenyc.org**

〉〉

DORIAN VAN DER BREMPT 〉 Dorian Van Der Brempt a étudié en philologie romane, en tourisme et en histoire de l'art, avant de diriger des agences de voyages et des hôtels en Belgique, au Pays-Bas et en Espagne. En 1980, sa rencontre avec Axel Enthoven marque le début de sa carrière en design. Il fonde Enthoven Associates Italia, à Padoue, en 1995, et occupe le poste d'administrateur délégué du bureau à Anvers jusqu'en 1999. Il a été commissaire de l'exposition Drawing The Film à la Cinémathèque québécoise, à Montréal, en 1987, et il a participé au projet New Math Gallery, à New York, en 1984. Passionné du livre, il est l'auteur de *Monologues* avec *Jan Hoet* (Van Halewyck, 1987) et directeur de Boek.be, un organisme à but non lucratif qui réunit les éditeurs et libraires flamands. Depuis 1999, il enseigne à la Design Academy d'Eindhoven aux Pays Bas. Il est aussi membre du conseil d'administration d'Ultima Vez, la compagnie de danse de Wim Vandekeybus. Conseiller en lettres, arts plastiques, architecture et design du ministre flamand de la Culture jusqu'en juin 2004, il a été président d'Antwerp Book Capital 2004.

〉〉

JOHN THACKARA › John Thackara is the director of Doors of Perception, a design futures network with offices in Amsterdam and Bangalore. Founded as a conference in 1993, Doors now connects together a worldwide network of visionary designers, thinkers, and grassroots innovators. In addition to its conferences and an award-winning Web site, Doors develops connectivity scenarios for clients; these currently include an airport, a university, and a children's hospital. A former journalist and publisher, Thackara was the first director (1993–99) of the Netherlands Design Institute. He is a member of Virtual Platform, a body which advises the Dutch government on cultural and innovation policy; he was on the start-up Steering Committee of Interaction Design Institute Ivrea, in Italy (a post-graduate research centre sponsored by Telecom Italia and Olivetti); he is on the Scientific Committee of the Interactive Institute in Sweden; he sits on expert groups advising the European Commission in its innovation policy; and he was on the co-ordinating group, responsible for vision building, in Convivio – the new European Union network for social computing.

› **www.thackara.com**

› **www.doorsofperception.com**

TIM TOMPKINS › Tim Tompkins has been the president of the Times Square Alliance (formerly the Times Square Business Improvement District) since mid-February 2002. Prior to that he was the founder and director of Partnerships for Parks, a public-private partnership that works to improve neighbourhood parks in New York City. In 2000, Partnerships won an Innovations in American Government Award from the Ford Foundation and the JFK School of Government. Tompkins was also the co-founder and co-campaign manager of Parks 2001, a citywide campaign to advocate for increased funding for New York City parks. In the late eighties, Tim Tompkins worked for the New York City Charter Revision Commission, and was then the special assistant to the executive director of the Charter Commission, chaired by Frederick A.O. Schwarz, Jr. He was the national editor at the *Mexico City News*, and later served as senior project manager for the 42nd Street Project at the New York City Economic Development Corporation. He has an undergraduate degree from Yale and an M.B.A. from Wharton.

› **www.timessquarenyc.org**

DORIAN VAN DER BREMP › Dorian Van Der Brempt did his studies in Romance philology, tourism, and art history, before directing travel agencies and hotels in Belgium, the Netherlands, and Spain from 1973 to 1985. In 1980, a meeting with Axel Enthoven started him on a long voyage into the field of design. He founded Enthoven Associates Italia in Padua in 1995 and worked as executive director of Design Enthoven Associates in Antwerp until 1999. He has been involved in numerous projects that have taken him to Europe, Asia, and North America. He curated the exhibition Drawing the Film at the Cinémathèque québécoise in Montreal in 1987 and took part in the New Math project at a New York Art Gallery in 1984. He directs Boek.be, a non-profit organization for Flemish publishers and booksellers, and published, in 1987, *Monologues with Jan Hoet* (Van Halewyck). Advisor on arts, letters, architecture, and design to the Flemish Minister of Culture until June 2004, he was president of Antwerp Book Capital 2004. He has taught at the Eindhoven Design Academy in the Netherlands since 1999. He is also a member of the board of Ultima Vez, the dance company headed by Wim Vandekeybus.

ENGLISH TRANSLA- TION

ANTWERP
DESIGN PORTRAIT
〉〉〉

POPULATION

Antwerp, with a population of 500,000, is located in the Greater Antwerp region, which has almost one million residents.

YEAR OF FOUNDATION AND IMPORTANT EVENTS

The city was founded during the Roman era, but it was not until the late twelfth century that it was protected by a wall. In the sixteenth century, Antwerp was a large city. With its port and strategic location, it had an obvious economic importance. ✕ Antwerp has always been a city of trade. Its port, 80 km from the North Sea, was essential to economic development. In the sixteenth century, Antwerp was one of the main economic and financial centres in Europe. Imports of English textiles and trade in German metal products and Portuguese spices were the port's main activities. Today, Antwerp is home to one of the three largest container ports in the world. The printer Christophe Plantin, whose mansion is now a museum open to the public, was a major promoter of the diffusion of ideas. The Belgian Congo exported a range of new and popular products: cotton, coffee, wood, and rubber. Petrochemicals, chemicals, and diamonds were the industrial stakes in Belgium's rise during the twentieth century. Creativity, particularly in fashion, is the most recently developed sector in Antwerp. ✕ Although it historically owes its prosperity to its port, the city's commercial activities have always been combined with cultural energy, as exemplified by Rubens, Jordaens, and Van Dyck. Antwerp has always had a reputation for being a city of pleasures, a city that likes to party. ✕ The Spanish pillaged Antwerp in 1576. The city surrendered and the Escaut, its river, was closed. Napoleon subsequently discovered its strategic value and made it a war port. In 1920, Antwerp hosted the seventh Olympic Games of the modern era. A few years later, a world fair expressed hope for the future. In 1945, more than one million European Jews boarded ships bound for North America from the port of Antwerp.

NUMBER OF DESIGNERS

Thanks to the city's excellent Fashion Academy, there are some one hundred fashion designers and ten times as many suppliers. The Higher Institute for Architectural Sciences has a solid reputation (see http://adsl.ontwerpwetenschappen.be/). ✕ A number of architectural offices have set up shop in Antwerp. This creative sector contains between 1,200 and 1,500 people.

FAMOUS DESIGNERS

There are several important designers on the sites mentioned below. One could say that the first "designer" was Rubens, for he was not only a Baroque painter but also a consultant to, and a decorator for, royalty. Today's Antwerp has a reputation that is linked mainly to fashion. Dries van Noten, Ann de Meulemeester, Walter van Beirendonck, Véronique Branquino, Raf Simons, and many others have become the city's ambassadors. One Antwerp "notable," Axel Vervoort, is the master of good taste in interior design—an antique dealer who entertains and an entertainer who decorates.

MAIN DESIGN EVENTS

Antwerp does not have, properly speaking, repeated and concerted design initiatives. In September, there is a "Laundry Day," when boutiques in the Kammenstraat (fashion design district) take over the street. In recent years, there have been "Design Weekends," but they have not met with the anticipated success. ✕ Although this is probably not a phenomenon unique to Antwerp, most design initiatives in the city are in private hands, rather than arising from a long-term policy, and they do not really share a common denominator. Given the competitive spirit and natural mistrust of Flemish designers, design is less animated by a group dynamic than it is by informal meetings and the absence of a precise plan. In light of design guerrilla warfare, chance, and necessity, the management of each initiative is not easy. × Recent events that might be repeated are Open Studios (September), Vitrine septembre, Vizo Ladders Zat (summer), and the autumn "Laundry Day."

INSTITUTIONS

MoMu (www.momu.be) is an excellent fashion museum. Every year it offers different thematic exhibitions. Its restoration workshop and fashion library are exceptional. The Flanders Fashion Institute (www.ffi.be) shares space with MoMu and the Fashion Academy. × The Diamond Museum (www.diamantmuseum.be) regularly offers displays of work by the city's jewellers. × Betet Skara is a design and weaving studio that is reviving Assyrian craft weaving. This initiative is supported by a socio-economic program (www.betetskara.com).

DESIGN SCHOOLS AND PROGRAMS

A master's degree in management is offered that focuses on the cultural industries and fashion (www.uams.be). This new master's program (to be launched in October 2006) is organized by the Universiteit Antwerpen Management School and is intended to train managers in fashion and design. The fashion sector supports this initiative because "Antwerp, Fashion City" is more representative and more spectacular these days than "Antwerp, Design City." × The Fashion Academy is an important part of an institute of higher learning that we do not call a "university" (the word "university" provoked a long and emotional debate over semantics) (www.academieantwerpen.ha.be/modeontwerpen). Within this Hogeschool are a number of programs grouped under the rubric "Creative Sciences" (Ontwerpwetenschappen). There are bachelor's programs in fashion, architecture, industrial design, and graphic design (www.ontwerpwetenschappen.ha.be/modeontwerpen).

DESIGN STRATEGIES

There is no specific design strategy. The province of Antwerp is perhaps the main promoter of design. MoMu, the Kasteel Rivierenhof, and the Diamond Museum have local initiatives. The City of Antwerp is very active on the communications level.

DESIGN PORTRAIT

INFORMATION PROVIDED BY DORIAN VAN DER BREMPT
> Professor, Eindhoven Design Academy

PATRICK JANSSES
MP AND MAYOR OF THE CITY OF ANTWERP SINCE 2003

>>>

Mr. Gérald Tremblay, Mayor of Montreal
Mr. Michel Thiollière, Senator and Mayor of Saint-Étienne

Antwerp, March 13, 2005

Dear Sirs:
I was pleased and grateful to learn about the interest that you have expressed in the city of Antwerp. I was happy to participate in the debate that you organized, during which I met excellent interlocutors from Montreal, New York, Lisbon, Saint-Etienne, and Glasgow. × Antwerp has always welcomed creative people and has often been the cradle of innovative projects, both political and cultural. The port of Antwerp is probably the metaphor for the generosity and tolerance of a city whose residents are known for having a particular personality ("together against the world"). Perhaps this trait comes from the Spanish era, when we inherited the title "Sinjoren" (Lords). × Today, Antwerp is a medium-sized city where 140 nationalities cohabit—newcomers, newborns, and the less young. I manage and organize this mélange of cultures. × The visual arts, theatre, and literature have always thrived in Antwerp.

Like all successful cities, Antwerp has always been liked, detested, and full of visitors. ✕ Antwerp is now a fashion capital, and I believe that this success is all the more valuable because it is not political. Aside from an excellent fashion department at the Academy of Fine Arts, it was the "Antwerp Six," the pioneers of the city's fashion movement in the 1980s, who put the city on the map. Their genius and hard work gained us the reputation that we enjoy today. ✕ One important initiative by the city was the creation of the Winkelhaak Design Centre (the Square). In this facility, young graduates of the schools of industrial and graphic design can find a first studio to rent at a reasonable price. ✕ I believe that making workspaces, exhibitions, and presentations available is very important for young creative artists and for the city. Antwerp is almost unaffordable by the square metre. It is essential that we act to retain this artistic presence—the symbol of a creative city. ✕ Antwerp has an impressive cultural life. The cultural centre of Flanders, it was named a world capital of books by UNESCO in 2004—a title that was awarded to Montreal the following year! Antwerp also has great tourist attractions. The museums and galleries, the theatre, the fashion designers and boutiques, and the fine dining that everyone enjoys offer a wealth of choice and quality. ✕ I am proud of the title Antwerp Design City. I believe it is deserved because the city has achieved this distinction with the eclectic range of talents that we have here, matching the many strata that are covered by the word "design." Antwerp offers many readings, which is why it is interesting to discover it gradually, from one angle, then another, and finally to see it in its totality. ✕ The truth is, Antwerp does not have a specific design policy. Good schools have educated good designers. The city tries to communicate with all of its citizens, and designers play and will continue to play their role in this enterprise. ✕ I invite you all to visit Antwerp, the city whose ambition is always to surprise, to tell a new story each time you come. ✕
Best regards

ANTWERP, NEW DESIGN CITY?

BY DORIAN VAN DER BREMPT
> **Professor, Eindhoven Design Academy, the Netherlands**

〉〉〉

Antwerp is a city in fashion and a city of fashion. In 2004, a Newsweek article listed Antwerp as one of the ten cities of cultural influence. I would say, rather, that it is one of the ten most surprising cities of the moment. I don't know exactly what the expression "design city" means. If this colloquium is about "new design cities," as opposed to "old design cities," the latter should have a special place in history. ✕ Therefore, I decided to take a look back and ask, What would an old design city look like? A short stroll through the history of Europe took me to what I would dare to call the first design cities. The Andalusian cities of the fourteenth and fifteenth centuries, even given their great age, were design cities in the modern sense of the term. ✕ The quality of life in Toledo, Cordoba, and Granada was, for the times, very refined and highly sensual. Well-chosen materials were combined with construction techniques that were propitious to fresh breezes and cool water in a region of tropical summers—technologies that promoted the highest aesthetics and hedonism. Architecture and the design of domestic objects in Andalusia combined Eastern and Western elements and juxtaposed a Moslem aesthetic against Christian imagery. Such architecture and design probably gave rise to the first multicultural communities—"multicultural" not in the sense of assimilation but in the sense of respect for the values and standards of all citizens. Long before Andalusia, Mesopotamia also had a cultural mix that puts the current barbarism in an even sadder perspective. Today, Antwerp is a city where more than 120 nationalities cohabit. This encounter between cultures, religions, and customs is not always easy, but it is a perpetual challenge. ✕ The main difference between Andalusia in the fourteenth and fifteenth centuries and, for example, the United States today is this: the advisors to the Andalusian kings were poets, artists, and scholars; at Bush's side are business people who do not understand or recognize the general interest. And this suggests a first definition or direction: a design city was and will be a city in which the general interest has a value that is equal to, or greater than, private interests. ✕ Design can be understood as a certain sensibility applied to both the container and the content of things. Well-designed public furniture is an invitation to encounter and dialogue. Design may have a political dimension. There are classic examples in the politics of our era. Kennedy and Mitterrand were two earlier heads of state noted for having received advice from designers—the former from Raymond Loewy and the latter from Starck. ✕ In my country, Flanders, there are cities that correspond to the idea of "old design cities." Bruges, Gand, and Antwerp were design cities from the fourteenth to the nineteenth century, before the expression "design city"—and even the word "design"—were defined as they are today. ✕ Not only was Rubens a painter and diplomat, but he was also a master of commercial ceremonies and gracious living. In this capacity, he decorated the palaces of kings and nobles, as well as the residences of the very wealthy traders who were already preparing to replace them. In today's Antwerp, memory and tradition mix with and inspire contemporary creativity. The city's Notre-Dame Cathedral receives 200,000 visitors per year who come to see, among other things, Rubens's Descent from the Cross. ✕ In the early twenty-first century, the new squires of Antwerp are Axel Vervoort, a master decorator and antique dealer who decorates both the houses of princes and princesses and those of the English pop musicians who move to Tuscany; Jan Fabre, visual artist, theatre director, and playwright; and Dries Van Noten, the famous fashion designer. As proof of their status, these three artists have acquired castles to live in. When nobility loses its fortune, "predatory" artists take its place. It is probably the first time in history that certain artists, creative people, and those who I call the great entertainers (athletes, pop musicians, movie actors) are reaping the extreme rewards generated by the capitalist system. Creativity—or, at least, a certain kind of creativity—has never been as profitable as it was in 2004. Since an ex-circus performer recently had china designed for his private jet, we can see this logic at work also in Quebec. The Cirque du Soleil, which is in Antwerp at this moment, proves that design is also a vector of export for cities. ✕ Explosive expansion in certain forms of commercial innovation does not occur without risks, of course. Oscar Wilde warned us that the day would come when we would know the price of everything and the value of nothing. Price defines the limit of value. When we speak of design, we speak of value and not of price. Design shopping is a major tourist attraction in Antwerp. The fashion boutiques around MoMu and the Fashion Museum are worth visiting. The specialized bookstore, Copyright, located inside the MoMu, offers an exceptional selection.

〉〉〉

In discussing the value called design, I would like to propose some ideas. First, design is a political act. Today's design city is a city that takes care of itself, that keeps up appearances. It's a city that plays sports, takes a shower, applies a delicate scent, and dresses itself with all the discreet charm of the bourgeoisie. It's a city that likes to entertain and has a reputation for well-organized generosity. A design city is a city that issues invitations and likes to be surrounded by friends. Packaging the city, outfitting it to be both beautiful and practical, both pleasant and safe, both friendly and resolute, are decisions of politics and of design policy. Public space, public transit, cultural offerings, and educational and health-care services (and the communication between all these good things and the inhabitants) are areas in which a proper and judicious dose of design can make a difference. It is up to politicians to understand this. It is up to us to explain to them that a poor choice of lighting fixtures is as costly as a good choice, that well-thought-out and well-made street furniture is no more expensive than the banal variant. The public sector, from the local to the national level, is the greatest consumer of goods and services. It goes without saying that effective discipline and methodology in public commissions are a guarantee that the quality of our human biotope, too often urban, will be improved. × This is why I have cautiously suggested that we envisage the creation of a "master designer" in city administration. Today, everyone understands that a city has the right to an administration that concentrates on architecture and urban planning, but few politicians consider the creation and development of products sufficiently important. To achieve the creation of big brother "Architecture," little sister "Design" must be manifest and influential. × If "design city" is synonymous with "high-quality city," it is obvious that within a few years we will see a new university program that will offer a "master of public design" degree. Designers whose classical training is combined with social sciences will be able to contribute to the creation of products and services whose purpose it is to serve the general interest of the city as much as the user's private interest. As an aside, I would say that the public designer takes care of users while the private designer takes care of consumers.

〉〉〉

Design is the melding of good taste and good sense. A design intervention should be a "normal" intervention. It does not mean an artificial search for visibility at any price. Good design interventions are often discreet. The intelligent choice of materials is as important as the choice of shapes. Excess is allowed from time to time. When, in 1935, Baron Louis Empain imported steel window frames from Belgium to be installed in the shopping centre that he built in Sainte Marguerite du Lac Masson (said to be the first of its kind in North America), it certainly made news in his home country. But his decision was, above all, a design intervention. Certainly, it was a bit more "good taste" than "good sense"; in this family of extravagant entrepreneurs and decision makers worthy of the title, a certain dose of wild imagination was permitted. We mustn't forget that Baron Empain was also the inventor of "snow tourism." × Let's talk about Antwerp. Thanks to fashion and to the Antwerp Academy, our city is seen today as a design city. Twenty years ago, six young designers, all in their final year of studies, combined all the qualities required to put Antwerp on the design map. And it was really no coincidence: each was a hard worker, very ambitious, very different from the others, and had an excellent mix of pragmatism and flair. Politicians were quickly made aware of their existence, and soon afterward the Flanders Fashion Institute was created. × The mandate of the Flanders Fashion Institute, which is housed in the MoMu, is to combine the cultural and the commercial. Fashion is one of the most fickle sectors of creativity. Twice a year, distributors gather to pronounce, in a few moments, the judgments that will decide the next six months or year for designers. This high tension, and the obligation to succeed to survive, is one of the "third rails" of this cultural industry. × I tell you this as if it's coincidence or sheer luck, because I am convinced that luck is as important as necessity. I believe that one can stimulate, encourage, and facilitate creativity or design, but the first sign must come from those who create. It is they who must step forward and convince political, financial, and commercial circles that an opportunity is presenting itself. Dries van Noten is probably the most remarkable fashion designer of his generation; he is continuing a family tradition and adding a new dimension. The international recognition of van Noten and others has given Antwerp a new reputation as a design city.

〉〉〉

Design is sometimes the cultural expression of the nouveau riche, the false code of the avant-garde bourgeoisie. Fifteen years ago, a small New York theatre company transformed Molière's Bourgeois Gentilhomme into an avant-garde maniac who surrounded himself with "design" objects, visited conceptual-art exhibitions (which he didn't like), and lived in a house that pleased only the architect and decorators who had advised the poor gentleman. In Houston, I saw well-designed buildings with elegant silhouettes. Concrete, steel, and glass stretched in a filigree to the horizon. But these pearls of architecture were occupied by gentlemen who wore boots and hats, and I wanted to look for the spot where they had parked their horses. When one went to the sixteenth or twenty-sixth floor, one found offices furnished with false fireplaces blazing with fake wood fires. When design cheats, the result is sad. Design is a method and a tonic, not an antibiotic. We need to take small doses regularly and constantly. A quick fix will always be a superficial fix.

〉〉

Design goes beyond identity. It provides a cosmopolitan dimension for the women and men of tomorrow. In a world of increasing globalization, it goes without saying that there are global influences. Taste is not international but global. This means that there are new communities forming. Belonging to these communities means sharing a particular interest or taste. A hundred thousand fans of a particular piece of music, visual expression, or text do not have to live in the same city, or the same country. New communications allow for sharing remotely the intimacy of taste. I mention these communities because we cannot forget that those who are participating directly in the design festival are a small number of privileged people. ╳ Design is also a language that goes beyond words. It's a means of communication and a vector of exchange. Thanks to their own magazines and electronic communications, Japanese fashion addicts, who are very well informed, land in Antwerp and find the fashion district, which they have in fact seen to the last detail before they come. "Design" has the very particular quality of inspiring individuals from different cultures to reach out to each other, to mix together, without losing themselves in the other. Design is also respect for, and cultivation of, difference; a celebration of the "marvellous stranger." ╳ I could never be a cynic because life does not allow me to be, but today, the dominant political party in Belgium, which is forcing all others into a coalition, is, alas, an extremely right-wing formation. In my nice "new design city," one Antwerp resident out of three voted for a party that preaches values that are not mine, that are not ours. I have no precise response to this shameful fact. I'm looking for a response. I am wondering how I can bring back the "disappointed," the fanatical, and the furious. ╳ Because that's the true challenge: how to transform "new design cities" into simply "new cities." Design must be a method, a mode, and a path, but never a goal. "Art for art's sake" should not be followed today by the postmodern paraphrase "design for design's sake." ╳ Designers must transform the world and change the city. Their sensitive approach is called for because their only ambition is to enhance quality of life. But although this is an ambitious goal, the designers and politicians who are nurturing it will not be able to talk of triumph, or even of success, if most of the residents of design cities cannot take part in this transformation, in this lovely feast of good taste and good sense. ╳ Antwerp is worth visiting. Standing here is a semi-chauvinist who is saying, "I am an Antwerpian, happy and satisfied because I realize that I am spoiled. I have not yet found another city that is as easy and pleasant to live in, and that has so much to offer. Both contemporary and classic art are represented in the city's museums and galleries. The stage arts, which have blossomed under an excellent Flemish policy, offer great dance and theatre performance." ╳ Antwerp is a city for hedonists. You have to visit to understand.

AXEL ENTHOVEN
〉 Industrial designer
〉 President of Enthoven Associates design consultants, Antwerp, Belgium.

〉〉

WHAT DESIGN IMPROVEMENTS WOULD YOU LIKE TO SEE?
That sponsors/clients be better educated so that they can give more accurate descriptions in their orders and commissions.

WHAT WOULD YOU LIKE TO SEE BUILT OR IMPROVED IN YOUR CITY?
Right now, there's something missing in Antwerp: a signature building. The new Courthouse aspires to this status, but it was much more attractive as a model than in reality.
It is clear that we need a powerful bridge to link the two parts of the city, rationally and emotionally, as an alternative to our tunnels. It would certainly become my favourite place.

SVEN GROOTEN
› B-architecten, Antwerp, Belgium

〉〉〉

B-ARCHITECTEN

In November 1997, Evert Crols, Dirk Engelen, and Sven Grooten founded B-architecten, an independent design firm, in Antwerp, Belgium.

The three architects met when they were students in Antwerp and Amsterdam. While studying at the Berlage Institute, an international laboratory for advanced architectural studies in the Netherlands, they discovered their common interest in design.

B-architecten is a firm that brings innovation to its work on various projects: construction, design competitions, and studies. These projects are produced in partnership with other firms, as needed.

SVEN GROOTEN

1971 › born in Beveren-Waas.

1995 › graduated in architecture from Henry van de Velde Instituut, Antwerp.

1995 to 1997 › advanced studies at the Berlage Institute, Amsterdam.

1997 › Architect in the firm of Driesen-Meersman-Thomaes, Antwerp.

1997 › Opening of design firm B-architecten with Evert Crols and Dirk Engelen.

WHAT ARE YOUR FAVOURITE PUBLIC PLACES IN ANTWERP?

My first choice is the Linkeroever (the left bank of the Schelde River). From there, you have an extraordinary view of the city's skyline. For many people today, the Linkeroever isn't really part of the city. ✕ Second, I would choose the port, one of the largest in the world. Moving through it in a boat at night, in the middle of enormous ships, millions of lights, gigantic flames leaping from industrial plants—it's fantastic!

WHAT DESIGN IMPROVEMENTS WOULD YOU LIKE TO SEE?

The docks on the river. Today they are covered with huge parking lots for cars, trucks, and buses. It is shameful that these areas aren't treated as public spaces.

WIVINA DEMEESTER
› Former minister of Belgium and Flanders, Antwerp.

〉〉〉

—A design city is an uncompleted city that is searching for itself and sometimes reinvents itself. The creative people, both young and old, who live and work in Antwerp give the city a new dimension that I would call a 'permanent questioning.'

—Antwerp is home to a Gothic cathedral, to the Carolus Borromeus Baroque church, and to Rubens's house. But there is also contemporary architecture, such as the new courthouse by Richard Rogers, and the new library, in the middle of a disadvantaged neighbourhood. Locating the library here was daring and risky, yet reasonable and successful.

MONTREAL
DESIGN PORTRAIT

〉〉

POPULATION

The metropolitan area has a population of 3.5 million, 34.3 percent of which is composed of more than 150 ethno-cultural communities.

YEAR OF FOUNDATION AND IMPORTANT EVENTS

Founded in 1642 by French military men and priests. Conquered in 1760 by England. ✕ In the late nineteenth century, Montreal was the uncontested metropolis of Canada. Its wealth was due to the development of the transcontinental railway, as well as the presence of major shipping companies trading with Europe and Asia, some quickly growing banks, and a group of large companies (fur, tobacco, flower, sugar, iron, etc.). The Second World War provided an opportunity for the development of strong aeronautics, optics, biochemicals, and other industries. ✕ A post-war decline in traditional industries led to the departure of many head offices and much financial activity for Toronto, which became Canada's new metropolis. ✕ A pick-up in the late twentieth century, centred around the new information and communications technologies, advertising agencies, and the movie industry, revived contemporary Montreal. Also contributing were the recreation and tourism industries, which had grown in response to the presence of international-calibre arts festivals and the city's reputation for fine dining. ✕ The 1967 World Fair, Expo 67, the construction of the subway, and the 1976 Olympic Games were key moments for design in Quebec. Montreal, and its artists and designers, benefited from work opportunities and unprecedented media attention. ✕ The design professions, which had started to become more structured, acquired new visibility and credibility. Some European designers relocated to Montreal to pursue a career or to teach. ✕ Highlights in the history of Montreal as a design city include:

1933 〉 Founding of the Interior Decorators Association of Quebec; in 1948, it becomes the Interior Decorators' Society of Quebec, then in 1992, the Société des designers d'intérieur du Québec. Since 2003, it has been known as the Association des professionnels en design d'intérieur.

1951 〉 Founding of the Art Directors Club of Montreal, followed in 1974 by the Société des graphistes, which, twenty years later, changes its name to the Société des designers graphiques du Québec.

1958 〉 Founding of the Association des designers industriels du Québec.

1966 〉 Opening by the National Design Council of a design centre in Montreal to promote Canadian design (it closes in 1970).

1973 〉 Opening of an industrial design section within the urban design faculty of the Université de Montréal; in 1974, programs in graphic design and environmental design (architecture, industrial design, and urban design) are created at the Université du Québec à Montréal (UQAM).

1979 〉 Founding of the Canadian Centre for Architecture (CCA) by Phyllis Lambert.

1981 〉 Founding by a group of professors of the Centre de design at UQAM.

1983 〉 Launch of Via Design, the first commercial design—including fashion—exhibition. It lasts only three years.

1984 〉 Launch by the Société des graphistes du Québec of the competition Graphisme Québec, which is replaced in 1997 by the Grafika Awards run by a private company, Éditions Infopresse.

1986 › Creation in Montreal of two design centres (exhibition windows for industry suppliers): Centre Infodesign, founded by a design promoter Ginette Gadoury (closed in 1988), and the Centre international de design, initiated by a furniture promoter (closed in 1989). With the publishing of the Picard Report in 1986, design became one of the seven high-priority axes for economic development in the Montreal region. The governments of Canada, Quebec, and the city of Montreal were mobilized around the objective of making Montreal an international-calibre design centre. ✕ Acting on the recommendations in the report:

1989 › Ginette Gadoury and the Société des décorateurs-ensembliers du Québec launches the Salon international du design d'intérieur de Montréal (SIDIM).

1989 › Agence Liaison Design, an agency that dispenses information and links up supply and demand for design, is founded by Marie-Josée Lacroix with the support of the professions. Liaison Design is integrated with the Institut de Design Montréal in 1995.

1991 › The city of Montreal becomes the first city in North America to create a position of commissioner of design, devoted exclusively to the development and promotion of design in the city.

1992 › The Institut de Design Montréal, directed by Eleni Stavridou, is set up by the Board of Trade of Metropolitan Montreal, with funding from the federal, provincial, and municipal governments.

1995 › The Design Commission of the city of Montreal launches the Commerce Design Montréal competition. ✕ Founding of the École supérieure de mode by UQAM and the Groupe Collège Lasalle.

1998 › Creation of Émission d., devoted to design in all its forms, which is produced by TVMaxPlus and broadcast on TV5 (Sylvie Berkowicz and François Guenet) and other networks.

Late 1990s The Centre de design at UQAM takes Quebec design onto the international stage. Thanks to support from the three levels of government, *Montréal 5 – portrait de cinq designers montréalais* (directed by Georges Adamczyk) and a series of touring exhibitions (directed by Marc H. Choko) are presented, starting in 1998, in North America, Latin America, Europe, and China.

2005 › Opening of the head office of the International Design Alliance (IDA – combining ICSID and ICOGRADA). This is a major step in the opening of the city to the international scene and the recognition of Montreal in the design sector.

NUMBER OF DESIGNERS

Montreal is home to about 20,000 designers and architects working in all aspects of design. After some creative people left the city during the economic crisis of the 1980s, there was a turnaround, and in the last ten years the city has seen a rise of almost 50 percent in the number of designers.

RENOWNED DESIGNERS

Moshe Safdie, architect of the Habitat 67 complex, is certainly the best-known architect internationally. Dan Hanganu has designed a number of major Montreal institutions, including the emblematic Musée d'histoire et d'archéologie de Montréal Pointe-à-Callière. The architects Saucier + Perrotte, designers of the Cirque du Soleil's future facilities in Tokyo, have been building a reputation, notably at the 2004 Venice Biennale. ✕ In product design, Michel Dallaire, designer of the furnishings at the Bibliothèque nationale du Québec and the street furniture for the Quartier international de Montréal, is the dominant figure. ✕ In graphic design, young agencies such as Orangetango and Paprika stand out for their high-quality, often audacious creatives in both the cultural and commercial sectors. ✕ In interior design, Jean-Pierre Viau stands out as the leader in commercial design, as evidenced by the many prizes awarded to him by Commerce Design Montréal. ✕ Finally, mention should be made of fashion designer Philippe Dubuc, landscape architect Claude Cormier, and the exhibition design firm GSM design.

ANNUAL DESIGN EVENTS

A number of design events take place in May, baptized by the Institut de Design Montréal as "design month." Among the activities are exhibitions by students from all the design schools, the Salon international du design d'intérieur de Montréal (SIDIM), and the handing out of the Commerce Design Montréal and Design Montréal competition awards. Since 2004, the Biennale Internationale de Montréal (visual arts and architecture) has also included a design section.

DESIGN INSTITUTIONS

With regard to design exhibitions and promotion, Montreal has one of the largest collections of contemporary design from 1935 to the present (textiles, table arts, and furniture), acquired by the Stewart Foundation for the Montreal Museum of Decorative Arts, now integrated with the Montreal Museum of Fine Arts. ╳ With its unique archives, the Canadian Centre for Architecture (CCA) is among the most prestigious institutions for research on and promotion of architecture in the world. ╳ The Centre de design at the Université du Québec à Montréal has been presenting and/or producing exhibitions (some of which tour) in all areas of design since 1981. ╳ The architecture gallery Monopoli has been presenting thematic exhibitions since 2003.

DESIGN SCHOOLS

The Design Art Department at Concordia University offers a three-year program that accentuates the interdependence between design, the arts, and the social and applied sciences. It also offers a graduate diploma in design and digital technologies, as well as a bachelor's degree in digital image and sound. ╳ The industrial design school at the Université de Montréal offers two design programs: one in industrial design (four years) and one in interior design (three years). The master's program in design and complexity and the doctoral program in urban design are aimed at those who wish to pursue more advanced research in design. The schools of architecture at the Université de Montréal and McGill University offer a four-year program recognized by the Order of Architects. Finally, the Université de Montréal has also offered, for more than thirty years, the only degree program in landscape architecture in Quebec. ╳ The design school at the Université du Québec à Montréal, founded in 1974, offers three three-year bachelor's programs: graphic design, environmental design, and, in collaboration with Collège Lasalle, fashion design. It also offers one-year graduate diploma programs in knowledge and preservation of modern architecture, event design, and design of transport equipment, and it organizes a summer session in international design.

DESIGN STRATEGIES

Municipal strategies are focused mainly on improving the design of the city and on promotion of Montreal as a design city. ╳ Since 1991, through its Design Commission, which combines active communication of exemplary productions and a supporting role in design commissions (competition for the furnishings at the Casino de Montréal and the Grande bibliothèque du Québec, workshop on an identity for the theatre district, etc.), the city makes private and public stakeholders aware of the benefits of high-quality design. After major awareness-raising campaigns among businesses (retailers, restaurateurs, hotel owners, craftspeople) from 1995 to 2004 through the Commerce Design Montréal program—a concept that the organization instigated and that is now being adopted by other cities all over the world—the city is formulating its new integrated strategy, "Design de ville | ville de design," aiming to introduce the notion of design innovation in all of its decisions and actions affecting the built environment and also to intensify the international circulation of Montreal design.

DESIGN PORTRAIT BY MARC H. CHOKO

> **Full professor, École de design, and Director, Centre de design,
Université du Québec à Montréal**

GÉRALD TREMBLAY
MAYOR OF MONTREAL SINCE 2001

〉〉

DO YOU CONSIDER MONTREAL TO BE A NEW DESIGN CITY?

First of all, I believe that to be a design city it is not enough simply to announce it. You have to be very careful when you adopt slogans like "Montreal, capital of" this or that. Although it may be useful and important for consolidating a city's reputation, it must nevertheless reflect reality. ✕ I would therefore prefer to call Montreal a *young* design city, an *emergent* design city on the international scene. Why? Because design and designers represent a dynamic force in the culture and economy of Montreal, and the city is constantly gaining a better understanding of how this creative power can be used to serve the quality of its living environment. ✕ Propelled onto the international stage by the 1967 World Fair, Montreal is a modern city that draws both the curious and those interested in culture and design; they move here or come as tourists. People who choose to make Montreal their home like the access to a high-quality life style, while visitors are stimulated by the ambient creativity or attracted by the diversity of the retail offerings. All of these factors led to the recent decision by the International Design Alliance (the joint secretariat of ICSID and ICOGRADA) to establish its head office in Montreal. This choice was made from among some thirty candidate cities, and we are very proud of it. ✕ Montreal has some major assets to offer—numerous designers, high-quality educational institutions, and well-known exhibition centres—but I think that our main strength, and our distinction as a design city, is linked to the dissemination of creative design and architecture throughout the city, without regard to size or nature of the project. There is a subtle omnipresence of creativity—discreet or dazzling—resulting from the increased accessibility of design, which in too many cities is reserved for the elite or confined to downtown areas. ✕ Thanks to initiatives such as Commerce Design Montréal and similar awareness-raising campaigns by a number of partners, design in Montreal is not simply for show but a source of daily well-being, and it is becoming a basic value for Montrealers. As its citizens begin to accept this fact, Montreal will inevitably assert its status as a design city.

WHAT HAS YOUR PERSONAL CONTRIBUTION BEEN TO FACILITATING THE EMERGENCE OF YOUR DESIGN CITY?

First, I would say that I believe profoundly in the importance of design. And this conviction was not born yesterday. When I was minister of industry, science, and technology of Quebec, from 1989 to 1994, I instituted the tax credit for design, a fiscal measure that was decisive in stimulating private investment in research and innovation in design; it is still in force today. This incentive expanded the market for Quebec designers, almost two thirds of whom are concentrated in Montreal. Under the initiative of Bernard Lamarre, I also supported the creation of the Institut de Design Montréal, whose mission is to promote design as an economic value and to make Montreal an international-calibre design centre. ✕ As mayor, I make decisions every day that have an impact on design in the city. It is my responsibility to be aware of this and to surround myself with people with the skills necessary to inform my judgments. We have therefore created a number of bodies that have this advisory role, including the Heritage Council and, especially, the Design Commission. ✕ Montreal is the only Canadian city to have a commissioner devoted exclusively to promoting design. This position, created by my predecessors fifteen years ago, has greatly contributed to the development of design in Montreal. My own contribution, no doubt, will have been to immediately recognize the strategic importance of this position within the municipal government and to support its actions and interventions. The challenge now is to broaden the scope of the commission's involvement with design in the city for an integrated approach to highlighting design in all our actions within our borders. The city, as an institution, must provide an example and be innovative in what it does. Being a better client for designers can help us better shape the city.

WHY DO YOU BELIEVE THAT POSITIONING YOUR CITY THROUGH DESIGN IS IMPORTANT?

Design has meaning only when it enables human beings to live well and thrive. Design is important because it has an immense impact on our lives. Think, for example, of the design of products of all sorts, work environments, houses, parks, streets. ✕ Thus, aspiring to become a design city means above all being concerned with the well-being of the citizens. It means advocating a better quality of life in a perspective of sustainable development. ✕ In fact, design is an extraordinary tool of social inclusion. Western cities are in a phase of restoring quality (recycling, reusing, restoration, rehabilitation) in a context of unprecedented socio-cultural change, which implies a completely new cohabitation of points of view and a plurality of values. ✕ Recently, a design workshop was organized to choose a team of designers to develop an identity for the Quartier des spectacles de Montréal. This exercise in contextual design, which led to the selection of Swiss designer Ruedi Baur and Montrealer Jean Beaudouin of the Intégral international network, was more than simply a process of selecting professionals. Above all, it offered a forum for enriching the reflection on the expectations and needs of the different, sometimes divergent, interest groups that exist in the city, which generate an inclusive common vision indispensable to the project's success. ✕ To see design as essential to the future of Montreal is to seize the opportunity that this powerful design process offers us to [re]shape the city and everyone who lives in it.

WHAT EXAMPLES OF DESIGN PROMOTION STRATEGIES DEVELOPED IN OTHER CITIES HAVE INSPIRED YOU?

Montreal is a member of various international networks of cities (Metropolis, Association Internationale des Maires Francophones [AIMF], United Cities and Local Governments [UCLG]), and we have signed partnership agreements with cities all over the world. These relationships constantly feed into our thoughts and enhance our practices. Design has a cross-disciplinary aspect that touches many dimensions of municipal life, so we were inspired by the many actions taken by our colleagues in other cities, such as the lighting plan for Lyon. ✕ The Biennale Internationale Design in Saint-Étienne has also been an important source of inspiration for us. Because we are highly motivated to make design accessible, we would like to use certain basic principles of Saint-Étienne's concept to create a similar biennale in Montreal focusing on the Americas. ✕ More recently, as we have been looking for ways to provide Montreal with an integrated strategy for highlighting design articulated around the idea of an "innovative platform in design," the British CABE (Commission for Architecture and the Built Environment) model has inspired us enormously. We are convinced, among other things, that it would be very useful to form "design champions" as essential conduits through which to promote design quality in all boroughs of Montreal.

WHAT SHOULD THE ROLE OF THE CITIZEN, THE DESIGNER, AND THE POLITICIAN BE IN THE DEVELOPMENT OF A DESIGN CITY?

Citizens must be critical and demanding. They must know how to recognize, appreciate, and ask for high-quality design and architecture. They must also have a sense of responsibility for their living environment. ✕ Designers must initiate new ideas and be mediators. They are experts who must inspire and fully assume leadership. They must know how to translate, put into concrete form, and project the aspirations of the elected officials and citizens. ✕ As for elected officials, they must have a unifying vision and take the risk of innovation both in choosing projects that are presented to them and in the implementation of processes.

COMMERCE DESIGN MONTRÉAL: IMPACTS ON THE CITY

BY MARIE-JOSÉE LACROIX
> Design commissioner, City of Montreal.

〉〉

The city of Montreal is interested in design primarily for its contribution to the living environment, a decisive factor in attracting new businesses. But design also provides an important point of differentiation and a means of drawing tourists. ✕ Municipal actions therefore focus on encouraging participation by designers in shaping the face of the city and encouraging the efforts of developers, both public and private, to incorporate high-quality design. Their projects define and shape our built environment and can serve as showcases for experimentation and the promotion of designers in Quebec and abroad. ✕ Commerce Design Montréal, the program that I am describing here, was created ten years ago, precisely out of the city's desire to encourage high-quality design throughout its territory. It targets businesses, which, because they are everywhere in the city, have an enormous impact on the image of Montreal.

〉〉

WHY TARGET BUSINESSES?

If there is one sector that influences our daily experience of the city—whether we live or work or are visiting there—it is that of retail businesses and restaurants. These places where people meet and communicate are always the soul of a city. When they are attractive and lively, so is the city… and vice versa. ✕ The city, as an institution, has very few obvious means at its disposal to encourage businesses to adopt high-quality design. In Montreal, as everywhere in North America, the notion of public interest differs greatly from that in Europe. Here, individual rights tend to dominate. ✕ In addition, businesses here tend to come and go. The notion of a business continuing for generations does not exist. A butcher shop might succeed a drugstore in a given storefront, and may in turn be succeeded by a bistro. Retail spaces are constantly changing owners, vocation, and décor at a frenetic pace. To some extent, individuals can do what they want within the walls of their own establishment, even though, in many cases, the storefront—sometimes all too transparently—has as much visual impact on the street, at least for pedestrians, as does the façade as a whole. ✕ In such a liberal, individualistic environment, it may be difficult to regulate the quality of architecture and design. Design quality thus becomes a matter of culture, and for it to develop people must be exposed to it. Personally, I do not believe in promoting "beauty," "good taste," or "absolute excellence"— especially in a patchwork city such as Montreal, whose interest and identity lie precisely in its heterogeneous character—its diversity of approaches, styles, and viewpoints. ✕ To develop a culture that values design and architecture in this context, I have confidence in the immense power of leading by example—accessible examples that will inspire the greatest possible number. I believe in learning by mimicking others. If what is promoted as an example makes sense culturally and socially, innovation will follow. ✕ Quebecers have made giant steps in areas in which meaning and taste are important, such as fine dining and wines. The achievements of Commerce Design Montréal over the last ten years and the recent public debates over beauty and ugliness in the city indicate that we are indeed developing a taste for architecture and design.

COMMERCE DESIGN MONTRÉAL—THE CONCEPT

Commerce Design Montréal is a competition that we launched in 1995 to stimulate collaboration between design professionals and Montreal merchants. The basic idea was to reward those who, with their talents and judicious investments in commercial architecture and design, make the city a stimulating, unique, and attractive place for both residents and visitors. But our objective was, of course, not only to reward these innovators but also to encourage many others to follow their example. × As a veritable laboratory for experimenting with design communication strategies, this colloquium offers a wonderful opportunity for us to share some main points of what we have learned with those who are working in cities elsewhere in the world to develop a culture of design and architecture. And because Commerce Design Montréal is celebrating its ten-year anniversary this year, it's a good time to take stock. × After one decade and almost $7 million invested in this program, mainly from public funds, we wanted to measure its effects as precisely as possible, and we had compiled a unique and abundant body of information over the years for this purpose. The program has always adjusted its strategies by looking back on what it has accomplished. Our annual performance evaluations and reviews of our promotional tools and actions have enabled us not only to adapt the concept and make it more effective, but also to document its impacts. × We have summarized and analyzed the documentation accumulated over the last ten years in a report titled *Commerce Design Montréal 1995–2004—Rapport décennal d'activités, octobre 2004.* The goal is to conduct a review and make it public. Here are some highlights.

GUIDING PRINCIPLES

The primary objective of the competition is to start a ripple effect—to convince other merchants of the fundamental value of design to their commercial success and to structure the revitalization of commercial arteries. × The principle of the competition is to raise the awareness of as many people as possible through the promotion of exemplary cases. Consequently, the promotional and advertising campaign for winning businesses is at the core of the organizers' strategy. The winners are widely promoted as success stories in the media in order to demonstrate to neighbouring merchants that investing in design quality is profitable. × The selection of the winning businesses is crucial to attaining the awareness-raising goals. Each year's winners must reflect certain commercial realities so that most merchants can identify with one or more of them. The selection must be made in such a way as to dispel misconceptions and to show that design is not simply a look (modern, hip), but that it is affordable and profitable for all businesses, whatever their products or services, size, location, and target market. The idea is to present not one award for absolute excellence in commercial design, but twenty prizes on an equal footing that take into consideration the urban context, the kind of business, and the resources available. Indeed, the competition is based on the idea that a city is built on the sum of individual efforts and not exceptional cases. Accordingly, Commerce Design Montréal rewards both spectacular, big-budget, extremely innovative projects and much more modest projects showing a concern for design quality—the kind that we would like to see more of in all neighbourhoods and commercial sectors. × The winning businesses are good ambassadors among their peers, but consumers are just as effective in this, if not more so. In fact, for merchants to invest in the quality of the design of their establishments, they must feel the need, and this means that their customers must ask for it. This is why the competition introduced a "People's Choice" award in 1998 that complements the jury awards. Members of the public are invited to evaluate the competing businesses, take a critical look at the designs, and choose their favourite.

CHOOSING THE WINNERS

In short, twenty grand prizes on an equal footing are awarded every year by a jury composed of professionals from the different disciplines involved in businesses of design—architecture, interior design, graphic design, urban planning—chaired by a well-known personality from the business world (2004: Louise Roy, international consultant), communications (2001: Jean-Jacques Stréliski, advertising professional; René Homier-Roy, morning host on Radio-Canada), the arts (Denys Arcand, director, *The Barbarian Invasions*), or culture (Lise Bissonnette, president of the Grande Bibliothèque du Québec; Claude Gosselin, general and artistic director of the Biennale de Montréal). ✕ Then, the general public is invited to choose a favourite business from among the jury's twenty winners to win the People's Choice award.

〉〉

PROMOTING THE WINNERS

Commerce Design Montréal is a design-promotion activity based on communications aimed at the general public. ✕ The competition does not give out cash prizes to the winning merchants or design and architectural professionals. Rather, it invests in a campaign to promote the winners as examples to follow. It thus helps increase their visibility and boost their sales while maximizing the ripple effect. ✕ The success of the program rests essentially on the promotion surrounding the twenty design "ambassadors" and on our capacity to reach business people as well as the public, both the neophyte and the well informed. The promotional campaign has two sections: one for local communications with Montrealers and one for an international audience. Both are intended to reach a general public as well as experts. A number of communications tools have been developed and refined over the ten years. ✕ At first, the competition was limited to the awarding of prizes and honourable mentions to emphasize commercial design quality. The program grew quickly, however, as a variety of complementary activities were added: the People's Choice award, publication of a design guide, a Web site, guided tours, street sales, national and then international press relations. These tools and strategies enhanced the effectiveness of the promotion of the winning businesses, expanding their influence on other businesses, boosting public awareness so that people would demand better design quality, confirming and showcasing the talents of Quebec designers, and positioning Montreal as a design city. Ten years later, Commerce Design Montréal has become one of the largest design-promotion operations in Quebec, and cities elsewhere are taking up the standard.

〉〉

FUNDING

Commerce Design Montréal is an initiative of the city of Montreal's Design Commission. Directed by a five-person executive team, the program has in the last few years involved more than thirty consultants who take on specialized temporary mandates. This human capital, a pool of talent in commercial design and, more generally, in design communications that developed over a number of years, is at the core of the program's growth and success.

〉〉

INVOLVEMENT OF DIFFERENT SECTORS

The project quickly drew the lasting support of the professional and business networks targeted by its actions. Professional associations, chambers of commerce, and groups of retailers support the activity through financial or services sponsorship and have been, since the beginning, the main conduit by which Commerce Design Montréal has become known and recruited entries for the competition.

〉〉

GOVERNMENT AND PRIVATE MOBILIZATION

Commerce Design Montréal is based on two main forms of partnership: funding and promotion. Both have played essential and complementary roles in developing the program by encouraging its growth and optimizing its returns. ✕ This partnership system is an integral part of the strategy of Commerce Design Montréal. Generally, partners are recruited with an eye to their potential contribution in the context of the program's objectives. ✕ The search for relevance and synergy between partners does not limit in any way the range of sectors to which they belong. On the contrary, diversity is the order of the day: Hydro-Québec, Société des alcools du Québec, Société de transport de Montréal, Air Canada, Tourisme Montréal,

Musique Plus, and others. ✕ Similarly, the strategic positioning of Commerce Design Montréal at the crossroads of urban, economic, and cultural issues has been well received by the government of Quebec. The cross-disciplinary nature of the program has led to the co-ordinated involvement of three ministries directly involved with the promotion of commercial design in Montreal: the ministry of economic and regional development and research; the ministry of municipal affairs, sports, and leisure; and the ministry of culture and communications.

〉〉〉

THE BUDGET

Commerce Design Montréal has grown constantly, generating investments in design promotion of almost CA$7 million, of which about $2 million ($1,973,465) comes from the city of Montreal and about $5 million ($4,907,304) from external partners. ✕ In 1995, the city of Montreal, the instigator of the competition, alone supplied the initial effort by financing all direct and indirect costs of its production. For the second edition, the program began to diversify its funding sources. On average over the ten years, the para-public sector has funded 39 percent of the costs of producing Commerce Design Montréal, governments 21 percent, and the city of Montreal 41 percent. However, since 2000, investments by governments and the city of Montreal have balanced out to stabilize at around 30 percent each. ✕ Since 1995, the annual budget of the program has been multiplied by a factor of fifteen; it has been over $1 million since 2001.

〉〉〉

COMMERCE DESIGN MONTRÉAL—THE IMPACTS

Ten years is not a long time to develop a culture of design quality among merchants, to change mentalities, dispel misconceptions, make people aware, and "educate" all the target markets. On the other hand, ten years is a long time for a public design-promotion initiative with such specific goals; it is also a rare opportunity. Few programs in Quebec have lasted so long. Generally, programs are abandoned prematurely; the funding bodies—governments and sponsors—gradually withdraw (they don't fund the same program twice, or they diversify their support, or they fail to renew projects); newly elected politicians look for a different focus; organizers run out of steam and their experts disperse in search of more stable employment. The strength of Commerce Design Montréal is definitely that it has managed to survive all this time, while retaining its team, partners, and sponsors and also bringing in new ones. ✕ Because the program has lasted since 1995, it is important now to evaluate its spin-off effects. Have we achieved the objectives that have motivated the annual event since the beginning? Has it had the desired impact?

Impact on Merchants

Decentralization of Design Projects

While the entries to the competition in the early years were located mainly in and around downtown Montreal, mapping of the participation over the ten years shows that there has been a gradual decentralization of projects toward outlying districts. Consumers are increasingly interested in design and looking for distinctive environments, and they are encouraging merchants in the suburbs to offer sales environments that are competitive with those downtown.

A Localized Ripple Effect

Quality attracts quality. Innovative businesses, whether or not they win awards, have a real impact on their immediate environment by encouraging, simply by example, their competitors to invest in quality in design; 40 percent of the award-winning businesses feel that they have been a source of inspiration for their neighbours.

From Atypical to Mainstream

Today, design is not the sole prerogative of downtown businesses, but is extended to the types of businesses for which design quality was far from being a priority ten years ago. Some kinds of businesses, termed "atypical" from 1995 to 2000, are now among those that most often turn to design—telephone boutiques, bookstores, financial institutions, and convenience stores. ✕ This diversification in kinds of participating businesses shows that the program has broadened the market for business design by making breakthroughs into commercial sectors previously unconcerned with design quality.

Good Design "At Any Price/At All Prices"

Similarly, despite the still widespread misconception that design is expensive, since 2001 the highest proportion (39%) of entries in the competition have been low-budget projects, at less than $70 per square foot, even though, with the growing popularity and visibility of the competition, designers and merchants have a tendency not to enter if they feel that their project is too modest. Commerce Design Montréal has gone a long way toward overcoming this prejudice by rewarding businesses that show that good design is possible at a reasonable cost.

Design Pays

Finally, the competition creates a ripple effect among merchants, as increasing numbers of them realize that good design pays off:

> 46 percent have seen an increase in customer traffic
> 40 percent have seen an increase in sales
> 51 percent say that they have attracted new customers

Impacts for the Design Sector

Tangible Business Benefits for Professionals

Over the past ten years, Commerce Design Montréal has helped increase merchants' awareness and dispel their prejudices about design. More of them now feel that designing a store or restaurant requires specific skills and is a job for experts. New commercial sectors are now concerned with design quality for both low and high-budget projects. As a consequence, Commerce Design Montréal has had a positive impact on the development of new markets for commercial design professionals.

> 80 percent of professionals who have won Commerce Design Montréal awards say that they have gained new business contacts as a result
> 46 percent of these professionals say that these contacts have led to contracts generating new sales (between $50,000 and $200,000)

More Designers, Better Known, Greater Recognition

The competition also helps identify, encourage, and confirm new Quebec talent in commercial design on both the national and international scenes. Every year, almost half (46%) of the projects submitted come from professionals—architects and interior designers—who have never entered before. And the competition does not always reward the same people; therefore, on average, almost 60 percent of the professionals rewarded every year are winning for the first time. This helps to bring in younger designers, and to renew and enhance the community of Quebec commercial design professionals.

Impact on the Public

A Growing and Diversifying Public

When the People's Choice award was introduced in 1998, 3,847 people voted. Since then, the number has constantly risen, reaching 58,725 in 2004. In that year, even though no change was made to the previous year's campaign, an additional 20,000 people voted. Such skyrocketing participation clearly shows the public's growing interest in design in general and in the competition in particular. ✕ Not only are more people voting in the People's Choice award, but this facet of the competition is attracting and educating new consumers each year. On average, over the last two years (2002 and 2003), 77 percent of voters were casting ballots for the first time.

Media Impact: The Numbers

Public awareness of design is also measured by the interest that the media show in the subject and the number of people affected by the media spin-offs of the competition. ✕ Relatively realistic, even conservative, evaluations made on the basis of monetary equivalent coefficients of the press coverage obtained reveal that the media impact of the competition is growing remarkably and has reached more than 12 million people per year since 2001 (12,562,155 in 2003), including almost 2 million outside of Quebec (rest of Canada, United States, Europe), who are individually exposed to the quality of design in Montreal businesses.

Impact on Montreal

It is a natural mission for a city to highlight the quality of the living environment through better commercial design, by emphasizing, encouraging, and rewarding efforts deployed in this direction that contribute directly to making it more competitive. With this in mind, the city of Montreal has devoted considerable professional and material resources to Commerce Design since 1995. After investing $2 million in municipal funds in this program, what are the benefits to Montreal today?

Improved Living Environment

The first benefit of the program has been to generate investments in commercial design, and these have had an obvious impact on enhancing and revitalizing commercial streets.

Return on Investment

For the city of Montreal, Commerce Design Montréal has generated external investments of more than $626,000 per year on average. These revenues have improved substantially the annual municipal budget allocated to communications with citizens. And thanks to this activity, the city of Montreal now has a vast, strong, well-informed, and reliable network of partners on which it can depend in pursuing, extending, and strengthening its mission of promoting design quality.

Montreal: A Design Destination

Commerce Design Montréal has contributed to positioning the city as a destination of interest for design enthusiasts. ✕ Among other things, by sending the Montréal Design Guide to 15,000 subscribers of the American magazine *Metropolis* for the last three years, Commerce Design Montréal has raised the city's visibility from the point of view of commercial design. In addressing the public specializing in design on the eastern seaboard of the United States, the goal was to position Montreal as a design city and a desirable destination. ✕ Commerce Design Montréal has invested in international promotion since 1998 (materials on Air Canada flights, partnership with Tourisme Montréal, hosting foreign journalists, creating a Web site). In addition, a distinction awarded by the International Downtown Association in 2002 (Washington, D.C.) and licences granted to other cities in 2003 have clearly strengthened the attraction of Montreal as a design city in the international media.

〉〉〉

AN EXEMPLARY DESIGN STRATEGY

Although the Commerce Design concept has been adopted by only one city in Quebec (Trois-Rivières, in 2002—Séduction Design competition), it is now being exported. ✕ In 2003, three complete or partial licences were accorded at the request of the city of Saint-Etienne (the first European city to adopt the concept), the Lyon chamber of commerce and industry, and the Times Square Alliance of New York. Bratislava, Zagreb, Geneva, and Paris are also studying the possibility of adopting the concept of the competition. ✕ These agreements are generating demand for skill transfers and creating opportunities for partnerships that are advantageous for the international networking of Montreal.

〉〉〉

TEN YEARS OF COMMERCE DESIGN MONTRÉAL IN PERSPECTIVE

The founding principles of the Commerce Design Montréal concept (making design more accessible, rewarding merchants for investment in design, and increased public awareness) are behind the success of the program, which is now recognized throughout Quebec and abroad. ✕ The data confirm that the city's initial objectives have been achieved: stimulating a tangible ripple effect among merchants, creating new markets for designers, generating interest and higher standards among the public, and increasing the attraction for tourists. Thus, the initiative, based on educating merchants and the public, perseverance, and the repetition of a single message over a number of years, has clearly borne fruit. ✕ Commercial design is becoming a durable and deep-rooted part of Montreal's culture, and a decisive factor in the city's economic competitiveness, quality of life, and urban identity. It is already a valuable part of the city's public image. ✕ In other words, Commerce Design Montréal has had a far-reaching, tangible effect on both the city itself and the city's image, and thus has made an important contribution to positioning Montreal as a young design city.

PHYLLIS LAMBERT
› **Founding Director and Chair of the Board of Trustees,**
  Canadian Centre for Architecture (CCA)
› The Canadian Centre for Architecture (CCA) was founded in 1979 to build public
  awareness of architecture, promote scholarly research in the field, and stimulate innovation
  in design practice.

››

WHAT IS YOUR DEFINITION OF A DESIGN CITY?
A design city requires a municipal policy that touches on all aspects of daily life: transportation, patrimonial issues, graphics, signage, streetscapes and furnishings, lighting, and so on.
IN ORDER FOR A CITY TO EMERGE AS A DESIGN CITY, DOES IT NEED A PARTICULAR SOCIAL HISTORY, A SPECIFIC POLITICAL OR INDUSTRIAL TRADITION?
A design city cannot exist without creative people. Cities no longer depend on industry for revenue; instead, they rely on services and cultural sectors. They can grow and mature only in an open and democratic political atmosphere. A city must nurture a tradition of creativity.
HOW DO YOU THINK DESIGN CAN HELP IMPROVE THE QUALITY OF LIFE IN THE CITY?
Recently there have been discussions about light—not only about streetlight but also about the use of light at night to help create places of public gathering. Public places must be understood as "inspiring places," which allow for both contemplation and stimulation and give unique identities to different sectors of the city. We need a city-wide strategy that will generate a continuity of public spaces, diversified and scattered through the island, thus giving an overarching structure to the entire city. I presented that concept of the need of "inspiring places" at the Montréal 2017 symposium, held at the Chamber of Commerce in May 2002.
WHAT ARE THE ROLES OF THE CITIZEN, THE DESIGNER, AND THE POLITICIAN IN THE DEVELOPMENT OF A DESIGN CITY?
The role of the citizen is to militate for good design. Public consultation through well-structured open public hearings has proved the citizen to be the most effective proponent of urban issues. Ideas come from the ground level up. The designer works with citizens and politicians to assess the program, the conditions, the constraints and possibilities. The ensuing design is subject to public hearings; politicians establish the policy, and the cycle begins all over again.
HOW HAS THE CITY OF MONTREAL MOST BENEFITED FROM THE CCA?
The CCA has brought the constant presence and a civic and critical understanding of architecture in today's society. Thanks to its rich exhibition and conference programs, its concerts linking architecture and music, its active study centre, and its collaboration with schools, it has put Montreal on the international map again. Some of the changes in the city would not have happened without the CCA.
WHAT HAVE BEEN THE MAIN OBJECTIVES OF THE CCA'S PUBLIC PROGRAMS?
The exhibitions and publications have raised a series of urban issues (what I call "hot spots"), while using the city, and the evolution of its urban landscape, as an open book from which to read the culture of our country. Major issues dealing with the environment were addressed through our public programs, such as the future city, urban preservation and evolutionary process (from the colonial past to the 1960s), social vs. natural sustainability, and other ques-

tions raised by major twentieth-century architects (from Mies to Frank Lloyd Wright) as well as contemporary figures such as Peter Eisenman. ✕ Whether through the architectural photo commissions, our permanent architectural toy collection, or the children's programs, the CCA looks at the city through a wide spectrum of viewpoints, always thinking about the formation of the idea of architecture.

WHAT DO YOU CONSIDER THE CCA'S MOST IMPORTANT ACHIEVEMENTS?

It is probably the quality and wealth of collaborations that we've been able to establish with high-ranking universities, such as Columbia University, McGill, and UQAM, to name a few. The Study Centre is an international institute devoted to research in architectural theory and practice, which brings in ten scholars at the master's and post-doctoral levels per year. ✕ Basically, we have managed to create a sort of permanent agitation; we are piloting a laboratory here, as we've put forward experimental research and opened a public forum to make people more aware of architecture. I believe the CCA has fostered the subliminal role of Montreal as a city concerned with architecture.

WHAT IS YOUR FAVOURITE BUILDING AND/OR PUBLIC SPACE IN MONTREAL, AND WHY?

I think of two places of total design in Montréal: the Quartier International de Montréal (QIM) and the CCA (Canadian Centre for Architecture), both the building and the garden. Importantly, both examples have interior and exterior public spaces in which people can meet.

RALPH DFOUNI
> Creative director, president, and founder, Bluesponge, Montreal.
〉〉

WHAT ARE YOUR FAVOURITE PUBLIC PLACES IN YOUR CITY?

The Mountain as a whole, including the cemetery, and especially the Purple Trail: it's so removed from the city it's unreal. ✕ Montreal's side streets are eclectic in their diversity and in the homey feeling that they convey to the walker. Also, the nicest architectural details are found there, for those who look up from time to time.

WHAT WOULD YOU LIKE TO SEE IMPROVED DESIGN-WISE?

Access to water. Of course, this implies that the water would have to be cleaned first. But Montreal is an island whose citizens are so removed from the surrounding water that it becomes absurd to think about the city as an island. Water should be brought into the soul of the city, and that could be achieved by letting people access the waterfront in various ways and at different entrance points.

WHAT WOULD YOU LIKE TO SEE BUILT IN YOUR CITY?

A pyramid. Or, if that's too far fetched, please rehabilitate the tramway. Montréal is not a landmark city, and its conviviality and charm come from small things, details. It gives it a village feel, and makes living in it a comfortable thing.

HOW DOES MADEINMTL ADDRESS DESIGN IN THE CITY?

MadeinMTL.com is an attempt to re-create and represent aspects of a city (Montreal in this case) on a computer screen, within a set of tools that make its content accessible to the user. At once a space and a tool, MadeinMTL conveys the spirit and ambience of Montreal by highlighting its most interesting and picturesque places, sonorities, imageries, and colours. The poetry of the city is counterbalanced by the pragmatism of navigation on the site. Using an algorithmic engine called "Itinerator," users can create customized Itineraries within the city, and the rich media content of the site gives viewers a virtual experience of dwelling in the city on screen before being physically in it.

FRANÇOIS CARDINAL
› **Editorialist, La Presse (daily newspaper), Montreal.**

〉〉

"Montreal has been in a process of beautification for twenty years. Megalomaniacs crazy about concrete and cars have given way to designers concerned with leaving their mark on projects that improve the urban landscape—and this is not a small task, given the heterogeneity of the city. Unlike republican cities that display a large degree of homogeneity (Paris), Montreal has an architectural intensity that is found in few places in the world. It is an asset, but also a challenge for designers, urban planners, and architects."

SAINT-ÉTIENNE
DESIGN PORTRAIT

》》》

POPULATION

With some 185,000 inhabitants, Saint-Étienne is the second-largest city in the Rhône-Alpes region, in the heart of an urban area with a population of 400,000. The metropolis of Saint-Étienne contains 43 communes.

YEAR OF FOUNDATION

Saint-Étienne entered the portals of history in the thirteenth century with the parish name "Sanctus Stephanus de Furano." ✕ In the fifteenth century, Saint-Étienne was a tiny town of peasants and blacksmiths. In the sixteenth century, it began to grow as industries took root: manufacturers of bladed weapons, firearms, hardware, and trimmings. The Manufacture Royale d'Armes was founded in 1764.

STRENGTHS AND CHALLENGES

Saint-Étienne's great epoch was the nineteenth century, when its industrial expansion was centred around mining (coal), metallurgy, and the manufacture of cycles, arms, machinery, and trimmings (an industry that was in its golden age). At the time, Saint-Étienne was at the heart of the largest industrial area in France. ✕ Saint-Étienne was ambitious; it was the first city to welcome the railway (trains started running between Saint-Étienne and Andrézieux in 1827, then between Saint-Étienne and Lyon in 1832) and to provide its citizens with a tramway. Saint-Étienne's inventiveness was also demonstrated in mail-order sales by Manufrance, and its famous catalogue, and by Casino's general retail business. ✕ In the middle of this period, in 1857, the École des Beaux-Arts was built; in 1889, the Musée d'Art et d'Industrie, the expression of the city's desire for a diverse culture, was opened. ✕ Economic crises in the second half of the nineteenth century forced the city to develop new economic axes and poles of excellence: the optics industry, machinery, medical technologies, higher education, and design.

IMPORTANT EVENTS

1947 〉 Inauguration of the Comédie de Saint-Étienne, Centre Dramatique National, directed by Jean Dasté, who worked his entire life to bring high-quality theatre to the public in the provinces

1968 〉 Opening of the Maison de la Culture

1987 〉 Opening of the Musée d'Art Moderne

1991 〉 Opening of the Musée de la Mine

1998 〉 Saint-Étienne hosts the Soccer World Cup

1998 〉 1st Biennale Internationale Design Saint-Étienne

2000 〉 2nd Biennale Internationale Design Saint-Étienne

2002 〉 3rd Biennale Internationale Design Saint-Étienne

2004 〉 4th Biennale Internationale Design Saint-Étienne

2005 〉 Les Transurbaines, city-wide festival

NUMBER OF DESIGNERS

Two hundred designers and communications agencies, among them 150 architects, practise their trade in Saint-Étienne.

RENOWNED DESIGNERS

In the Saint-Étienne region is a site unique in Europe: the architectural grouping by Le Corbusier at Firminy-Vert, including a housing block, a cultural centre, a stadium, a swimming pool, and a church. Construction on the Saint-Pierre church will be completed in 2005 by Le Corbusier's former apprentice, the Franco-American architect José Oubrerie. ✕ Daring to have strong, exemplary, and audacious architecture is a recent choice for Saint-Étienne.

Didier Guichard designed the Musée d'Art Moderne, and Jean-Michel Wilmotte renovated the Musée d'Art et d'Industrie. ✕ A number of projects are underway:

> The Zénith by Foster and Partners
> The Cité du Design, by Finn Geipel and Giulia Andi of LIN Agency
> The head office of Casino, conceived and designed by Architecture Studio

Among Saint-Étienne's designers are François Bauchet, Eric Jourdan, Laurent Gregori, Sylvie Fillère, Jean-François Dingjian, Céline Savoye, Patrick de Glo de Besses, and Bertrand Voiron. ✕ The Atelier Espace Public, directed by Jean-Pierre Charbonneau, brings together young designers, architects, and artists, who work with the city's technicians on renovating neighbourhood spaces.

ANNUAL DESIGN EVENTS

Founded in 1998, the Biennale Internationale Design Saint-Etienne is the largest public international design event in France. Under the aegis of the city of Saint-Étienne, it is organized by the Ecole Régionale des Beaux-Arts de Saint-Etienne with numerous partners. This overview of the diversity of design in the world, illustrated through a profusion of objects, enables participants to decipher the thinking and issues of our times. ✕ The first edition of the Commerce Design Saint-Etienne competition was organized in 2003 in partnership with the city of Montreal.

DESIGN INSTITUTIONS

The Musée d'Art et d'Industrie, founded in 1889, featured industrial products and art. Famous for France's largest collection of cycles, ribbons, and weapons, this museum was renovated by Jean-Michel Wilmotte in 2001. ✕ Inaugurated in 1987, the Musée d'Art Moderne has the second largest collection, after the Centre Pompidou, of modern French design and art. It also offers a schedule of original exhibitions. ✕ In the near future, the Le Corbusier site in Firminy will permanently house the design collections of the Musée d'Art Moderne. ✕ Finally, the Cité du Design is scheduled to open in 2007.

DESIGN SCHOOLS

The École Régionale des Beaux-Arts de Saint-Étienne was founded in 1857 to train artists and respond to of manufacturers' need for greater decorative diversity in their products. ✕ This school, which has municipal status, is an institution of higher learning under the pedagogical supervision of France's ministry of culture. Its five-year bachelor's programs in art, communications, and design have acquired an international reputation. ✕ The focus of the design department, "global design," involves a project-oriented, interdisciplinary approach. Research contracts are signed with companies for the development of both everyday and technologically innovative products. ✕ The École Régionale des Beaux-Arts also offers graduate and post-graduate programs:

> Post-graduate program in design and research, created in 1989. As part of their research, students participate in production of the design magazine *AZIMUTS*.
> "Dual Design" specialized master's program, given jointly by the École Régionale des Beaux Arts de Saint-Étienne and the École Nationale d'Ingénieurs de Saint-Étienne (ENISE), and created in 2002.
> Professional master's program, "Public Space: Design, Architecture, Practice." Educational program given jointly by Université Jean Monnet, the École d'Architecture, and the École Régionale des Beaux-Arts, and created in 2004.

Complementary programs have been instituted at Université Jean Monnet (master's degree in territory, patrimony, environment), the École des Mines (sustainable development), CNAM (design and innovation), and the École de Commerce (marketing). A doctoral degree in design at Université Jean Monnet and in partnership with the École Régionale des Beaux-Arts is currently under development.

DESIGN STRATEGIES

The formidable dynamic that is developing around design in Saint-Étienne demonstrates the spirit that must reign over this aspect of urban, cultural, and economic development. ✕ For Saint-Étienne, this new identity as a French capital of design is based on a natural legitimacy linked to the city's history and its current potential, reinforced by political and financial support from the government, which is seeking to create French metropolises that are attractive on the European scale.

DESIGN PORTRAIT
INFORMATION PROVIDED BY ÉCOLE RÉGIONALE DES BEAUX-ARTS DE SAINT-ÉTIENNE, BIENNALE INTERNATIONALE DESIGN ST-ÉTIENNE

MICHEL THIOLLIÈRE

SENATOR OF THE LOIRE SINCE 2001. MAYOR OF SAINT-ÉTIENNE SINCE 1995.

〉〉〉

DO YOU CONSIDER SAINT-ÉTIENNE TO BE A NEW DESIGN CITY?

More than two centuries ago, art and industry were united in Saint-Étienne through the invention of objects that were functional but created with a concern for artistry. Thus, Saint-Étienne sowed the roots of French design, and in having this forerunner status it anticipated its own future. ✕ Today, Saint-Étienne is considered to be among the international design capitals thanks to the Biennale Internationale Design, created in 1998; this event is now considered a must on the international design scene. ✕ Also, there is consensus that the Cité du Design project, beyond being a new site for research, training, and exhibitions, will be a symbol of Saint-Étienne's ability to always bounce back and constantly innovate. ✕ So, I would say that Saint-Étienne can never forget that it has always been a design city.

WHAT HAS YOUR PERSONAL CONTRIBUTION BEEN TO DEVELOPING THE NEW DESIGN CITY?

Since 1995, the city of Saint-Étienne has been involved in a renewal of its urban patrimony, treating neighbourhood projects and large-scale developments with the same close attention. ✕ This desire to transform the city is accompanied by a new way of working with modern methods that we have tested and use today in each project: plans made in consultation with users, more rapid ways to plan projects, increased involvement by artists with the urban design. ✕ During the first phase of transformation, we proceeded to make high-quality, welcoming, creative improvements. ✕ The work of the Atelier d'Espace Public, created by Jean Pierre Charbonneau, is one aspect of this success: this innovative studio was the result of close co-operation between residents, technicians, consultants, and young artists, which is the practice in Saint-Étienne but not in Toulouse, Paris, or Lyon. ✕ I wanted our young architects and designers (trained right here at the École Régionale des Beaux-Arts ou d'Architecture) to be responsible to create, little by little, our urban environment with the special warm and creative stamp of Saint-Étienne and respect for the traditions of our city. ✕ Then, in 1998, the idea of a design biennale was born. The immediate success of this event gave a new impetus to our city and proved that we had made the right choice. This event, unique in France, has become a must-see for design professionals and design lovers. ✕ And so, I decided to work on this project with Jacques Bonnaval, who was the director of the Biennale Internationale Design and the director of the École Régionale des Beaux-Arts. What followed was a long adventure and lots of detailed work. We had to convince our partners, and we managed to do so. On 25 May 2003, the French government officially confirmed the merit of our approach by providing support for the Cité du Design in Saint-Étienne. ✕ We still had to entice the best architects in the world to come and work on the future Cité, and we chose the talented architecture firm LIN. This Berlin firm, founded by Finn Geipel and Giulia Andi, has been responsible for such prestigious projects as the Contemporary Art Gallery in Rome, the covering of the arena in Nîmes, and the Zénith theatres in Tours and Nantes. For the Cité du Design, the team proposed a design that is intelligent and futuristic, combining technical prowess, creativity, and sustainable development. Through these three fundamental elements, we were able to convey our desire to build a future that combines identity and modernity. ✕ Meanwhile, the well-respected Sir Norman Foster is currently working on the design of the first Zénith theatre in the Rhône-Alpes region. ✕ I am happy to know that the great architects of the world have wanted to participate in projects such as the Zénith and the Cité du Design. Their strong interest proves indisputably that our project is equal in quality to those in cities such as Bilbao and Glasgow. ✕ Finally, with the reopening of the construction site for the church in Firminy, a work by Le Corbusier, in conjunction with the two major projects designed by Finn Geipel and Sir Norman Foster, we are developing a new centre of tourist attraction.

WHY DO YOU BELIEVE THAT POSITIONING SAINT-ETIENNE AS A DESIGN CITY IS IMPORTANT?

Last week, I was reading an article about what technologies might be developed by Silicon Valley in 2010. On the list of new technologies and services under development were creative services and design—at the same level of importance as biotechnology and nanotechnology. The article stated that the development, production, marketing, and sales of technological products will necessarily entail a need for creative services. Design will become truly complementary: it will enhance the thinking about and multiply the capacities of the technology of which it is the creative partner. ✕ It is a fact that design is a vector of industrial development. As proof, in the Saint-Étienne region there are ninety-two design firms working in the areas of the environment, packaging, industrial design, inter-disciplinary design, multimedia, and visual identity. Our city's landscape has been enhanced by the development of these innovative small and medium-sized businesses.

HAVE YOU BEEN INSPIRED BY OTHER CITIES' PROMOTION STRATEGIES? IF YES, WHICH ONES AND HOW?

Montreal was an inspiration. During the 3rd Biennale Internationale Design Saint-Étienne, the city of Montreal was asked to present the "Commerce Design" competition that it had launched in 1995. The enthusiasm with which this initiative was met led to the signing of a dynamic and multi-faceted partnership between our two cities. Saint-Étienne, already "the source of French design," has become the first city in Europe to adopt an original idea developed in Canada. ✕ This operation planted new seeds in our already fertile soil and confirmed our strong desire to adopt design as a unifying element in the development of our territory. ✕ But we have already created a broad international network based on the Biennale, and we have become a flagship for international design cities. As proof, more and more cities are asking to join the network of design cities. Nagoya, Pasadena, Glasgow, Eindhoven, and Courtrai are among the partner cities that we have had the pleasure of communicating with. ✕ Our biennale concept has also inspired many cities—some with which we already have partnerships, and others, in Spain, Hungary, and even South Africa, are interested in adopting the concept. There is also talk of sharing our expertise with Montreal to create a Biennale of the Americas.

WHAT ARE THE ROLES OF THE CITIZEN AND THE POLITICIAN IN THE DEVELOPMENT OF A DESIGN CITY?

If the Musée d'Art et d'Industrie, the Biennale Internationale Design, and the plan for the Cité du Design exist here in Saint-Étienne, it is because there is a real political will. Other French cities have made vague moves toward design, since it is now a fashionable thing to do. But here in Saint-Étienne, politicians have ardently promoted this project because it is already deeply rooted in our city. ✕ One must have a strong conviction to be able to transmit the idea that a project may be important for a territory. But it is the role of the politician to be a visionary for his city, to be able to look beyond a single mandate to imagine his city ten or fifteen years from now, and thus to prepare the future for our children. ✕ The role of the politician consists of bringing to the attention of his fellow citizens a field of possibilities in such a way that they will understand and accept change and that they themselves will design the future face of their city. ✕ Design is also a policy of image. To bring our city to the forefront, to show that it is alive and evolving, we must be able to attract foreign visitors and show them that we have entered the twenty-first century with all the evidence and lessons of our past intact. ✕ We need large-scale projects to gain media coverage, but also to bring together our residents, to energize them and make them love their city. The Soccer World Cup in 1998 is an excellent example of an event that triggers a sense of solidarity. Similar events on a city-wide scale are the Biennale Internationale Design, the Cité du Design, the Zénith, and the Fête de la Ville "les transurbaines" taking place 10–21 June 2005. ✕ A city is always an unfinished story, it must always be moving forward, and Saint-Étienne is no exception to the rule.

THE CITÉ DU DESIGN IN SAINT-ÉTIENNE

〉〉

The minute you arrive in Saint-Étienne, you immediately sense how redolent this city is of the history of the nineteenth and twentieth centuries. Makers of trimmings, guns, and cycles— each in his own domain—contributed to the development of industrial design and helped to forge its definition in the noblest way possible thanks to their ingenious, inventive, and creative craftsmanship. ✕ Initially centred on manufacturing products, the exercise of "shaping a way of thinking," as the designer and architect Sylvain Dubuisson put it, then turned to the marketing of objects. In this regard, I want to mention Manufrance for catalogue (or mail) sales, and especially Casino for general retailing. The concept store and new head office that Casino is planning to open in 2008 will be designed by the Architecture Studio group and built in the city's new business district. ✕ This ineluctable march to modernity has been marked by a number of important steps. The first one took place in 1857, when the École Régionale des Beaux-Arts de Saint-Etienne was asked by industrialists to improve the products in their catalogues and to invent others. ✕ Today, several institutions commemorate this industrial heritage: the Musée d'Art et d'Industrie, the Musée de la Mine, and the Musée d'Art Moderne, which houses a remarkable design collection. There is also the architectural legacy of Le Corbusier, who, upon invitation by mayor Eugène-Auguste Petit, designed a cultural centre, a stadium, a church, and a housing block in Firminy. This patrimony, the reflection of urban construction in the twentieth century, endures.

〉〉

Since 1995, the city of Saint-Étienne has been updating its urban patrimony, paying just as much attention to neighbourhood undertakings as to large-scale projects. The renewal of local spaces is one facet of Saint-Étienne's urban policy launched by Michel Thiollière, senator and mayor. This policy is unique in two ways: it treats all of the city's "ordinary" spaces with the same attention, and its projects are designed by a studio of young Saint-Étienne designers who are graduates of the architecture and fine-arts schools. ✕ For example, a second tramway line is under construction and the Gare de Chateaucreux train station is being refurbished; both projects are under the masterful supervision of Jean-Marie Duthilleul, chief architect of the SNCF (the French national railway). ✕ Another major construction site in Saint-Étienne is the Zénith, a 7,000-seat concert hall. The architect was chosen through an international competition to which a number of renowned teams made design submissions; the project was awarded to Sir Norman Foster. ✕ In response to all of these projects, and to stimulate participation by residents of Saint-Étienne, the city also had to create dynamic cultural institutions that could keep abreast of the dash to modernity. ✕ The École Régionale des Beaux-Arts de Saint-Étienne meets this need. This institution of higher learning has the vocation of creating a context favourable to creativity, as well as being a prestigious location for teaching design. Today, it is the top design school in France, with five hundred students. It will be acting as the training and research centre for the Cité du Design. ✕ In the school's design department, which defines its approach as "global design," the students are exposed to all design disciplines. It offers:

› A post-doctoral program: Design &Recherche.
› A specialized master's degree, "Dual Design," in conjunction with the École Nationale d'Ingénieurs de Saint-Étienne.
› A professional master's degree, "Public Space," in conjunction with the École d'Architecture de Saint-Étienne and Université Jean Monnet.

It also publishes the design magazine AZIMUTS. ✕ The École Régionale des Beaux-Arts has created an international exchange network for students, exhibitions, and workshops; this led to the organization of the first Biennale Internationale Design Saint-Étienne in 1998. ✕ The Biennale Internationale Design is a major international event; in 2004, it featured more than 80 countries, 2,500 designers, and 20,000 objects, and attracted 200,000 visitors. By last November, 1.5 million visitors to its Web site had been recorded. ✕ This brilliant success has made the Biennale a must-see on the international design circuit, confirming Saint-Étienne as a world design capital and ensuring its project, the Cité du Design, a lasting place in history. It represents a strategic stake in the city's development, as it consolidates what already exists and provides a catalyst for the future. ✕ It will complement the site where a new vocation for a city that is emblematic of two centuries of industrial revolution is under construction. Education, creativity, and research are its cornerstones. ✕ In 2007, the Cité du Design will rise in the heart of the city on an eighteen-hectare industrial lot that was once the site of the GIAT arms factory. Among its objectives will be to make businesses aware of design culture and to keep them informed of trends and the evolution of concepts and materials. ✕ This objective will be pursued by providing assistance with design, with networking, with distribution to encourage the launch of new products, and with increasing visibility by means of trade shows and exhibitions. ✕ In general, the Cité du Design will provide businesses with both basic structural activities and timely activities for important events. It will also offer some thirty residencies to French and foreign designers. ✕ The architectural plan designed by Finn Geipel and Giulia Andi of the Berlin firm LIN, winners of the international architecture competition, is for "a contemporary site that is flexible, open, and evolving."

› Flexible, so that the spaces can accommodate a program of varied disciplines: concerts, fashion shows, and various events.
› Open, to attract the public and contribute to the city's dynamic image.
› Contemporary, to convey an image of modernity that fits with the purpose of design and creativity.
› Evolving, in anticipation of its extension to retailers and tertiary activities.

The Cité du Design will present major cultural exhibitions, as well as exhibitions on current design issues. It will have a resource centre and a training and research centre with close ties to industry, universities, and engineering schools. Graduate training in industrial design will be offered. In addition, some thirty foreign designers will be hosted in residence at the Cité de Design. ✕ The Cité du Design will operate on the international scale, as partnership agreements are currently being negotiated with major design institutions in Montreal as well as the United States, England, Denmark, Italy, Spain, Japan, and China. ✕ The Cité du Design is intended to boost the image of unique expertise, positioning the city of Saint-Étienne as a major player in the context of international competitiveness. Our goal is to make Saint-Étienne the capital of effervescent inventiveness.

THE BIENNALE INTERNATIONALE DESIGN SAINT-ÉTIENNE — AN INNOVATIVE CONCEPT

BY JOSYANE FRANC

> Public and International Relations Manager, École Régionale des Beaux-Arts de Saint-Étienne. Biennale Internationale Design Saint-Étienne

〉〉

The Biennale Internationale Design Saint-Étienne is unique because it was conceived and brought to reality by an art school. This adventure was born of the meeting of two visionaries: Jacques Bonnaval and Michel Thiollière. ✕ Jacques Bonnaval, in 1989 director of the École Régionale des Beaux-Arts de Saint-Étienne, oriented the development of his institution around training in design, new technologies, and industrial partnerships, while opening its activities to the international scene. An adopted son of Saint-Étienne, Bonnaval was fascinated by the city's history, which is interwoven with that of industrial modernity—as exemplified by the Manufrance catalogue, an emblematic example of the advent of the culture of daily objects. Bonnaval proposed to organize an international design biennale to pay permanent tribute to the dynamic of a city in which culture transcends ingeniousness. ✕ Michel Thiollière, mayor of Saint-Etienne, had already begun an urban renewal project for his city. Concerned with designing and inventing the city of the future, which would be able to meet both the daily aspirations and the imaginations of the men and women living in it, he supported Bonnaval's dream and committed the city to meeting the challenge. ✕ In its first edition, in 1998, the Biennale Internationale Design Saint-Étienne immediately established itself as a professional level show where the commercial successes of the moment were displayed. But today it is more than that: it is a crossroads, an international design forum, with meetings and debates that investigate the object in all its sociological resonance and all of its diverse cultural identities (50 countries in 1998, 100 countries in 2000, and 80 countries in 2002 and 2004). ✕ Here, objects made with traditional savoir-faire sit side by side with commercially successful objects, the work of students with that of professional designers, objects by young talents with those by famous designers, and objects made in countries where design is integrated into the culture with those from countries where design is in its infancy. ✕ Even though this display may seem confusing to visitors wishing for clear formulas, it deliberately poses thought-provoking questions.

〉〉

THE BIENNALE HAS A NUMBER OF OBJECTIVES:

> To present the only event in France in which international creativity from North and South is gathered, based on a mingling of ideas and exchanges
> To debate the acceleration of technological, ecological, architectural, and cultural changes
> To demonstrate the dynamics of international industries that consider design as an essential part of their identity
> To emphasize the responsibility of designers' involvement in economic and cultural debates
> To encourage research and imagination
> To convince corporate executives of the diversity of issues in design
> To meditate on the wealth of cultural mixings
> To show the public that there is no single design "attitude" but as many points of view as thinking approaches and designers
> To provoke interest among professionals, companies, students, and the general public

The École Régionale des Beaux-Arts de Saint-Étienne organizes this event and thus provides a learning experience for its students through workshops and meetings with international designers, through creating set designs, signage, the catalogue, and the Web site, and through setting up and dismantling the exhibition. An improvised forum is created in which designers, students, industrialists, stylists, and intellectuals debate and form connections through the colloquia, exhibitions, fashion shows, and moments shared in bars and at the festivities accompanying the event. ✕ This event also brings together those involved in the political, cultural, economic, and higher-education issues in the Saint-Étienne region. The passion and enthusiasm of the entire team from the school and the city have contributed to the success of this "human adventure."

LAURENT GREGORI AND NADINE CAHEN

› Designers, Atelier Cahen & Grégori, Saint-Étienne, France.

››

Partnership between a colourist and a designer. ✕ Nadine Cahen, colourist and visual artist, born in Saint-Étienne, and Laurent Grégori, designer, born in Geneva, combined their specific talents in 1998 with a common aspiration: to design environments whose surfaces have meaning, emotion, and information. Through colour, texture, and motif, they question the senses, encouraging people to touch and seek the depth of the surface. ✕ Sectors of activity: Art direction, creation of motifs and colour charts, set design, signage, environmental design. ✕ References: Abet Laminati, Print-France, Groupe SEB, Groupe ✕ Michelin, Grosfillex, RATP, Gaz de France, Chaumont-sur-Loire, BHV Paris.

EXHIBITIONS

2002 › Festival des jardins de Chaumont-sur-Loire
2003 › Designers' Week, Tokyo
2003 › Habiter c'est vivre, Parc de la Villette, Paris
2004 › Institut Français de Valence et Galerie Papyrus, Spain
2004 › Centre de design UQAM, Montreal
2005 › Cité du design, Triennale de Milan
2005 › Designers' Week, Bangkok

WHAT ARE YOUR FAVOURITE PUBLIC SPACES IN SAINT-ÉTIENNE?

The neighbourhood around Place Louis Comte, the first spot where you can breathe south of downtown. This group of small squares, between the "rue du tram," the Mélies movie theatre, Les Halles, and the Musée d'Art et d'Industrie, offers one of the most harmonious views of the city: the urban space is spread before you so that you can appreciate the true architectural quality of buildings that have a similar style identity—a rare sight in Saint-Étienne. This space has nothing that stands out, that focuses attention on it, and that is perhaps what makes it interesting. Here, the city presents a "naturally beautiful" façade, the property of elegance. ✕ Parc Montaud: one kilometre from downtown, the largest park in Saint-Etienne looks more like a piece of countryside than an urban park. And yet, it borders very industrial neighbourhoods. In contrast to the first space, it telescopes all the façades of the city—its stories and its parallel realities. It is an invitation to zoom in, to frame views, to recompose a different city each time you look.

WHAT WOULD YOU LIKE TO SEE BUILT OR IMPROVED BY DESIGN IN YOUR CITY?

We don't wish to see anything in particular built, in the architectural sense of the term. Many facilities have already been built or are about to be, such as the Zénith and the Cité du design. What remains to be built—or improved by design—is a real "heart of the city"; because it stretches along the main street, the downtown area does not have the energy, fluidity, or coherence that one expects in a medium-sized city. In particular, the Town Hall square, a no-man's-land of banks and insurance companies, literally cuts the living fabric into two separate zones, instead of being a point of convergence. Redefining the role of this space in the heart of the city is a major challenge.

MARINE LECOINTE
> Independent designer, Saint-Étienne, France
>>>

WHAT ARE YOUR FAVOURITE PUBLIC PLACES IN SAINT-ETIENNE?
Place Jules Guesde, for three aspects of the quality of its layout:
> The aesthetic and functional connection with the spirit of the place
> The quality of production
> The very special ambience that results from this
Place Raspail, for its incongruity. It is an intimate spot in the Beaubrun neighbourhood (downtown), corresponding perfectly to the needs of residents, who use it enthusiastically and exploit all its possibilities. However, the intervention of a designer could improve the space, because it has the fussy, obsolete layout of the suburbs and is therefore enclosed, and isolated, within the city.

WHAT WOULD YOU LIKE TO SEE IMPROVED DESIGN-WISE?
Urban improvements require a threefold commitment: politicians, designers, and population. The ambitions of one group are often pushed back in favour of the others, which means that the humanist values conveyed by urban design projects are compromised. An emphasis on and support for the work of designers and appropriate communications with (and I emphasize "with") the population would no doubt allow for a better match between projects' goals and their results. For this to happen, politicians must learn to work with designers and the population, rather than using designers to manipulate the population.

WHAT WOULD YOU LIKE TO SEE BUILT IN YOUR CITY?
Gardens (not green spaces). Gardens are always a reflection, either figurative or abstract, of society. We live in an era when cities, like human communities (both urban and rural), are in a period of major change. Gardens, visible and practicable milestones, help us comprehend who we are and where we are going. They are exemplary, expressive areas, articulating our desire to become more human, and thus social. Yet, in Saint-Etienne, they are woefully few and far between.

STÉPHANE LAURIER
> Owner and chef, Restaurant Nouvelle, Saint-Étienne.
>>>

—Saint-Etienne is a city with an industrial past, with a wealth of working-class tradition. Today, it is looking to the future and giving priority to urban design. There has been much renovation to make its public squares, streets, and buildings more attractive and contemporary. This has made the city "lighter," and one feels good in it. ✕ Design is a reflection on modernity, which follows invention. We have obviously "swallowed" technology. Today, we need to appropriate it, use it, and take advantage of it differently in a "design" city.

LIVING IN THE CITY: FROM THE NEIGHBOURHOOD TO THE TERRITORY

BY FRANÇOIS BARRÉ
> Consultant on urban and cultural issues, Paris

>>

What is a "design city" given the complexity of the city? There certainly are design cities, just as there are coal cities, banking cities, textile cities, and chocolate cities! But these cities are, above all, cities of architecture, passion, production, conflict, art and history, relations and exchange, urbanity, festivals and rituals, cultures and communities. The part that design plays in all this is completely relative.

Industrial designers' theories about the city are often pure statements of principle. Adopting the old dream of the "total work of art," Gio Ponti wanted to control everything, "from the dessert spoon to the city." Later, Archizoom and, especially, Superstudio showed a true awareness (mainly graphical) of the territorial dimension of the city. Andrea Branzi, in *Nouvelles de la métropole froide*, his projects *Non-stop city* and *Agronica*, and his master plan for Philips in Eindhoven, wanted to erase the distinction between metropolitan world and domestic world, between interior—the domain of design—and exterior. Invoking Walter Benjamin and Louis Kahn, Branzi considered the city an interior that had to be furnished. The world of objects was held up in opposition to architecture, which, according to Branzi, would be abolished. "What is taking shape at present," he writes, "is a metropolis of objects without an exterior, which is invading the entire material world, the entire territory of humankind."

It is important to me personally to inhabit the city rather than to furnish it. Would a "furniture city" correspond to Satie's "furniture music"? What a sad prospect. In design cities, urban design is the product of the city and not the reverse. I will therefore refer to a process of planning and production of the built environment that enables an ecosystem of relationships to be defined and the formal organization of urban growth to be established and controlled through permanence and change. For this, I will favour culturalist urban planning, as taught at the architecture school at Université Laval under the title "Forme urbaine et pratiques culturelles" (Urban form and cultural practices), and I will discuss the joint action of urban planners, architects, designers, landscape architects, artists—in contrast to confining the city within a single discipline. The city is beyond disciplines.

My concern with emphasizing culture, narrative, emotion, and pleasure, rather than economy and function, is not about forgetting the present but about being attracted to a culture of project. What project? To act in order to transform. To be of the world and from somewhere. To design today's cities without denying what is already there or expanding them into historicist mimicry or generalized standardization. Will we be condemned to live in a hundred-times-reproduced world city or will we be of our times and our place? The cities that are emerging, cities with populations of more than ten million, generic cities for generic inhabitants and generic societies, exert the fascination of numbers and quantities—rarely of quality. Whether old or new, they are often uninhabitable. We should remember Gaetano Pesce, who hailed mass production and made each product a different object. Let us learn the project of living in the city, with all its singularities.

THE DESIGN OF THE CITY: ITS FORM AND TERRITORIES

According to Yves Chalas,[1] the figures of mobility, territory, nature, polycentrism, choice, emptiness, and continuous time are replacing the figures of yesterday's cities based on classical harmony, formal unity, minerality, density, fixity, a single centre, defined contours, separation from nature—and thus creating new spaces. The binary opposites of centre/periphery, continuity/discontinuity, mixity/separation, homogeneity/heterogeneity, and emptiness/fullness are giving way to the paradoxical city of everything at once in a world divided between the global and the local. But between multiple places and multiple times, between ubiquity and simultaneity, we are faced with the question of everything at once and its possible crumbling into utter nothingness, wherein everything equalling everything, its meaning would be reduced to nothing. Is reality something we experience or something we construct? Could this be the end of the project? The form and nature of cities is never the result exclusively of destiny or of plans. But in all things, planning seems, to me, preferable to destiny. Can we still talk of the form of a city?

During the 1914 edition of the *Deutscher Werkbund* exhibition that they had founded, the architects and designers Hermann Muthesius and Henry van de Velde held their "Cologne debate." Muthesius, arguing in favour of standardization, won out over van de Velde, who advocated variation. This famous debate, marking a new connection of rationalism and functionalism with industrial development, promoted the universal dissemination of a scientific model. Can these notions be applied to the city and its form? How can we live in and give order to an urban form? By a standard, declared Ildefonso Cerda in 1859 with his plan to extend Barcelona. By urban composition or urban art, responded Camillo Sitte in 1889 in *City Planning According to Artistic Principles*. Twenty years later, Raymond Unwin continued the battle in terms that I find touching: "Our cities lack the vivifying touch of art which would have given completeness and increase their value tenfold; there is a need for just that imaginative treatment which would transform the whole... It is the lack of beauty, of the amenities of life, more than anything else that forces us to admit that our work of town building in the past century has not been well done. Not even the poor can live by bread alone; and substantial as are the material boons which may be derived from such power for the control of town development as we hope our municipalities will soon possess, the force which is behind this movement is derived far more from the desire for something beyond these boons, from the hope that through them something of beauty may be restored to town life."[2]

Aldo Rossi, in *L'architectura della citta* (1966), then Carlo Aymonino (1975) addressed the issues of urban morphology and typology of the built environment. Disagreeing with the proponents of an exportable model that could be imposed everywhere, Rossi advanced the idea of an autonomy of the urban form, which, like an underground river, would continue to well up and flow across epochs.

What is happening today, in an era of globalization, when we are passing from a city of goods to a city of flows? Carefully balanced between fullness and emptiness, our cities of the past often grew unpredictably depending on the price of real estate and the search for individual habitats, which became less remote as travel got easier. The diffuse city, *la citta diffusa*, studied by the Italian urban planner Bernardo Secchi, spreads without boundaries. It is not a city centre, or the official city, or even suburbs and periphery, but a "beyond" that includes these territories without really defining them: an informal territory full of empty spaces. Empty spaces are what it is full of; in fact, they form its true structure. Half of the population of Europe live in diffuse cities. They live neither in the city nor in the country; Secchi calls them "dispersed urbanites," jealous of their individual withdrawal. This is how the city becomes informal and fragmented, spreading without response to a plan. This is the true challenge for design.

Giving the city a form that everyone can read is democratic, according to Secchi. "I am able," he says, "to use a city if I am able to read it... to understand where things are, to understand the form of the city." But how do we design the open, informal space of the great empty areas that are illegible holes in the fabric of the city? By turning toward non-urban realities: nature and art. Secchi proposed to study "what agriculture has designed in our landscapes, [as] we can see formidable designs there." Similarly, Peter Cook undertook to find shapeless traces in nature, which he used in his plans. The example of Emscher Park, reconstituting an urban landscape with the cities of the Ruhr, is a hopeful sign.[3] Art may also provide answers: collage, decoupage, montage, seriality, uprooting, mixing, framing, morphing, and sampling have engendered improbable and remarkable forms. With regard to cities, if we concur with Giulo Carlos Argan that "the form is the result of a process whose point of departure is not the form itself," then we must find our way back to this process. Research and experimentation are necessary to stitch the diffuse city back together and provide its vast territoriality with elements of dignity and urbanity. Artists have already experimented with territorial coverage of the landscape in order to make the form of a territory intelligible. This is what Christo[4] did with wrapping, Felice Varini with lines, and Llorenc Barber with the spatialization of sound. Even shapelessness may be planned. Cy Twombly has demonstrated it brilliantly.

THE CITY IS A STORY: IT IS WRITTEN OVER TIME

The time of stories. Once upon a time…

The city is built on top of itself. It is both record and direction. We must read the traces of its past to pronounce its future. The city was once organized to obey the prerogatives of defence and display of power. Public space and great urban works of art celebrated the city as a mirror and allowed for a cohabitation of domination, ostentation, and familiarity. The earliest of these spaces, the agora and the forum, allowed for public exchange, the founding expression of the city (the *polis*) and of politics. Today, no one dares to credit the space and its monuments with portraying the values of the social contract: justice, homeland, education, administration, surveillance/punishment. Have we lost the political vision that made us citizens? Have we become no more than consumers, living in a marketplace and a spectacle, rather than in the city and its communal spaces? And if new values have appeared, we must give them an urban existence.

Was the story the sense of history coming to an end announced by Francis Fukuyama? Was the story the ideologies of a separate world? According to Jean-François Lyotard, the disappearance of ideologies has opened up an era of postmodernity propitious to anamnesis and quotation. The time span of the city outlasts us. It precedes us and survives us. But this long time span seems threatened. Fernand Braudel distinguished three time spans: the long term of history, the medium term of trends, and the short term of current events. This tidy trilogy has shifted. We are in a time of news reports, and we live by what we remember. When the future is lacking, memories flow freely: memory becomes the plan. This is what François Hartog calls presentism.[5] The city once combined a long time span and a space, a history and a geography, all legible and memorable. Now, we must invent shorter, quicker narratives. Architects must forget eternity (Rem Koolhaas is correct to say that urban planning consists of managing uncertainties), and we all must forget the conviction that there are immutable identities. Paul Ricœur perceived this and questioned the permanence of the collective identity, which is currently being strengthened due to intimidation and insecurity. Ricœur calls upon the story-telling and its variations: "I'd like to contrast the idea of an immutable identity against the idea of a narrative identity: living communities have a history that can be recounted, and I will consider the story one of the paths… along which cultures are spread and intermingled.

I wanted to introduce the idea of variations of horizon: within a given culture, the horizons of value vary in rhythm, they do not all advance or retreat at once, but they are spaced out at intervals.

I will use the metaphor of the countryside seen from a moving train: there are short horizons, which move rapidly; medium horizons, which change more slowly; and, finally, the ultimate horizon of the landscape, which is almost unchanging. Thus, we are not faced with an alternative between the unchanging and the moving: the idea of the horizon implies the idea of variation of horizons at an evolutionary pace."[6] New symbols and rhythms are marking out the time span and the story of cities. Power, as celebrated by the monument, is being replaced by values linked to economics, culture, and events.

Culture connects fragments of reality and provides the stories about speed and production with the depth of field that they are lacking. And they need it! Cultural facilities are the figureheads of today's urban plans. This is true for Utzon's Opera House in Sydney; for Piano and Rogers's Centre Pompidou in Paris; for Gehry's Guggenheim Museum in Bilbao; for Ando's Fondation Pinault at Ile Seguin in Boulogne-Billancourt; for Foster's Zénith and Finn Geipel's Cité du Design soon to be built in Saint-Etienne; for Paul Andreu's opera house in Beijing; and so on.

Beyond this celebration, which approaches the status reserved for the sacred, appears a variant linked to new rhythms: the event. The presentist city is programmatic before it is historic. The architect Bernard Reichen has analyzed what he calls a society of pretext. The event, he says, has become an essential component of the city and a response to the population's expectations. Individualization valorizes the present and an urban plan of flow. This idea of pretext—there are pre-Bilbao and post-Bilbao pretexts—takes various forms. For example, there is the event of events: the Olympic Games. The Sydney Opera House was built for the Melbourne Games of 1956. For the Games of 1976, Montreal created many facilities, including the Olympic Park, the Stadium with its leaning tower, and the Velodrome. Barcelona was spectacularly restructured for the 1992 games. Great architects were invited to participate, and whole new neighbourhoods were created. Athens was profoundly transformed in 2004, notably with the "butterfly" vault by Santiago Calatrava. And Beijing is inviting the aristocracy of architecture to transform the city for 2008. Even being on the list of finalists has become a trigger in itself. The two largest urban projects in Paris today, the Nord-Est and the Batignolles, were launched even though there was no guarantee that Paris would ultimately be chosen.

World fairs have a similar effect. It all started with London's Crystal Palace in 1851. In Montreal in 1967, a major metamorphosis took place on Île Notre-Dame and Île Sainte-Hélène and in the Cité du Havre; Fuller's geodesic dome, Safdie's Habitat 67, and Archigram's lovely Montreal Tower—which never made it past the paper stage—are still with us.

The spread of festivals, such as the "nuits blanches" in Paris, Montreal, Rome, and Brussels, is generating new forms of use of space and urbanity. The dance parade and the festival of lights at Lyon, the Montréal en Lumière festival, the Biennale de Design and Biennale de la ville/les TransUrbaines in Saint-Etienne, and other such events put cities in motion and in the media.

PUBLIC/COMMUNITY/PRIVATE

A human multicultural entity, the city welcomes and protects intimacies and individualities, which may not in themselves reveal its global identity. Mixing, hybridization, and pluralism express a common trace/common place composed of the interdependent diversity and collective use of spaces that belong to everyone. We must challenge attempts to mute this natural chorus: privatization and "gated communities"—an exclusive form of voluntary ghetto and rejection of outsiders—as well as the folklorization of spaces dedicated exclusively to tourist excursions. Marne la Vallée Val d'Europe is a new city east of Paris that has been designed by

the Disney corporation. Its architecture and urban plan obey strict rules, and its aim is to create a city that complies with the ideas that visitors might have, including state-of-the-art information, which makes them imagine Paris as a subtle mélange of Toulouse Lautrec, the Moulin
Rouge, communists, sweet little old ladies, and restaurants where they can sample French
baguette and frogs' legs. The Web site of Val d'Europe delivers the keys to this fairytale:
"Friendly wrought-iron and glass architecture with a human face, inspired by Baltard, Eiffel,
and Haussmann," and neighbourhoods that offer "well-being, freedom, and pleasure... The
Traditional District (Serris Village)... reminiscent of the charming traditional Briard farm-
houses." Wherever you are in the world, international tourism, though necessary and benefi-
cial, may, over the long term, turn cities into display windows and disguise their inhabitants.

The public space of cities is both material and virtual, constituting the two faces of
exchange and debate. Richard Sennett was one of the first to discuss the dangers incurred by
public spaces whose design and use were not founded on a community: "Society remains
dominated... by the collapse of the *res publica*. We feel that social values are produced by
individuals. This belief has sown confusion in two areas of social life: I want to talk about
power and the city... Intimate idolatry keeps us from using our comprehension of the phenomena of power as a political weapon. The city is the instrument of impersonal life, the cru-
cible in which the diversity of interests, tastes, and human desires is transformed into social
experience. Yet the fear of impersonality tends to destroy this experience."[7] Sennett advo-
cates the creation of a secular material space that everyone can use to celebrate resem-
blances, not differences. The public space is also an immaterial space of conversations and
thoughts connecting individuals who are brought together by the general interest. In this
sense, the public space is, according to Jürgen Habermas, the conquest of the critical spirit
over the secrecy of the state.[8] The press and the media play an essential role in guaranteeing
the freedom of exchange. The risk that this space will be confiscated and commercialized
may be real if publicity (advertising) definitively loses its capacity to make public and becomes
simply the imposition of an imaginary of merchandises. When Paul Virilio writes, "The public
image becomes the public space," he is expressing the same fear: the city is dematerializing,
privatizing, and merchandising itself. Rem Koolhaas calls the continuum of interior spaces,
usually commercial, in which "there are no longer walls but partitions," *Junkspace*. Here, he
says, the public merges with the private, and "because it costs money, the conditioned space
becomes a conditional space."[9] This deprivation caused by the conditional may leave hospi-
tality in oblivion.

Although Sennett's radical analysis no longer corresponds to a reality in which public
and private interpenetrate, it is still useful to distinguish a familiar use of the public space that
gives it a form of social intimacy (manifest in the Mediterranean, for example) from a strict privatization that, in the name of hygiene and security, often wipes out the guarantee of free
access for everyone. Agora, the 2004 Montreal Biennale, was devoted to the study of public
space. The introduction highlighted the current issues: "The International District, the university districts, and the plan for a Dhow District in Montreal respond to our desire for easily accessible spaces on a city-wide scale. The city is gradually being divided into thematic bits, each
of which seeks to attract customers through banners and attractive street furniture. This new
design of the public space tends, however, to close the borders of these spaces to strollers,
vendors, and street artists—elements that might disturb the carefully stage-managed surroundings. An obsession with security separates these undesirable elements from the old
spaces and from public parks that have been embellished by city investments." This is precisely the risk of conditional access.

The public space must be prepared beforehand and designed so that it fulfils a plan
and is not a leftover. Free and welcoming as an interior city—an urban room, Louis Kahn

might have said—it must be opened up to everyone, especially the most disadvantaged. But it must not stay frozen in a model inherited, in large part, from old European cities. Shopping, recreation, culture, the desire to move around, and the ubiquity created by the Internet modify our living habits and spaces. Stadiums, shopping centres, airports, train stations, means of transportation and their stations, conference centres, exhibition halls, museums, commercial galleries, concert halls, festivals and festivities, billboards, street furniture, façades, media buildings—they all constitute the public space as much as do public squares, streets, malls, and parks. The city's design must master their conception and installation. New centres thus develop in the polycentric city. They are needed so that the old centres do not become overcrowded and the space for the majority become neglected. This essential attention to the majority living environment must take into account the components of a city and an everyday history.

ORDINARY/EXTRAORDINARY/SINGULARITY/SIMILARITY

Patrimony refers to the history of a few, almost never to the history of all—and even less so today. The monuments and great urban rooms edify in both senses of the term: to construct and to instruct, to bring to virtue. Pascal said, "The strength of a man's virtue should not be measured by his special exertions, but by his ordinary acts." In the city, the ordinary is glossed over by the sumptuous effects of power. Selective and eradicating memory. This institutional negligence reduces the value of most of the past and confiscates the space of celebration by ignoring the everyday and the creations of the present, spaces of sociability, crafts, shared uses. In Les lieux de mémoire,[10] Pierre Nora establishes, for France, an inventory of and pathway for these memories and these places. The time has come to give meaning to new paths and to perceive, beyond beautiful monuments, the entreaties of the everyday.

There are no small projects. Though monuments and urban rooms must delineate the space and provide its points of reference, secular space is just as important. The small urban forms, as urban planner Jean-Pierre Charbonneau calls them, are the necessary sparks for a shared consideration and use of the city. It is easier to build an Arc de Triomphe or an office building than to lay out a street or a neighbourhood. Architecture must escape the twin dangers of the expiatory monument (everything is ugly but our monuments save us) and the architecture of developers, "easy architecture." Between the two, the road is narrow toward a friendly and comfortable architecture of daily life that is local, global, contemporary, and ordinary. Can we be everything at once: of here, of the world, and of the present? Can we be universal without denying our roots; inventive without distancing ourselves from the ordinary; of today without forgetting yesterday? This is the mission that Kenneth Frampton[11] assigned to architects in his proposals for an architecture of resistance instituting a "critical regionalism." If, as Miguel Torga writes, "The global is the local without walls," it is a good idea to preserve the walls, while opening up to the great beyond. The architect of the city must express these inseparable truths. Identitary content will be specified not by confining history to a distant past but by recording within it the more recent developments and integrating the cultural diversity of inhabitants. Critical regionalism must therefore expand with exogenous contributions that become constitutive elements of the hybrid corpus of the city. All of this is complex. But nothing would be worse than the diversion of all ambitions to the market, the market for profit. Once again, we must reinvent stories, narrative horizons, policies. The design of the city is also about that. Such "ordinary" architecture would rediscover symbols and significances other than the poetry of the right angle, the magic of the skin, or the infatuation with size, and would no longer consider style, ornament, and the body as signs of a backward-looking degeneracy.

THE BODY OF THE CITY/ THE CITY OF BODIES/ THE RELATIONSHIP

With proxemy, Edward T. Hall shows that each of us has a sort of bubble that changes according to culture, use, and place.[12] He explains how spaces are organized as a function of different traditions and how new spaces can be planned integrating this hidden dimension of minds and bodies. Although architecture is, above all, light, we also live in a landscape of sound. Murray Schafer was the first to perceive and analyze this in his writings, in his teaching at Simon Fraser University,[13] and in the development since the late 1960s of his *World Soundscape Project*. His lectures and works on sound have gradually come to be seen as inherent to the knowledge and shaping of cities. Much remains to do, however, for these analyses to be integrated into cities' development—and even more, if we follow the inventory of our senses. The urban space is a space that our bodies play, as they are sensitive to temperature, air, shadow, movement, noise, colours, and other bodies. We should be very attentive to the physical aspects of the city, to the way that its paths, its architectures, its flows, its topography, and its materials interact with our bodies, enter us, and unconsciously create an inventory of affects and perceptions[14] that give rise to the enjoyment and richness of the space. The city of accumulated knowledge and tastes is situated between sense and sensitivity. Reason is not its only empire and space is not decreed in it. "Space is a poetry that is felt instead of being measured," declared Antoine Pevsner. We must resist in the name of sensitivity and introduce into the design of the city the rich composite of our sensations, a subtle and essentially unused resource. To do this, we must control the relationship between ambience, light, sound, warmth, odour (smell-scape), tactility, and kinetics. We must combine the objective and the subjective, what Jean-François Augoyard calls "paradoxical unity," in order to make an aesthetic founded on the contextualized organization of the sensations.

The sensitive world is created through the relationship with the body. The city is a fabric; relationships are formed there—between bodies, between spaces, between fullness and emptiness. "Let us forget things and think only of relationships," recommended Georges Braque. In the fragmented city even more than in the official city, it is important to weave ties and provide a place. This linking of coherence and meaning that makes the city intelligible and inhabitable is both form and background, an urban ecology, a design of relationships.

Design must take into account the sponsor's commission and words in order to appreciate their nature, to determine the share of desire and the share of need, to connect rootedness and projection, and to design and produce a plan. Who is the sponsor of the city, and is there no place for a new control, not just by the master contractor and master client but by the master user as well? Thus, the voice of inhabitants should be mixed with the voices of power and of design. The voice that various groups have, the "low-energy speech" that Belgian architect and urban planner Lucien Kroll speaks about, is no doubt the basis for a local plan that would not suffer the consequences of globalization but would respond without ignoring or denying it. The "local plan," says Alberto Magnaghi,[16] is a globalization from below, a dynamic management of conflicts, and the networking of cities in response to their divestiture.

The design of the city is the organization of its governance and a subtle balance of political representation and associative life. We are, according to François Ascher, torn among different, and perhaps opposed, axioms: that of performance in the economy, that of justice in the social context, and that of ethics in the environment. It would be distressing if the loss of a collective story and project led to a division of governance among specialized expertises. Politics, like the city, crosses and abolishes segmentations and states the generalist nature of our lives and their spatial and symbolic framework. Politics must reinvent the *polis*: the city must become our horizon. It is thus essential to give cities more power and more real representation within international, economic, social, and cultural bodies.

Cities are different. Between being out of bounds and losing identity, between simplistic autonomy and amnesiac dependence, they designate an agreed-upon world of relationships and interdependence.

They make us similar and fraternal by stating the possible stories of a future and a plan that will enrich us through our diversities.

〉〉〉

1. Yves Chalas, *Villes contemporaines* (Paris: Cercle d'art, 2001), pp. 7, 8, 9. ✕ 2. Raymond Unwin, *Town Planning in Practice: Introduction to the Art of Designing Cities and Suburbs*. Published in London in 1909, this book was one of the very first textbooks on the "science of cities." ✕ 3. The "urban exhibition" *Internationale Bauausstellung (IBA)* on the Ruhr included seventeen cities in an 803 km^2 area that were in a steelmaking or mining crisis. In 1990, seventy-six plans were selected with the following themes: rural park in Emscher Park starting from the original landscape; ecological restructuring of the canal in Emscher Park; use of the Rhin-Herne canal as a recreational space; development of industrial and tertiary spaces in the industrial hinterlands on the theme of work in the park (five hundred hectares of activity zones integrating seventeen technological centres); restoration and conversion of industrial buildings as cultural spaces; construction of new housing projects and rehabilitation of working-class districts. ✕ 4. *The Umbrellas*, Japan and United States, 1984–91; *The Wrapped Coast*, Australia; *The Valley Curtain of Colorado*; *Surrounded Islands off the coast* of Miami. ✕ 5. François Hartog, *Des régimes d'historicité— présentisme et expérience du temps* (Paris: Seuil. 2003). ✕ 6. Paul Ricœur, "Cultures, du deuil à la traduction," Le Monde, 25 May 2004 (our translation). ✕ 7. Richard Sennett, *Les tyrannies de l'intimité* (Paris: Ed. du seuil, 1979), p. 275 (our translation). Originally in English: *Fall of Public Man: On the Social Psychology of Capitalism* (New York: Vintage, 1977). ✕ 8. Jürgen Habermas, *L'espace public, Archéologie de la publicité comme dimension constitutive de la société bourgeoise* (Paris: Payot, 1978). The original German-language edition was published in 1962. ✕ 9. Rem Koolhaas, *Mutations Actar* (Arc en rêve centre d'architecture, 2000), pp. 743–57 (our translation). ✕ 10. Pierre Nora (ed.), *Les lieux de mémoire*, 3 vols. (Paris: Gallimard, 1984–92). ✕ 11. Kenneth Frampton, "Pour un régionalisme critique et une architecture de résistance," *Critique : L'objet architecture*, No. 476–77. ✕ 12. Edward T. Hall, *The Hidden Dimension* (Garden City, NY: Doubleday 1966). See also Hall's *The Silent Language* (Garden City, NY: Anchor Press/ Doubleday, 1959). ✕ 13. R. Murray Schafer, *Soundscape: Our Sonic Environment and the Tuning of the World* (Rochester, VT: Destiny Books, 1994). ✕ 14. "Characters can exist, and the author can create them, only if they do not perceive but are passed in the landscape and are themselves part of the composite of sensations... Affects are precisely these non-human fates of man, just as perceptions [including the city] are non-human landscapes of nature." Gilles Deleuze and Félix Guattari, *Qu'est-ce que la philosophie?* (Paris: Editions de Minuit, 1991) (our translation). ✕ 15. Alberto Magnaghi, *Le projet local* (Mardaga, 2003). First published in Italian, 2000.

〉〉〉

QUOTES

—I say 'yes' to design as a tool for better living and a better existence in the city, and as a means of cultural and economic expression at street level and among citizens. Although design is adopted in daily life through small interventions that are appreciated and used by everyone, this should never impede its audacity, innovation, modernity, or humour.

Sylvie Berkowicz, design reporter, Émission d., MusiquePlus, Montreal

〉〉〉

—A design city, and not a designed city, is a diverse city in which citizens may find a new ambience by turning a street corner. However, a design city is, above all, endowed with a common thread that may be defined by a standardized layout of the public right-of-way and its furnishings. The lampposts, trashcans, bus shelters, and other items are discreet; they subscribe to the concept of zero visual pollution and contribute to the city's identity, and they allow the architecture of buildings to be revealed.

Mario Brodeur, architect, Montreal.

》》

—A city may be a new design city because among its driving forces is a strong awareness of the potential of design. Also, the quality of life that a design city offers its residents is improved through major transformations of the living environment: the quality of buildings and their interiors, public spaces and street furniture, private outdoor spaces, public transit, signage and signalling, and so on.

Marc H. Choko, full professor, École de design at the Université du Québec à Montréal.

》》

—Those involved in the new design cities share a common quest to improve their environment and their citizens' quality of life. They must balance the increasingly complex processes associated with the production of interventions with a concern for aesthetics, accessibility, and sustainability.

Pierre Deschênes, project director, Quartier des Spectacles, for the enhancement of the territory and patrimony of the city of Montreal.

》》

—To a certain extent, our quality of life is determined by the objects that are placed at our disposal. In a city, these objects are often public facilities, and so their comfort, safety of use, durability, ease of maintenance, and beauty all contribute, directly or indirectly, to that quality of life.

Koen De Winter, industrial designer, president, HippoDesign, Montreal.

》》

—It is essential that designers have as an objective the humanizing of the city. The greatest fault that I see among some designers is that they want to create a work of art that attracts attention, to the point of fatigue rather than repose. Good design isn't seen, it is felt.

Marc Kandalaft, art director, Paris.

》》

—The process of decentralization that started in France in the 1980s gave local communities the possibility of developing policies that more directly reflect the expectations of their residents, who have stamped their cities with distinct identities. Nantes, Lille, Bordeaux, and Lyon are perfect illustrations of this.

Florence Michel, independent journalist specializing in architecture, urban planning, design, and interior design.

》》

—A design city is not a "theme city." If it were, it would be analogous to an amusement park or an eighteenth-century "cabinet of curiosities." A true "design city" is a city concerned with its well-being — a city that actively constructs its identity, its soul, and its living environment. Moreover, it's a city whose design is diverse. The intention of "shaping the city" should be to renew the basis of such a destiny.

Philippe Poullaouec-Gonidec, UNESCO Chair of Landscape and Environment, Université de Montréal.

》》

—Cities that have been bogged down in the past for too long are now searching to be contemporary. Their citizens are demanding that their cities be in the present, offering the extraordinary every day, so that situations both fleeting and immutable may intermingle. Cities must imprint their territories with new expressions and impressions to feed the expectations of a rapidly changing urban culture that is subjected to great environmental challenges.

Philippe Poullaouec-Gonidec, UNESCO Chair of Landscape and Environment, Université de Montréal.

—If I were a politician, a high priority for me would be raising awareness among residents, since the quality of public life cannot improve if they do not feel like "citizens." I would encourage them to feel responsible for the public space. This space must belong to someone, or else it will die.

Siglinde Spanihel, industrial designer by training, full professor at the Offenbach Academy of Applied Arts, Germany.

—To take a stroll, to meet someone by chance or by prearrangement, to observe, to run from one place to another, to cross the public space or to stop in it — these activities should be the point of departure for composition of the public space."

Siglinde Spanihel, industrial designer by training, full professor at the Offenbach Academy of Applied Arts, Germany.

— NOTRE QUALITÉ DE VIE EST EN PARTIE DÉTER- MINÉE PAR LES OBJETS MIS À NOTRE DISPOSITION. DANS UNE VILLE, CES OBJETS ÉTANT SOUVENT DES PIÈCES D'ÉQUIPEMENT PUBLIC, LEUR CONFORT, SÉCURITÉ D'UTILISATION, DURABILITÉ, FACILITÉ D'ENTRETIEN ET BEAUTÉ Y CONTRIBUENT, DIRECTE- MENT OU INDIRECTEMENT.

Koen De Winter, designer industriel, président de la firme HippoDesign, Montréal

Direction
Direction
MARIE-JOSÉE LACROIX

Interviews, gathering of texts and images
Entrevues, cueillette des textes et de l'iconographie
MARIE-JOSÉE LACROIX
LAETITIA WOLFF
Éditions Infopresse : MICKAËL CARLIER, MÉLANIE RUDEL-TESSIER
GENEVIÈVE ANGIO-MORNEAU
AMÉLIE BILODEAU

Writing and editing
Rédaction et mise au point
MARIE-JOSÉE LACROIX
LAETITIA WOLFF with **avec** CORINNE BRIVOT, RYAN BRUNETTE
Éditions Infopresse : MICKAËL CARLIER, ANDRÉANNE LECLERC,
MÉLANIE RUDEL-TESSIER

Translation **Traduction**
French > English **Français > anglais** : KÄTHE ROTH
English > French **Anglais > français** : STÉPHANIE CLAUSMANN

Copy editing **Révision linguistique**
English **Anglais** : JOAN IRVING, KÄTHE ROTH, THÉRÈSE BROWN
French **Français** : FRANÇOIS PERREAULT

Publishing **Édition**
Éditions Infopresse
Pyramyd

Coordination and production **Coordination et production**
Éditions Infopresse : SANDRINE ARCHAMBAULT, LOUISE GOUDREAULT

Graphic Design **Conception graphique**
orangetango

Distribution **Diffusion**
In America **En Amérique** : Éditions Infopresse
In Europe **En Europe** : Pyramyd

Printing **Impression**
K2 impression, Canada

Acknowledgments **Remerciements**
The City of Montreal and the Ville de Saint-Étienne would like to
thank the authors and other contributors who provided articles,
interviews, and visuals, making this publication possible. ✖
We also thank the partners of Commerce Design Montréal—in
particular, the Gouvernement du Québec—for their financial
support for the symposium Nouvelles villes de design and for this
book. We are also very grateful to the Centre Jacques Cartier and
its director, Alain Bideau, for the assistance provided to this project
in the context of the 17th Entretiens. ✖ Finally, a huge thank-you
to the entire design and production team whose talent,
enthusiasm, and professionalism have contributed to the quality
of this publication. ✖ **La Ville de Montréal et la Ville de
Saint-Étienne tiennent à remercier, en premier lieu, les
nombreux auteurs et collaborateurs qui nous ont fourni les
textes, les entrevues et l'iconographie et ainsi rendu possible
cette publication. ✖ Nous remercions également les partenaires de Commerce Design Montréal, et en particulier le
gouvernement du Québec, pour leur appui financier au
colloque Nouvelles villes de design et à ce livre. De même, nos
sincères remerciements au Centre Jacques Cartier et à son
directeur, monsieur Alain Bideau, pour l'aide accordée à ce
projet dans le cadre des 17ième Entretiens. ✖ Enfin, un
immense merci à toute l'équipe de conception et de production pour avoir contribué par leur talent, leur enthousiasme
et leur professionnalisme à la qualité de cette publication.**

— UNE VILLE PEUT ÊTRE UNE NOUVELLE VILLE DE DESIGN
PARCE QU'IL EXISTE PARMI SES FORCES MOTRICES UNE
FORTE PRISE DE CONSCIENCE DU POTENTIEL DU DESIGN.
ÉGALEMENT, PARCE QUE LA QUALITÉ DE VIE QU'ELLE OFFRE
À SES HABITANTS S'AMÉLIORE PAR D'IMPORTANTES TRANS-
FORMATIONS DU CADRE DE VIE : QUALITÉ DES BÂTIMENTS ET
DE LEUR INTÉRIEUR, ESPACES PUBLICS ET MOBILIER
URBAIN, ESPACES EXTÉRIEURS PRIVÉS, TRANSPORTS EN
COMMUN, AFFICHAGE ET SIGNALÉTIQUE...

Marc H. Choko, professeur titulaire à l'École de design de l'Université du Québec à Montréal

— LES ACTEURS DES NOUVELLES VILLES DE DESIGN PARTAGENT CETTE QUÊTE D'AMÉLIORER LEUR ENVIRONNEMENT ET LA QUALITÉ DE VIE DE LEURS CITOYENS PAR LA MAÎTRISE DES PROCESSUS ASSOCIÉS À LA PRODUCTION D'INTERVENTIONS DE PLUS EN PLUS COMPLEXES DANS UN SOUCI D'ESTHÉTISME, D'ACCESSIBILITÉ ET DE DURABILITÉ.

Pierre Deschênes, directeur du projet Quartier des spectacles, Service de la mise en valeur du territoire et du patrimoine de la Ville de Montréal

— SI J'ÉTAIS POLITICIENNE, JE RÉALISERAIS SURTOUT UN TRAVAIL DE SENSIBILISATION AUPRÈS DES HABITANTS, CAR LA QUALITÉ DE LA VIE PUBLIQUE NE PEUT S'AMÉLIORER SI CEUX-CI NE SE SENTENT PAS "CITOYENS". JE LES ENCOURA-GERAIS À PRENDRE LEURS RESPONSABILITÉS FACE À L'ESPACE PUBLIC. CE DERNIER DOIT APPARTENIR À QUELQU'UN, SINON IL MEURT.

Siglinde Spanihel, designer industriel de formation et professeur titulaire à l'Académie des Arts Appliqués, Offenbach, en Allemagne

— LA DÉCENTRALISATION ENGAGÉE AU DÉBUT DES ANNÉES 80 EN FRANCE A DONNÉ AUX COLLECTIVITÉS LOCALES LA POSSIBILITÉ DE DÉVELOPPER DES POLITIQUES PROCHES DES ATTENTES DES HABITANTS, QUI ONT CON-FÉRÉ À CHAQUE VILLE SON IDENTITÉ. NANTES, LILLE, BORDEAUX OU LYON EN SONT DE PARFAITES ILLUSTRATIONS.

Florence Michel, journaliste indépendante spécialisée en architecture,urbanisme, design et aménagement intérieur, Paris

—AS RECENTLY AS 1985, THERE WAS NO GENERAL IDEA OF WHAT DESIGNERS DID OR WHAT THEY MIGHT BE USEFUL FOR. SOMETHING HAPPENED IN THE LAST DECADE THAT HAS RADICALLY CHANGED HOW DESIGN AND ARCHITECTURE ARE PERCEIVED IN CANADA. I THINK IT BOILS DOWN TO GLOBALIZATION. JUST FIVE YEARS AGO THERE WAS NOWHERE NEAR THE NUMBER OF FOREIGN MAGAZINES ON CANADIAN NEWSSTANDS THAT WE NOW FIND. THIS MORE DIVERSIFIED RANGE IN PRINT MEDIA HAS HELPED TO OPEN UP THE NORTH AMERICAN PUBLIC TO A WIDER RANGE OF OPTIONS IN TERMS OF LIFESTYLE PRODUCTS AND POPULARIZING MODERN DESIGN.

Nelda Rodger, editor of the design magazine Azure, Toronto

— TROP LONGTEMPS ENLISÉES SUR CE QU'ELLES ONT ÉTÉ, LES VILLES SONT EN QUÊTE DE CONTEM-PORANÉITÉ.

LEURS CITOYENS EXIGENT QU'ELLES SOIENT LEUR PRÉSENT, LEUR QUOTIDIEN EXTRAORDINAIRE, OÙ SE MÊLENT FUGA-CITÉ ET IMMUABILITÉ DES SITUATIONS. LES VILLES DOIVENT MARQUER LEUR TERRITOIRE DE NOUVELLES EXPRESSIONS ET IMPRESSIONS POUR NOURRIR LES ATTENTES D'UNE CULTURE URBAINE EN RAPIDE MUTATION SOUMISE À DE GRANDS DÉFIS ENVIRONNEMENTAUX.

Philippe Poullaouec-Gonidec, titulaire de la Chaire UNESCO en paysage et environnement, Université de Montréal